D0939673

READINGS IN
BAPTIST HISTORY

Four Centuries
of Selected Documents

JOSEPH EARLY JR.

ACADEMIC
NASHVILLE, TENNESSEE

Copyright © 2008
by Joseph Early Jr.
All rights reserved
Printed in the United States of America

978-0-8054-4674-6

Published by B&H Publishing Group
Nashville, Tennessee

Dewey Decimal Classification: 286.09
Subject Heading: BAPTISTS—HERITAGE\BAPTISTS—
HISTORY\BAPTISTS—BIOGRAPHY

4 5 6 7 8 9 10 • 22 21 20 19 18
VP

CONTENTS

Readings (continued)

Born in 1609, the Baptist denomination has grown from a handful of members hiding in a self-imposed exile in Amsterdam, Holland, under the persecution of their own monarch, King James I of England, to a twenty-first century worldwide membership that exceeds eighty million. Over these four hundred years many documents have been written in the United States and Britain detailing the Baptist story. In the last decade of the twentieth and into the twenty-first century, the most employed manuscript outlining Baptist history has been H. Leon McBeth's *Baptist Heritage: Four Centuries of Baptist Witness* (1987). With more than eight hundred pages of text, this book has been the primary textbook for many college, university, and seminary Baptist history professors. Since the publication of McBeth's text, several new Baptist history books have been written. Using many of the same sources as McBeth while adding material from before and after 1987, these books have made contributions to many different aspects of the Baptist story. Because these texts often take different approaches and emphasize different areas of Baptist history, each book contributes to a better understanding of who Baptists are, where Baptists came from, and where Baptists appear to be going.

While many new histories have been written, no major Baptist primary sourcebook has been compiled since McBeth's *A Sourcebook for Baptist Heritage* (1990). Access to the primary sources is the key to a deeper understanding of the events in question. By examining the primary sources, the reader has the opportunity to delve further into an issue and see it in its original context and through the eyes of the writer.

Even the most casual reader knows that many significant changes have occurred in Baptist life since 1990. Among the more important are the organization of the Cooperative Baptist Fellowship, Calvinism's assumption of a prominent station in Baptist higher education, and publication of a new edition of the Baptist Faith and Message by the Southern Baptist Convention. Each of these events is a milestone in Baptist life. Much material on these and other events is available, but is scattered in a myriad of locations. Selected documents that were and continue to be important in understanding these more recent events are contained in this manuscript.

Along with these new materials, seminal older documents are also included. Because of the antiquated language of many of these documents, I have updated the language of the more difficult passages, particularly the seventeenth-century English Baptists, to aid the modern reader's comprehension. The spelling of words such as *neighbour* and *Saviour* have been changed to the current American orthography. Other examples of words that have been replaced by their modern equivalents are *ye, thou, thro*, and other words of similar syntax. In no way have any of these changes altered the meaning of the word, phrase, or document. Some historians may disagree with even this limited modernization of the language, but the purposes of these passages are to convey their historical and theological importance, not to create an exercise in the translation of early modern English. With this in mind, I have eliminated as much of the cumbersome verbiage as possible so the reader can comprehend the meaning with the least possible confusion. I did not, however, correct grammar. In contrast to their language, the grammar of our Baptist predecessors, although flawed by current standards, is comprehendible.

In order to provide as broad a scope and be as inclusive as possible, representative materials concerning British Baptists, Black Baptists, American Baptists, Southern Baptists, Russian Baptists, Landmark Baptists, and Fundamental Baptists have been incorporated into the text. Several confessions of faith allow the reader to trace the development of Baptist theology and ecclesiology. Other materials discuss ethical issues, the development of Baptist organizations, home and foreign missions, theologians, pastors, women, and many other aspects of Baptist life. Some documents deal with controversial issues that have led to internecine fighting and upon occasion outright schism. In these documents, I have attempted to be fair in choice, number, and representation to all parties involved.

Unlike many sourcebooks that arrange the materials by topic, I have arranged the documents in a general chronological order. In some cases the date used to place the document is the date when the document was written and in other places the date selected is when the event written about occurred. My goal is to help the reader to see the flow of history and more easily discern the development of the Baptist denomination. When two or more documents fall under the same heading, the first document provides the date for their chronological placement.

I am sure that not everyone will agree with the inclusion or exclusion of one or more of documents for this manuscript, but this book is intended to be a streamlined and affordable sourcebook. My selections were made based on two criteria. First, as always, I was limited by the ever-present issue of word count and, second, the audience for this text is first and foremost students of Baptist history. Thus, as I made choices, I made every effort to eliminate my personal bias and consider what documents give the broadest and most understandable basis for our rich heritage.

Since this is a sourcebook of primary materials, the documents are the central aspect of the book. For this reason, I have added no introductory comments that might color the interpretation of the documents. This format allows the book to serve as a companion to virtually any of the Baptist history texts that are now available.

Baptists have a great story to tell. More often than not, the story is best told by those who participated in it. I hope the reader will be aided by this text to develop a deeper understanding of Baptist history.

Joseph Early Jr.
Assistant Professor of Religion
University of the Cumberlands

1

THE CHARACTER OF THE BEAST, 1609

John Smyth

T O EVERY ONE THAT LOVETH THE Truth in sincerity Salutations.

It may be thought most strange that a man should often times change his Religion. It cannot be accounted a commendable quality in any man to make many alterations and changes in such weighty matters, as are the cases of conscience. . . .

This must be true, (and we confess it) if one condition is admitted, that the Religion which a man changed is the truth. Otherwise to change a false Religion is commendable, and to retain a false Religion is damnable. For a man of a Turk to become a Jew, of a Jew to become a Papist, of a Papist to become a Protestant are all commendable changes though they all befall one and the same person in one year, nay, if it were in one month. So that not to change Religion is simply evil. Therefore that we should fall from the profession of Puritanism to Brownism, and from Brownism to true Christian baptism, is not simply evil or reprovable in itself, unless it is proven that we have fallen from true Religion. If we, therefore, having been formerly deceived in the way of Pedobaptistry, now do embrace the truth in the true Christian Apostolic baptism, then let no man impute this as a fault unto us. This therefore is the question, whether the baptism of infants is lawful, yes or no and whether persons baptized as infants must not renounce that false baptism, and assume the true baptism of Christ which is to be administered upon persons confessing their faith and their sins? This is the controversy now between us and the Separation commonly called Brownists. . . . Let the indifferent reader judge the whole and give sentence without partiality and I do not doubt but he shall be constrained to give glory to God in acknowledging the error of baptizing infants, to have been a chief point of Antichristianism, and the very essence and constitution of the false Church, as is clearly discovered in this treatise. . . .

Herein, therefore, we do acknowledge our error, that we retaining the baptism of England which gave us our constitution, did call our mother England a harlot, and upon a false ground made our Separation from her. Although it was necessary that we Separate from England, yet no man can Separate from England as from a false Church unless he also Separate from the baptism of England, which gives England her constitution. Whosoever retains the baptism of England does retain the constitution of England, and cannot without sin call England a harlot as we have done. . . . For if they retain the baptism of England, viz. the baptism of infants as true baptism, they cannot Separate from England as from a false Church though they may Separate for corruptions. Whosoever does Separate from England as from a false Church must Separate from the baptism of England, as from false baptism. The baptism of England cannot be true and be retained, and the Church of England false and be rejected. Neither can the Church of England possibly be false unless its baptism is false, unless a true constitution could be in a false Church, which is as impossible as for light to have fellowship with darkness. . . .

But the Separation, they say England has a false constitution, and is a false Church and is to be Separated from. Yet they also say England has a true baptism (that is a true constitution) which is not to be Separated from. For a true constitution and true baptism are one and the same. So is a false constitution and a false baptism. So the speeches and actions of the Separation are contradictory in this particular.

Finally, they that defend the baptism of infants cannot with any truth or good conscience Separate from England as from a false Church though they may separate for corruptions. They that do Separate from England as from a false Church must out of necessity Separate from the baptism of England, and account the baptism of England false, and so account the baptism of infants a false baptism. Therefore the Separation must either go back to England or forward to true baptism and all that shall in time come to Separate from England must Separate from the baptism of England. If they will not Separate from the baptism of England there is no reason why they should separate from England as from a false church. . . . Now concerning this point of baptizing infants we do profess before the Lord and before all men in sincerity and truth that it seems to us the most unreasonable heresy of all Antichristianism. For considering what baptism is, an infant is no more capable of baptism than is any unreasonable or insensible creature. For Baptism is not washing with water, but it is the baptism of the Spirit, the confession of the mouth, and the washing with water. . . .

Now that an infant cannot be baptized with the Spirit is plain, 1. Pet. 3: 21 where the Apostle said that the baptism of the Spirit is the question of a good conscience into God, & Heb. 10. 22, where the baptism which is inward is called the sprinkling of the heart from an evil conscience. Seeing, therefore, infants neither have an evil conscience, nor the question of a good conscience, nor the purging of the heart, for all these are proper to actual sinners. Hence it follows that infant baptism is folly and nothing. . . .

Lo, we protest against them, to be a false Church falsely constituted in the baptism of infants and their own unbaptized estate. We protest against them to have a false worship of reading books. We protest against them to have a false government of a triformed Presbytery. We protest against them to have a false Ministry of Doctors or Teachers. Finally, we protest against them that seeing their constitution is false, therefore there is no one ordinance of the Lord true among them. These things we have published, and of these things we require an answer. For we proclaim against them as they proclaim against their own mother England. The Separation, the youngest and the fairest daughter of Rome, is a harlot. For as is the mother so is the daughter. . . .

Briefly to conclude, let the Separation be advertised that whereas they do so confidently through their self love and self-conceit fill their mouths with heresy and heretics, as if thereby they would fear babes. Herein they tread in the steps of all the Antichristians their predecessors. Do not the Papists call the Protestants heretics and call for fire and fagot? Do not the Protestants proclaim the Separation Schismatics and Heretics and judge them worthy of the gibbet? Not the affirmation of men without proof, but the evidence of willful obstinacy in error makes men heretics. Let them take heed that they notwithstanding their Siren songs prove not to be cages full of the most ugly and deformed Antichristian Heretics. Thus desiring the Separation not to be wise in their own eyes through pride, but to become fools that they may be made wise through humility, and desiring the forwardest preachers and professors of the English nation to weigh well what is the true constitution of the Church, and what is the subject of true Christian baptism, and accordingly to measure a true and a false Church. I cease, wishing the light and love of the truth to everyone that Reads.

John Smyth

John Smyth, *The Character of the Beast*, or *the False Constitution of the Church* (1609); repr. W. T. Whitley, ed., *The Works of John Smyth*, 2 vols. (Cambridge: Cambridge University Press, 1915), 2:564–74.

2

LETTER TO SIR WILLIAM HAMMERTON, 1609

Hughe and Anne Bromheade

GRACE WITH INCREASE OF GRACE, peace even from the father and god of peace, with all true comfort and consolation in Jesus Christ be with you beloved Cousin and all yours, and that forever. Beloved Cousin we received A letter from you dated the xiii of July wherein you write that you expect an answer from us of the said letter. The first part of your letter is, that leaving our Country we removed to Amsterdam, which in removing was, you hope, but to make a trial of the Country. . . . A second part of your letter is that you would persuade us to return home to England, which you make no Question would be much pleasing to God. But we make a great Question there of you. We hold it without all Question, the same should be much and highly displeasing unto our good God and father, that has in his merciful providence brought us out of Babylon the Mother of all abominations, the habitation of devils and the hold of all foul spirits, and A cage of every unclean and hateful bird. . . .

Concerning the fourth part of your letter wherein you seem to desire to know wherein your church might be reformed although I know not herein, where to begin or where to end. The corruptions are so many and Infinite, yet, in some measure to satisfy your request, I will give you a view and taste of them, but before I will give you A brief Sum of the causes of our Separation and of our purpose in practice. First, we seek above all things the peace and protection of the most high and the kingdom of our lord Jesus Christ. Secondly, we seek and fully purpose to worship god Aright according as he has commanded in his most holy word. Thirdly, we seek the fellowship of his faithful and obedient servants and together with them to enter a Covenant with the lord, and by the direction of his holy Spirit to proceed to A godly free and right choice of Ministers and other officers by him ordained to the Service of his church. Fourthly, we seek to establish and obey the ordinances and laws of our Savior Christ left by his last will and testament to the governing and guiding of his church without altering, changing, innovating, wresting, or leaving out any of them that the Lord shall give us sight of. Fifthly, we purpose (by the assistance of the holy ghost) in this faith and order to lead our lives, and for this faith and order to leave our lives if such is the good will of our heavenly father. And sixthly, now that our forsaking and utter abandoning of these disordered assemblies as they generally stand in England, may not seem strange or offensive to any that will Judge or be judged by the word of god, we allege and affirm that heinous guilt in these 4 principal transgressions. 1. They worship the true god after A false Manner in their worship being made of the Invention of Man, even of that Man of Sin, erroneous and Imposed upon them. 2. for that the profane, ungodly . . . without exception of any one person, are with them received into, and retained in the Bosom of the church. 3. For that they have A false and Antichristian ministry imposed upon them, retained with them, and maintained by them. 4. For these churches are ruled by and remain in subjection under an Antichristian, and ungodly government, contrary to the institution of our Savior Christ. . . . As the prophet Isaiah spoke of the people of the Jews so may we speak of the church of England, from the Sole of the foot to the head, there is nothing whole therein but wounds, and swelling and sores, full of Corruptions, the whole head is heavy . . . your church of England therefore has an Antichristian constitution and is A false church. And can there be anything true in A false church but only the Scriptures and the truths therein contained. But your church has a false constitution, or false ministry, a false worship, a false government and A false Baptism, the door and entry into the church, and so all is false in your church. Wherefore beloved Cousin we wish you in the lord diligently and seriously to consider and weigh your universal state and standing, that it is most sorrowful and lamentable. And now at the last to harken to the lord's voice that sounded from heaven, sang go out of Babylon my people that you be not partakers with her in her Sins and that you do not receive her plagues.

Beloved Cousin concerning your request of A book of our present settled government, there is none extant though there are diverse books . . . the matters of controversy between the church of England and us, and touching the differences between us and the other churches here.

The order of worship and government of our church is. 1. We begin with A prayer, after we read some one or two chapters of the bible given the since thereof, and confer upon the same; that done we lay aside our books, and after a solemn prayer made by the first speaker, he propounds some text out of the Scripture, and prophesies out of the same, by the space of one hour, or three Quarters of an hour. After him stands up a second speaker who prophesies out of the said text in the like time and space, sometimes more sometimes less. After him the third, the fourth, the fifth &c as time gives leave. Then the first speaker concludes with prayer as he began with prayer, with an exhortation to contribute to the poor, with a collection being made and also concluded with prayer. This Morning's exercise begins at eight of the clock and continues to twelve of the clock. The like course of exercise is observed in the afternoon from 2 of the clock to 5 or 6 of the Clock. Last of all the execution of the government of the church is handled.

. . . I have by this Bearer sent unto you A book of . . . Mr. [John] Smith our pastor. I wish you diligently to peruse and with serious judgment examine the same. And if you . . . any more of this or any other argument written by him, either for yourself or for your friends to signify the same unto us by your letters, and we will (the lord willing) procure the same.

Yours In the lord at all times to use.
Hughe and Anne Bromheade.

Source: Champlain Burrage, *The Early English Dissenters in the Light of Recent Research, 1550–1641*, 2 vols. (Cambridge: Cambridge University Press, 1912), 2:172–77.

A Declaration of Faith of English People Remaining in Amsterdam in Holland, 1611

Thomas Helwys

T O ALL THE HUMBLE MINDED who love the truth in simplicity, Grace and peace.

A Declaration, Etc.

We Believe and Confess

1.

There are THREE which bear record in heaven, the FATHER, the WORD, and the SPIRIT. These THREE are one GOD in all equality, 1 John 5.7; Philippians. 2.5, 6. By whom all things are created and preserved, in Heaven and in Earth. Genesis 1.

2.

That this GOD in the beginning created all things from nothing, Genesis 1.1. and made man from the dust of the earth, Chapter 2.7, in his own image, Chapter 1.27, in righteousness and true Holiness. Ephesians 4.24. Yet tempted, fell by disobedience. Chap. 3.1–7. Through whose disobedience, all men sinned. Romans 5.12–19. His sin was imputed to all; and so death went over all men.

3.

By the promised seed of the woman, JESUS CHRIST, and by his obedience, all are made righteous. Roman 5.19. All are made alive, 1 Corinthians 15.22. His righteousness being imputed to all.

4.

That notwithstanding this, Men are by nature the Children of wrath, Ephesians 2.3. Born in iniquity and conceived in sin. Psalm 51.5. Wise to all evil, but they have no knowledge of good. Jeremiah 4.22. *The natural man does not perceive the things of the Spirit of God.* 1 Corinthians 2.14. And therefore man is not restored to his former estate, but that as man, in his estate of innocence, having in himself all disposition to good and no disposition to evil, yet being tempted might yield, or might resist: even so now being fallen, and having all disposition to evil, and no disposition or will to any good, yet GOD giving grace, man may receive grace, or may reject grace according to that saying; Deuteronomy 30.19. *I call Heaven and Earth to record. This day against you, I have set before you life and death, blessing and cursing. Therefore choose life, so that both you and your seed may live.*

5.

That before the Foundation of the World GOD Predestined that all who believe in him will be saved, Ephesians 1.4,12; Mark 16.16. and all that do not believe will be damned. Mark 16.16. all of which he knew before. Romans 8.29. And this is the Election and reprobation spoken of in the Scriptures, concerning salvation, and condemnation, and that GOD has not Predestined men to be wicked, and so to be damned, but that men being wicked will be damned, for GOD would have all men saved, and come to the knowledge of the truth, 1 Timothy 2.4. and would have no man perish, but would have all men come to repentance. 2 Peter 3.9. and does not will the death of him that dies. Ezekiel 18.32. And therefore GOD is the author of no man's condemnation, according to the saying of the prophet. Hosea 13. Your destruction O Israel is of yourself, but your help is from me.

6.

That man is justified only by the righteousness of CHRIST, apprehended by faith, Romans 3.28. Galatians 2.16. Yet, faith without works is dead. James 2.17.

7.

Men may fall away from the grace of GOD, Hebrews 12.15. and from the truth, which they have received and acknowledged, Chapter 10.26. after they have tasted of the heavenly gift, and were made partakers of the HOLY GHOST, and have tasted of the good word of GOD, and of the powers of the world to come. Chapter 6.4,5. And after they have escaped from the filthiness of the World, may be tangled again therein and overcome. 2 Peter 2.20. A righteous man may forsake his righteousness and perish Ezekiel 18.24,26. Therefore let no man presume to think that because he has, or once had grace, therefore he shall always have grace. But let all men have assurance, that if they continue to the end, they will be saved. Let no man then presume; but let all work out their salvation with fear and trembling.

8.

That JESUS CHRIST, the Son of GOD is the second Person, or substance in the Trinity, in the Fullness of time was manifested in the Flesh, being the seed of David, and of the Israelites, according to the Flesh. Romans 1.3 and 8.5. the Son of Mary the Virgin, made of her substance, Galatians 4.4. By the power of the HOLY GHOST overshadowing her, Luke 1.35. and being thus true Man was like us in all things, sin only excepted. Hebrews 4.15. being one person in two distinct natures, TRUE GOD, and TRUE MAN.

9.

JESUS CHRIST is the Mediator of the New Testament between GOD and Man, 1 Timothy 2.5, having all power in Heaven and in Earth given to him. Matthew 28.18. He is the only KING, Luke 1.33, PRIEST, Hebrews 7.24, and PROPHET, Acts 3.22. Off his church, he is also the only Law-giver, has in his Testament set down an absolute, and perfect rule of direction, for all persons, at all times, to be observed; Which no Prince, nor any whosoever, may add to, or diminish from, as they will avoid the fearful judgments denounced against them that will do so. Revelation 22.18,19.

10.

The church of CHRIST is a company of faithful people 1 Corinthians 1.2. Ephesians 1.1, separated from the world by the word and Spirit of GOD. 2 Corinthians 6.17. being knit unto the LORD, and one to another, by Baptism. 1 Corinthians 12.13. Upon their own confession of the faith. Acts 8.37. and sins. Matthew 3.6.

11.

That though in respect of CHRIST, the Church is one, Ephesians 4.4. yet it consists of diverse particular congregations, even so many as there will be in the World, every congregation, though they are but two or three, have CHRIST given to them, with all the means of their salvation. Matthew 18.20. Romans 8.32. 1 Corinthians 3.22. They are the Body of CHRIST. 1 Corinthians 12.27. and a whole Church. 1 Corinthians 14.23. And therefore may, and should, when they come together, to Pray, Prophesy, break bread, and administer all the holy ordinances, although as yet they have no Officers, or that their Officers should be in Prison, sick, or by any other means hindered from the Church. 1 Peter 4.10 and 2.5.

12.

As one congregation has CHRIST, so do all, 2 Corinthians 10.7. And that the Word of GOD does not come out from any one, neither to any one congregation in particular. 1 Corinthians 14.36. But to every particular Church, as it does to all the world. Colossians 1.5. 6. And therefore no Church should challenge any prerogative over any other.

13.

That every Church is to receive in all their members by Baptism upon the Confession of their faith and sins wrought by the preaching of the Gospel, according to the primitive Institution, Matthew 28.19. And practice, Acts 2.41. And therefore Churches constituted after any other manner, or of any other persons are not according to CHRIST'S Testament.

14.

That Baptism or washing with Water, is the outward manifestation of dying to sin, and walking in newness of life. Romans 6.2,3,4. And therefore in no way appertains to infants.

15.

The LORD'S Supper is the outward manifestation of the Spiritual communion between CHRIST and the faithful mutually. 1 Corinthians 10.16. 17. They are to declare his death until he comes. 1 Corinthians 11.26.

16.

That the members of every Church or Congregation should know one another so that they may perform all the duties of love one towards another both to soul and body. Matthew 18.15. 1 Thessalonians 5.14. 1 Corinthians 12.25. And especially the Elders should know the whole flock, of which the HOLY GHOST has made them overseers. Acts 20.28; 1 Peter 5.2, 3. And therefore a Church should not consist of such a multitude that they cannot have particular knowledge of one another.

17.

That the Brethren who are impenitent in one sin after the admonishment of the Church are to be excluded from the communion of the Saints. Matthew 18.17. 1 Corinthians 5.4,13. Therefore the committing of sin does not cut off any from the Church, but it is the refusing to hear the Church to reformation.

18.

Excommunicants in respect of civil society are not to be avoided, 2 Thessalonians 3.15. Matthew 18.17.

19.

That every Church should (according to the example of CHRIST'S Disciples and primitive Churches) upon every first day of the week, being the LORD'S day, assemble together to pray, Prophesy, praise GOD, and break Bread, and perform all other parts of Spiritual communion for the worship of GOD, for their own mutual edification, and the preservation of true Religion, and piety in the church. John 20.19. Acts 2.42 and 20.7, 1 Corinthians 16.2. They should not labor in their callings according to the equity of the moral law, which CHRIST did not come to abolish, but to fulfill. Exodus 20.8, &c.

20.

That the Officers of every Church or congregation are either Elders, who by their office do especially feed the flock concerning their souls, Acts 20.28, 1 Peter 5.2, 3. or Deacons, Men and Women, who by their office relieve the necessities of the poor and impotent brethren concerning their bodies, Acts 6.1–4.

21.

That these Officers are to be chosen when there are persons qualified according to the rules in Christ's Testament, 1 Timothy 3.2–7. Titus 1.6–9. Acts 6.3.4. By Election and approbation of that Church or congregation whereof they are members, Acts 6.3.4 and 14.23, with Fasting, Prayer, and Laying on of hands, Acts 13.3 and 14.23. And as there is but one rule for Elders, therefore there is but one sort of Elders.

22.

That the Officers of every Church or congregation are tied by Office only to that particular congregation where they are chosen, Acts 14.23 and 20.17. Titus 1.5. Therefore they cannot challenge by office any authority in any other congregation whatsoever except they would have an Apostleship.

23.

That the scriptures of the Old and New Testament are written for our instruction, 2 Timothy 3.16 and that we should search them for they testify of CHRIST, John 5.39. Therefore they are to be used with all reverence, as containing the Holy Word of GOD, which is our only direction in all things whatsoever.

24.

The Magistracy is a Holy ordinance of GOD, that every soul should be subject to it not for fear only, but for conscience sake. Magistrates are the ministers of GOD for our wealth, they do not bear the sword for nought. They are the ministers of GOD to take vengeance on them that do evil, Romans 13. It is a fearful sin to speak evil of them that are in dignity, and to despise Government. 2 Peter 2.10. We should pay tribute, custom, and all other duties. We are to pray for them, for GOD would have them saved and come to the knowledge of his truth. 1 Timothy 2.1.4. And therefore they may be members of the Church of CHRIST, retaining their Magistracy, for no Holy Ordinance of GOD debars any from being a member of CHRIST'S Church. They bear the sword of GOD,—this sword in all Lawful administrations is to be defended and supported by the servants of GOD that are under their Government with their lives and all that they have according to the first Institution of that Holy Ordinance. And whosoever holds otherwise must hold, (if they understand themselves) that they are the ministers of the devil, and therefore not to be prayed for nor approved in any of their administrations,—seeing all things they do (as punishing offenders and defending their countries, state, and persons by the sword) is unlawful.

25.

That it is Lawful in a just cause for the deciding of strife to take an oath by the Name of the Lord. Hebrews 6.16. 2 Corinthians 1.23. Philippians 1.8.

26.

That the dead shall rise again, and the living being changed in a moment,—having the same bodies in substance though diverse in qualities. 1 Corinthians 15.52 and 38. Job 19.15–28. Luke 24.30.

27.

That after the resurrection all men will appear before the judgment seat of CHRIST to be judged according to their works, that the Godly will enjoy Eternal life, the wicked being condemned will be tormented everlastingly in Hell. Matthew 25.46.

Source: Thomas Helwys, *A Declaration of Faith of English People Remaining at Amsterdam, Holland* (Amsterdam, 1611). The only known original copy is located in the York Minister Library, England.

A Short Declaration of the Mystery of Iniquity, 1612

Thomas Helwys

HEAR, O KING AND DO not despise the counsel of the poor and let their complaints come before you.

The king is a mortal man and not God, therefore he has no power over the immortal souls of his subjects, to make laws and ordinances for them and to set spiritual lords over them.

If the king has authority to make spiritual lords and laws, then he is an immortal God and not a mortal man.

O king, do not be seduced by deceivers to sin so against God whom you should obey nor against your poor subjects who should and will obey you in all things with body, life, and goods or else let their lives be taken from the earth.

God save you the king.

Tho: Helwys
Spittlefield near London. . . .

To the Reader

The fear of the Almighty (through the work of his grace) having now at last overweighed in us the fear of men, we have thus far by the direction of God's Word and Spirit stretched out our hearts and hands with boldness to confess the name of Christ before men. We are to declare to the prince and people plainly their transgressions, that all might hear and see their fearful estate and standing, and repent, and turn to the Lord before the decree comes forth, before the day of their visitation passes, and that the things that belong to their peace is altogether hid from their eyes. In this writing we have with all humble boldness spoken to our lord the king. Our defense for this is that we are taught especially by God to make supplications, prayers, intercessions, and give thanks for our lord the king. We are taught that the gracious God of heaven (by whom the king reigns) desires that the king should be saved and come to the knowledge of the truth. Therefore, we the king's servants are especially bound by all the godly endeavors of our souls and bodies to seek the salvation of the king although it puts our lives in danger. If we saw our lord the king's person in danger either by private conspiracy or open assault we were bound to seek the king's preservation and deliverance even if it meant the laying down of our lives. Which, if we did not do so, we should be readily and most worthily be condemned as traitors. How much more are we bound to seek the preservation and deliverance of our lord the king's soul and body as we see him in such great spiritual danger as we do. If any are offended by us for doing so, they do not love the king. If our lord the king should be offended at us his servants for doing so, the king does not love himself. If all men and the king are offended with us for this (which God forbid), yet we are sure that our God will be well pleased with us in that we have with our best strength and faithfulness obeyed him who commands and teaches us to admonish all men everywhere to repent. This is our sure warrant and our assured hope and comfort. . . .

The Principle Matters Handled in the Book

The declaration with proof that these are the days of greatest tribulation, spoken of by Christ (Matthew 24), wherein the abomination of desolation is seen to be set in the holy place.

That there has been a general departing from the faith and an utter desolation of all true religion.

That the prophesy of the first beast (Revelation 13) is fulfilled under the Romish spiritual power and government.

That the prophesy of the second beast is fulfilled under the spiritual power and government of archbishops and lord bishops.

How kings will hate the whore and make her desolate.

What great power and authority, honor, names and titles God has given to the king.

That God has given to the king an earthly kingdom with all earthly power against which none may resist but must in all things obey willingly, either to do, or suffer.

That Christ alone is king of Israel, and sits upon David's throne, and that the king should be a subject of his kingdom.

That none should be punished either with death or bonds for transgressing against the spiritual ordinances of the New Testament, and that such offences should be punished only with the spiritual sword and censures.

That as the Romish hierarchy says in words that they cannot err, so the hierarchy of archbishops and lord bishops show by their deeds they hold that they cannot err and in this they agree as one.

The false profession of Puritanism (so-called) and the false prophet is discovered.

Their two deceitful excuses for their undergoing of all those things they cry out against are made manifest.

The false profession of Brownism (so-called) is plainly laid open with their false prophets, and with their false supposed separation from the world.

The vanity of their most deceitful distinction between a false church and no church (whereupon their whole false building stands) is made evident.

Some particular errors of Mr. [John] Robinson's book concerning the justification of separation is laid open.

That no man justifying any false way, or any one error, though of ignorance, can be saved.

The perverting of those words of our Savior Christ (Matthew 10) "When they persecute you in one city, flee to another," is contrary to all the meaning of Christ is plainly showed. . . .

The Mystery of Iniquity

Our lord the king has the power to take our sons and our daughters to do all his services of war and of peace, yes, and all his servile service whatsoever. He has power to take our lands and goods of whatsoever sort or kind, or the tenth of it to use at his will. He has power to take our "men servants and maid servants and the chief of our young men and cattle," and put them to his work, and we are to be his servants. . . .

. . . Does the king not know that the God of Gods and Lord of Lords has under him made our lord the king an earthly king and given him all earthly power, and that he has reserved to himself a heavenly kingdom, "a kingdom that is not of this world" . . . "neither are the subjects of his kingdom of this world?" . . . Yet this king was in the world and his subjects are in the world, and that with this kingdom our lord the king has nothing to do (by his kingly power) but as a subject himself; and that Christ is King alone, only high priest and chief bishop; and there is no king, no primate, metropolitan, archbishop, lord spiritual, but Christ only, nor may be, either in name or power to exercise authority one over another. . . .

We bow ourselves to the earth before our lord the king in greatest humbleness, beseeching the king to judge righteous judgment herein whether there is so unjust a thing and so great a cruel tyranny under the sun as to force men's consciences in their religion to God. Seeing that if they err, they must pay the price of their transgressions with the loss of their souls. O let the lord king judge, is it not most equal that men should choose their religion themselves, seeing that they only must stand them-selves before the judgment seat of God to answer for themselves? It will be no excuse for them to say we were commanded or compelled to be of this religion by the king or by them that had authority from him. . . .

Let our lord the king in all happiness and prosperity sit on his own princely throne of that mighty kingdom of Great Britain, which God has given to the king and to his posterity. May the Lord give the king a most wise heart to rule and judge his people. And may the Lord give all his people faithful hearts to love and obey him. Let all those who are the king's enemies that do not want him to reign over them be slain before him.

Let our Lord Jesus Christ in power and majesty sit upon David's throne, the throne of the kingdom of Israel, which his Father has given to him. Let Christ according to his own wisdom judge his people Israel. Let our lord the king be his subject, which our lord the king yielding himself to be. The king must grant that as he is an earthly king, he can have no power to rule in the spiritual kingdom of Christ, nor can he compel any to be subjects thereof, as a king, while the king is but a subject himself. There may be but one king in Israel. . . .

Do not let our lord the king be angry now, and his servants will speak of this but once. Will our lord the king, being himself but a subject of Christ's kingdom, take upon himself by his kingly power to make pri-mates, metropolitans, archbishops, and lord bishops to be lords in the kingdom of Christ and over the heritage of God? Will our lord the king do this against the whole rule of God's Word, wherein there is not one tittle to warrant our lord the king to do this? Will our lord the king not be supplicated by the humble petition of his servants to examine his power and authority therein? Far is it from the hearts of us, the king's servants, to move the king to depart from the least tittle of his right that belongs to his royal crown and dignity. Far be it from the king to take from Christ Jesus any one part of that power and honor which belongs to Christ in his kingdom. . . .

We still pray our lord the king that we may be free from suspicion, for having any thoughts of provoking evil against them of the Romish religion, in regard of their profession, if they are true and faithful subjects to the king. For we do freely profess that our lord the king has no more power over their consciences than over ours, and that is none at all. For our lord the king is but an earthly king, and he has no authority as a king but in earthly causes. If the king's people are obedient and true subjects, obeying all human laws made by the king, our lord the king can require no more. For men's religion to God is between God and themselves. The king will not answer for it. Neither may the king be judge between God and man. Let them be heretics, Turks, Jews, or whatsoever, it appertains not to the earthly power to punish them in the least measure. . . .

Source: Thomas Helwys, *A Short Declaration of the Mystery of Iniquity* (Amsterdam: n.p., 1612). Facsimiles of the original, usually in microform, are available at various libraries in the United States and Great Britain. In matters of capitalization, I followed Thomas Helwys, *A Short Declaration of the Mystery of Iniquity,* ed. Richard Groves (Macon, GA: Mercer University Press, 1998).

5

THE BEGINNINGS OF THE
PARTICULAR BAPTISTS AND THE
BIRTH OF IMMERSION, 1633

[1633] SUNDRY OF THE CHURCH where Mr. Jacob and Mr. John Lathrop had been Pastors, being dissatisfied with the Churches owned by English Parishes to be true Churches desired dismission and Joined together among themselves, as Mr. Henry Parker, Mr. Tho. Shepherd, Mr. Sam. Eaton, Marke Luker, and others with whom joined Mr. William Kiffin.

[1638] Mr. Tho. Wilson, Mr. Pen, and H. Pen, and three more being convinced that Baptism was not for Infants, but professed Believers joined with Mr. Jo. Spilsbury the Churches favor being desired therein.

[1640] 3d MO: The Church became two by mutual consent just half being with Mr. P[raisegod] Barebone, and the other half with Mr. H. Jessey Mr. Richard Blunt with him being convinced of Baptism and that it also should be by dipping the Body into the Water, resembling Burial and rising again. Col: 2, 12. Rom. 6. 4. We had a sober conference about it in the Church and then with some of the forenamed who were also so convinced. After Prayer and conference about their so enjoying it, none having then so practiced it in England to professed Believers, and hearing that some in the Netherlands had so practiced they agreed and sent over Mr. Rich. Blunt (who understood Dutch) with Letters of Commendation, who was kindly accepted there, and returned with Letters from them, Jo: Batte a Teacher there, and from that Church to such that sent him.

They proceed on therein, viz, Those Persons who were yet persuaded Baptism should be by dipping the Body had met in two Companies, and did intend so to meet after this, all these agreed to proceed alike together.

And then Manifesting (not by any formal Words or Covenant) which word was scrupled by some of them, but by mutual desires and agreement each Testified. Those two Companies did set apart one to Baptize the rest. So it was solemnly performed by them.

Mr. Blunt Baptized Mr. Blacklock who was a Teacher among them, and Mr. Blunt being Baptized, he and Mr. Blacklock Baptized the rest of their friends that were so minded, and many being added to them they increased much. . . .

Those that were so minded had communion together were to become the Seven Churches in London.

Mr. Green with Cap. Spencer had begun a Congregation in Crutched Fryers, to whom Paul Hobson joined who was now with many of that Church; one of the Seven.

These being much spoken against as unsound in Doctrine as if they were Arminians, and also against Magistrates &c they joined together in a Confession of their Faith in fifty-two Articles which gave great satisfaction to many that had been prejudiced.

Thus Subscribed in the Names of the 7 Churches in London.

Wm: Kiffin		
Tho: Patience	Tho: Gun	Paul Hobson
	Jo: Mabbet	Tho: Goore
Geo: Tipping		
John Spilsbury	John Web	Jo: Phelps
	Tho: Kilcop	Edward Heath
Tho: Shephard		
Tho: Munden		

Original Source: Translations of the Baptist Historical Society (London: Baptist Union Publication Department), 1 (1908–9): 230–36.

6

THE BLOUDY TENNENT OF PERSECUTION, 1644

Roger Williams

... FIRST. THAT THE BLOOD OF so many hundred thousand souls of protestants and papists, spilled in the wars of present and former ages, for their respective consciences, is not required nor accepted by Jesus Christ the Prince of Peace.

Secondly. Pregnant scriptures and arguments are throughout the work proposed against the doctrine of persecution for cause of conscience.

Thirdly. Satisfactory answers are given to scriptures and objections produced by Mr. [John] Calvin, [Theodore] Beza, Mr. [John] Cotton, and the ministers of the New English churches, and others former and later, tending to prove the doctrine of persecution for cause of conscience.

Fourthly. The doctrine of persecution for cause of conscience, is proved guilty of all the blood of the souls crying for vengeance under the altar.

Fifthly. All civil states, with their officers of justice, in their respective constitutions and administrations, are proved essentially civil, and therefore not judges, governors, or defenders of the spiritual, or Christian, state and worship.

Sixthly. It is the will and command of God that, since the coming of his Son the Lord Jesus, a permission of the most Paganish, Jewish, Turkish, or anti-christian consciences and worships be granted to all men in all nations and countries: and they are only to be fought against with that sword which is only, in soul matters, able to conquer: to wit, the sword of God's Spirit, the word of God.

Seventhly. The state of the land of Israel, the kings and people thereof, in peace and war, is proved figurative and ceremonial, and no pattern nor precedent for any kingdom or civil state in the world to follow.

Eighthly. God does not require any uniformity of religion to be enacted and enforced in any civil state; which enforced uniformity, sooner or later, is the greatest occasion of civil war, ravishing of conscience, persecution of Christ Jesus in his servants, and of the hypocrisy and destruction of millions of souls.

Ninthly. In holding an enforced uniformity of religion in a civil state, we must disclaim our desires and hopes of the Jews' conversion to Christ.

Tenthly. An enforced uniformity of religion throughout a nation or civil state, confounds the civil and religious, denies the principles of Christianity and civility, and that Jesus Christ is come in the flesh.

Eleventhly. The permission of other consciences and worships than a state professes, only can, according to God, procure a firm and lasting peace; good assurance being taken, according to the wisdom of the civil state, for uniformity of civil obedience from all sorts.

Twelfthly. Lastly, true civility and Christianity may both flourish in a state or kingdom, notwithstanding the permission of divers and contrary consciences, . . .

To Every Courteous Reader

WHILE I plead the cause of truth and innocence against the bloody doctrine of persecution for cause of conscience, I judge it not unfit to give alarm to myself, and to all men, to prepare to be persecuted or hunted for cause of conscience.

Whether you stand charged with ten or but two talents, if you hunt any for cause of conscience, how can you say you follow the Lamb of God, who so abhorred that practice? . . .

Two mountains of crying guilt lie heavy upon the backs of all men that name the name of Christ, in the eyes of Jews, Turks, and Pagans.

First. The blasphemies of their idolatrous inventions, superstitions, and most unchristian conversations.

Secondly. The bloody, irreligious, and inhuman oppressions and destructions under the mask or veil of the name of Christ, &c. . . .

Who can now but expect that after so many scores of years preaching and professing of more truth, and amongst so many great contentions among the very best of protestants, a fiery furnace should be heated, and who sees not now the fires kindling? . . .

. . . Yet in the midst of all these civil and spiritual wars, I hope we shall agree in these particulars,

First. However the proud (upon the advantage of a higher earth or ground) overlook the poor, and cry out schismatics, heretics, &c., shall blasphemers and seducers escape unpunished? Yet there is a sorer punishment in the gospel for the despising of Christ than Moses, even when the despiser of Moses was put to death without mercy, Heb. x. 28, 29. *He that believeth shall not be damned*, Mark xvi. 16.

Secondly. Whatever worship, ministry, ministration, the best and purest, are practiced without faith and true persuasion that they are the true institutions of God, they are sin, sinful worships, ministries, &c. And however in civil things we may be servants unto men, yet in divine and spiritual things the poorest peasant must disdain the service of the highest prince. *Be ye not the servants of men*, 1 Cor. vii.

Thirdly. Without search and trial no man attains this faith and right persuasion. 1 Thes. v. *Try all things*.

In vain have English parliaments permitted English bibles in the poorest English houses, and the simplest man or woman to search the scriptures, if yet against their souls persuasion from the scripture, they should be forced, as if they lived in Spain or Rome itself without the sight of a bible, to believe as the church believes.

Fourthly. Having tried, we must hold fast, 1 Thes. v., upon the loss of a crown, Rev. iii; we must not let go for all the fleabitings of the present afflictions, &c. Having bought truth dear, we must not sell it cheap, . . .

SCRIPTURES AND REASONS,

WRITTEN LONG SINCE BY A WITNESS OF JESUS CHRIST,

CLOSE PRISONER IN NEWGATE,

AGAINST PERSECUTION IN CAUSE OF CONSCIENCE;

AND SENT SOME WHILE SINCE TO MR. COTTON

Whether persecution for cause of conscience is not against the doctrine of Jesus Christ, the King of kings. The scriptures and reasons are these.

1. BECAUSE Christ commands, that the tares and wheat, which some understand are those that walk in the truth, and those that walk in lies, should be let alone in the world, and not plucked up until the harvest, which is the end of the world. Matt. xiii. 30, 38, &c.

2. The same commands, Matt. xv. 14, that they are blind (as some interpret, led on in false religion, and are offended with him for teaching true religion) should be let alone, referring their punishment unto their falling into the ditch.

22

3. Again, Luke ix. 54, 55, he reproved his disciples who would have had fire come down from heaven and devour those Samaritans who would not receive Him, in these words: *"Ye know not of what Spirit ye are; the Son of man is not come to destroy men's lives, but to save them."*

4. Paul, the apostle of our Lord, taught, 2 Tim. ii. 24, *that the servant of the Lord must not strive, but must be gentle toward all men; suffering the evil men, instructing them with meekness that are contrary minded, proving if God at any time will give them repentance, that they may acknowledge the truth, and come to amendment out of that snare of the devil, &c.*

5. According to these blessed commandments, the holy prophets foretold, that when the law of Moses concerning worship should cease, and Christ's kingdom is established, Isa. ii. 4; Mic. iv. 3, 4, *They shall break their swords into mattocks, and their spears into scythes.* And Isa. xi. 9, *Then shall none hurt nor destroy in all the mountain of my holiness,* &c. And when he came, the same he taught and practiced, as before. So did his disciples after him, for *the weapons of his warfare are not carnal* (says the apostle), 2 Cor. x. 4.

But he charges straightly, that his disciples should be so far from persecuting those that would not be of their religion, that when they were persecuted they should pray, Matt. v. 44; when they were cursed, they should bless, &c.

And the reason seems to be, because they who now are tares, may hereafter become wheat; they who are now blind, may hereafter see; they that now resist him, may here after receive him; they that are now in the devil's snare, in adverseness to the truth, may hereafter come to repentance; they that are now blasphemers and persecutors, as Paul was, may in time become faithful as he; they that are now idolaters, as the Corinthians once were, 1 Cor. vi. 9, may hereafter become true worshippers as they; they that are now no people of God, nor under mercy, as the saints sometimes were, 1 Pet. ii. 10, may hereafter become the people of God, and obtain mercy, as they. . . .

THE ANSWER OF MR. JOHN COTTON,

OF BOSTON, IN NEW ENGLAND,

TO THE AFORESAID ARGUMENTS AGAINST PERSECUTION FOR CAUSE OF CONSCIENCE,

PROFESSEDLY MAINTAIND

PERSECUTION FOR CAUSE OF CONSCIENCE

The question which you put is, whether persecution for cause of conscience is not against the doctrine of Jesus Christ, the King of kings?

Now, by persecution for cause of conscience, I conceive you mean, either for professing some point of doctrine which you believe in conscience to be the truth, or for practicing some work which in conscience you believe to be a religious duty.

Now in points of doctrine some are fundamental, without right belief whereof a man cannot be saved; other are circumstantial, or less principal, wherein men may differ in judgment without prejudice of salvation on either part.

In like sort, in points of practice, some concern the weightier duties of the law, as, what God we worship, and with what kind of worship; whether such as, if it be right, fellowship with God is held; if corrupt, fellowship with him is lost.

Again, in points of doctrine and worship less principal, either they are held forth in a meek and peaceable way, though the things are erroneous or unlawful: or they are held forth with such arrogance and impetuousness, as tends and reaches (even of itself) to disturb the peace.

Finally, let me add this one distinction more: when we are persecuted for conscience's sake, it is either for conscience rightly informed, or for erroneous and blind conscience.

These things premised, I would lay down my answer to the question in certain conclusions.

First, it is not lawful to persecute any for conscience's sake rightly informed; for in persecuting such, Christ himself is persecuted in them, Acts ix. 4.

Secondly, for an erroneous and blind conscience, (even in fundamental and weighty points) it is not lawful to persecute any, till the admonition once or twice; and so the apostle directed, Tit. iii. 10, and gives the reason, that in the fundamental and principal points of doctrine or worship, the word of God in such things is so clear, that he cannot but be convinced in conscience of the dangerous error of his way after one or two admonitions, wisely and faithfully dispensed. And then, if anyone persist, it is not out of conscience, but against his conscience, as the apostle says, ver. 11, *He is subverted and sins, being condemned of himself*; that is, of his own conscience. So that if such a man, after such admonition, shall still persist in the error of his way, and be therefore punished, he is not persecuted for the cause of conscience, but for sinning.

But if a man holds forth, or professes, any error or false way, with a boisterous and arrogant spirit, to the disturbing of the peace, he may

justly be punished according to the quality and measure of the disturbance he has caused.

A REPLY

TO THE

AFORESAID ANSWER OF MR. COTTON,

IN A CONFERENCE BETWEEN TRUTH AND PEACE.

CHAP. II

Truth. Sweet Peace, what have you there?

Peace. Arguments against persecution for cause of conscience.

Truth. And what there?

Peace. An answer to such arguments, contrarily maintaining such
persecution for cause of conscience.

Truth. These arguments against such persecution, and the answer
pleading for it are written, as Love hopes, from godly intentions, hearts,
and hands, yet in a marvelously different style and manner—the arguments against persecution in milk, the answer for it, as I may say, in
blood.

The author of these arguments against persecution, as I have been
informed, being committed by some then in power a close prisoner to
Newgate, for the witness of some truths of Jesus, and having not the use
of pen and ink, wrote these arguments in milk, in sheets of paper brought
to him by the woman, his keeper, from a friend in London as the stopples
of his milk bottle.

In such paper, written with milk, nothing will appear; but the way of
reading it by fire known to this friend who received the papers, he transcribed and kept together the papers, although the author himself could
not correct, nor view what he himself had written. . . .

Peace. The answer, though I hope out of milky pure intentions, is
returned in blood—bloody and slaughterous conclusions—bloody to
the souls of all men, forced to the religion and worship which every
civil state or commonwealth agrees on, and compels subjects to, in a
dissembled uniformity:—

Bloody to the bodies, first of the holy witnesses of Christ Jesus, who
testify against such invented worships:—

Secondly, of the nations and peoples slaughtering each other for their
several respective religions and consciences.

CHAP. III.

Truth. In the answer, Mr. Cotton first lays down several distinctions and conclusions of his own, tending to prove persecution.

Secondly. Answers to the scriptures and arguments proposed against persecution.

Peace. The first distinction is this: by persecution for cause of conscience, "I conceive you mean either for professing some point of doctrine which you believe in conscience to be the truth, or for practicing some work which you believe in conscience to be religious duty."

Truth. I acknowledge that to molest any person, Jew or Gentile, for either professing doctrine, or practicing worship merely religious or spiritual, it is to persecute him; and such a person, whatever his doctrine or practice is, true or false, suffering persecution for conscience.

. . . So thousands of Christ's witnesses, and of late in those bloody Marian days, have chosen to yield their bodies to all sorts of torments, than to subscribe to doctrines, or practice worships, unto which the states and times (as Nebuchadnezzar to his golden image) have compelled and urged them. . . .

CHAP. IV.

Peace. The second distinction is this:—

"In points of doctrine some are fundamental, without right belief whereof a man cannot be saved; others are circumstantial and less principal, wherein a man may differ in judgment without prejudice of salvation on either part."

Truth. To this distinction I dare not subscribe, for then I should everlastingly condemn thousands, and ten thousands, yea, the whole generation of the righteous, who since the falling away from the first primitive Christian state or worship, have and do err fundamentally concerning the true matter, constitution, gathering, and governing of the church. . . .

CHAP. V.

Peace. With lamentation, I may add, how can their souls be clear in this foundation of the true Christian matter, who persecute and oppress their own acknowledged brethren, presenting light unto them about this point? But I shall now present you with Mr. Cotton's third distinction. "In points of practice," says he, "some concern the weightier duties of the law, as what God we worship, and with what kind of worship; whether such, as if it be right, fellowship with God is held; if false, fellowship with God is lost."

Truth. It is worth the inquiry, what kind of worship he intended: for worship is of various signification. Whether in general acceptation he means the rightness or corruptness of the church, or the ministry of the church, or the ministrations of the word, prayer, seals, &c. . . .

First, concerning the ministry of the word. The New English ministers, when they were new elected and ordained ministers in New England, must undeniably grant, at that time they were no ministers. . . . I apply, and ask, will it not follow, that if their new ministry and ordination is true, the former was false? and if false, that in the exercise of it, notwithstanding abilities, graces, intentions, labors, and, by God's gracious, unpromised, and extraordinary blessing, some success, I say, will it not according to this distinction follow, that according to visible rule, fellowship with God was lost?

Secondly, concerning prayer. The New English ministers have disclaimed and written against that worshipping of God by the common or set forms of prayer, which yet themselves practiced in England, notwithstanding they knew that many servants of God, in great sufferings, witnessed against such a ministry of the word, and such a ministry of prayer.

Peace. I could name the persons, time, and place, when some of them were faithfully admonished for using the Common Prayer, and the arguments presented to them, then seeming weak, but now acknowledged sound; yet, at that time, they satisfied their hearts with the practice of the author of the Council of Trent, who used to read only some of the choicest selected prayers in the mass-book, which I confess was also their own practice in their using of the Common Prayer. But now, according to this distinction, I ask whether or not fellowship with God in such prayers was lost? . . .

CHAP. VI.

Peace. The next distinction concerns the manner of persons holding forth the afore said practices, not only the weightier duties of the law, but points of doctrine and worship less principal:—

"Some," says he, "hold them forth in a meek and peaceable way; some with such arrogance and impetuousness, as of itself tends to disturb the civil peace."

Truth. In the examination of this distinction we shall discuss,

First, what is civil peace (wherein we shall vindicate your name the better),

Secondly, what it is to hold forth a doctrine, or practice, in this impetuousness or arrogancy.

First, for civil peace, what is it but *pax civitatis*, the peace of the city, whether an English city, Scotch, or Irish city, or further abroad, French, Spanish, Turkish city &c. . . .

Peace. Hence it is that so many glorious and flourishing cities of the world maintain their civil peace; yes, the very Americans and wildest pagans keep the peace of their towns or cities, though neither in one nor the other can any man prove a true church of God in those places, and consequently no spiritual and heavenly peace. The peace spiritual, whether true or false, being of a higher and far different nature from the peace of the place or people, being merely and essentially civil and human.

Truth. Oh! how lost are the sons of men in this point! To illustrate this:—the church or company of worshippers, whether true or false, is like unto a body or college of physicians in a city—like unto a corporation, society, or company of East India or Turkey merchants, or any other society or company in London; which companies may . . . wholly break up and dissolve into pieces and nothing, and yet the peace of the city not be in the least measure impaired or disturbed; because the essence or being of the city, and so the well being and peace thereof, is essentially distinct from those particular societies; . . .

CHAP. XLIV.

Peace. The next scripture produced against such persecution is 2 Cor. x. 4, *The weapons of our warfare are not carnal, but mighty through God to the pulling down of strongholds; casting down imaginations, and every high thing that exalts itself against the knowledge of God, and bringing into captivity every thought to the obedience of Christ: and having in a readiness to avenge all disobedience, &c.*

Unto which it is answered, "When Paul says, *The weapons of our warfare are not carnal, but spiritual,* he does not deny civil weapons of justice to the civil magistrate, Rom. xiii., but only to church officers. . . .

Truth. I acknowledge that herein the Spirit of God does not deny civil weapons of justice to the civil magistrate, . . .

Yet withal, I must ask, why he here affirms the apostle denies not civil weapons of justice to the civil magistrate? Of which there is no question, unless that, according to his scope of proving persecution for conscience, he intends withal that the apostle denies not civil weapons of justice to the civil magistrate in spiritual and religious causes: the contrary whereunto, the Lord assisting, I shall evince, both from this very scripture and his own observation, and lastly by that thirteenth of the Romans, by himself quoted.

First, then, from this scripture and his own observation. The weapons of church officers, he says, are such, which though they are spiritual, are ready to take vengeance on all disobedience; which has reference, says he, among other ordinances, to the censures of the church against scandalous offenders.

I hence observe, that there is in this scripture held forth a twofold state, a civil state and a spiritual, civil officers and spiritual, civil weapons and spiritual weapons, civil vengeance and punishment and a spiritual vengeance and punishment: although the spirit does not expressly speak here of civil magistrates and their civil weapons, yet, these states are of different natures and considerations, as far differing as spirit from flesh, I first observe, that civil weapons are most improper and unfitting in matters of the spiritual state and kingdom, though in the civil state most proper and suitable. . . .

CHAP. XLV.

. . . 2. I observe that as civil weapons are improper in this business, and never able to effect aught in the soul: so although they were proper, yet they are unnecessary; for if, as the Spirit here says, and the answerer grants, spiritual weapons in the hand of church officers are able and ready to take vengeance on all disobedience, that is, able and mighty, sufficient and ready for the Lord's work, either to save the soul, or to kill the soul of whomsoever be the party or parties opposite; in which respect I may again remember that speech of Job, *How have you helped him that has no power?* Job xxvi. 2. . . .

[*Truth*] Will the Lord Jesus (did He ever in his own person practice, or did he appoint to) join to his breastplate of righteousness, the breastplate of iron and steel? To the helmet of righteousness and salvation in Christ, a helmet and crest of iron, brass, or steel? A target of wood to His shield of faith? To His two-edged sword, coming forth of the mouth of Jesus, the material sword, the work of smiths and cutlers? Or a girdle of shoe-leather to the girdle of truth? &c. . . .

CHAP. XLVIII.

Peace. I pray now proceed to the second argument from this scripture, against the use of civil weapons in matters of religions, and spiritual worship.

Truth. The Spirit of God here commands subjection and obedience to higher powers, even to the Roman emperors and all subordinate magistrates; and yet the emperors and governors under them were strangers from the life of God in Christ, yes, most averse and opposite, yes, cruel and bloody persecutors of the name and followers of Jesus: and yet unto these, is this subjection and obedience commanded. . . .

Now then I argue, if the apostle should have commanded this subjection unto Roman emperors and Roman magistrates in spiritual causes, as to defend the truth which they were no way able to discern, . . .

Or else to punish heretics, whom then also they must discern and judge, . . . I say, if Paul should have, in this scripture, put this work upon these Roman governors, and commanded the churches of Christ to have yielded subjection in any such matters, he must, in the judgment of all men, have put out the eye of faith, and reason, and sense, at once. . . .

CHAP. L.

Peace. Which is the third argument against the civil magistrates' power in spiritual and soul-matters out of this scripture, Rom. xiii.?

Truth. I dispute from the nature of the magistrates' weapons, ver. 4. He has a sword, which he bears not in vain, delivered to him, as I acknowledge from God's appointment in the free consent and choice of the subjects for the common good.

We must distinguish of swords.

We find four sorts of swords mentioned in the New Testament.

First, the sword of persecution, which Herod stretched forth against James, Acts xii. 1, 2.

Secondly, the sword of God's Spirit, expressly said to be the word of God, . . .

Thirdly, the great sword of war and destruction, given to him that rides that terrible red horse of war, . . .

None of these three swords are intended in this scripture.

Therefore, fourthly, there is a civil sword, called the sword of civil justice, which being of a material, civil nature, . . . cannot extend to spiritual and soul-causes, spiritual and soul-punishment, which belongs to that spiritual sword. . . .

CHAP. LI.

Truth. A fourth argument from this scripture, I take in the sixth verse, from tribute, custom, &c.: which is a merely civil reward, or recompense, for the magistrate's work. Now as the wages are, such is the work; but the wages are merely civil—custom, tribute, &c.: not the contributions of the saints or churches of Christ, proper to the spiritual and Christian state. And such work only must the magistrate attend upon, as may properly deserve such civil wages, reward, or recompense.

Lastly, that the Spirit of God never intended to direct, or warrant, the magistrate to use his power in spiritual affairs and religious worship, I argue from the term or title it pleased the wisdom of God to give such civil officers, to wit, ver. 6, *God's ministers.* . . .

Truth. I conclude . . . that the Christian church does not persecute; no more than a lily scratches the thorns, or a lamb pursues and tears the wolves, or a turtle-dove hunts the hawks and eagles, or a chaste and a modest virgin fights and scratches like whores and harlots.

Source: Roger Williams, *The Bloudy Tennent of Persecution for Cause of Conscience Discussed* (London: n.p., 1644; repr., Hanserd Knollys Society, London, 1848), 1–2, 7–12, 19–21, 36–39, 41–45, 117–19, 126–27, 130–31.

7

THE WHIPPING OF OBADIAH
HOLMES, 1651

John Clarke

The Sentence of Obadiah Holmes of
Seacuck, the 31 of the 5th M. 1651.

FORASMUCH AS YOU OBADIAH HOLMES, being come into this Jurisdiction about the 21 of the 5th M. did meet at one William Witters house at Lin, and did hear privately (and at other times being an Excommunicate person did take it upon yourself to Preach and to Baptize) upon the Lord's day, or other days, and being taken then by the Constable, and coming afterward to the Assembly at Lin, did in disrespect of the Ordinance of God and his Worship, keep on your hat, the Pastor being in Prayer, insomuch that you would not give reverence in veiling your hat, till it was forced off your head to the disturbance of the Congregation, and professing against the Institution of the Church, as not being according to the Gospel of Jesus Christ, and that you the said Obadiah Holmes did upon the day following meet again at the said William Witters, in contempt to Authority, you being then in the custody of the Law, and did there receive the Sacrament, being Excommunicate, and that you did Baptize such as were Baptized before, and thereby did necessarily deny the Baptism that was before administered to be Baptism, the Churches no Churches, and also other Ordinances, and Ministers, as if all were Nullity; And also did deny the lawfullness of Baptizing of Infants, and all this tends to the dishonor of God, the despising of the ordinances of God among us, the peace of the Churches, and seducing the Subjects of this Commonwealth from the truth of the Gospel of Jesus Christ, and perverting the strait ways of the Lord, the Court does fine you 30 pounds to be paid, or sufficient sureties that the said sum shall be paid by the first day of the next Court of Assistants, or else to be well whipped, and that you shall remain in Prison until it is paid, or security given in for it.

By the Court, ENCREASE NOWELL
And now because of his sufferings, . . . the sense which his Soul felt of the Lord's Support, according to promise, is affectionately set forth, . . . in a Letter written with his own hand, and sent unto those that have obtained like precious faith in *London*. . . . The words of his Letter follow.

Unto the well beloved Brethren John Spilsbury, William Kiffin, and the rest that in London stand fast in that Faith; and continue to walk stedfastly in that Order of the Gospel which was once delivered unto the Saints by Jesus Christ: Obadiah Holm[e]s an unworthy witness, that Jesus is the Lord, and of late a Prisoner for Jesus sake at Boston, sends greetings.

Dearly Beloved and longed after,
My hearts desire is to hear from you, and to hear that you grow in grace, and in the knowledge of our Lord and Savior Jesus Christ, . . . I shall the rather import unto you some dealings which I have had therein from the Sons of Men, and the gracious support which I have met with from the Son of God, my Lord and yours, that so like Members you might rejoice with me, and might be encouraged by the same experience of his tender mercies, to fear none of those things which you shall suffer for Jesus sake.

I had no sooner separated from their assemblies, and from Communion with them in their worship of God, . . . but immediately the adversary cast out a flood against us, and stirred up the spirits of men to present myself and two more to *Plymouth* Court, . . . whereupon the Court straitly charged us to desist, . . . yet it pleased the Father of mercies (to whom be the praise) to give us strength to stand, and to tell them it was better to obey God rather than man. . . .

Not long after these troubles I came upon occasion of business to the Colony of the Massachusetts, with two other Brethren as Brother [John] *Clark* being one of the two can inform you, where we three were apprehended, carried to the prison at *Boston*, and so to the Court, and were all sentenced. . . . Upon pronouncing of which as I went to the Bar, I expressed myself in these words: I bless God I am counted worthy to suffer for the name of Jesus; whereupon *John Wilson* (their Pastor as they call him) took me before the Judgment Seat, and cursed me, saying, The Curse of God, or Jesus go with thee; so we were carried to the Prison where not long after I was deprived of my two loving Friends; at whose departure the Adversary stepped in, and took hold on my Spirit, and troubled me for the space of an hour, and then the Lord came in, and sweetly relieved me, . . .

I betook myself to my Chamber, where I might communicate with my God, commit myself to him, and beg strength from him; I had no sooner sequestered myself, and come into my Chamber, but Satan lets fly at me, saying, Remember yourself, your birth, breeding, and friends, your wife, children, name, and credit but as this was sudden, so there came in sweetly from the Lord as sudden an answer, 'tis for my Lord, I must not deny him before the Sons of men. . . . But then came in the consideration of the weakness of the Flesh to bear the strokes of a whip, though the Spirit was willing, and hereupon I was caused to pray earnestly unto the Lord, that he would be pleased to give me a spirit of courage and boldness, a tongue to speak for him, and strength of body to suffer for his sake, . . .

And when I heard the voice of my Keeper come for me, even cheerfulness did come upon me, and taking my Testament in my hand, I went along with him to the place of execution, and after common salutation there stood; there stood by also one of the Magistrates, by name *Mr. Encrease Nowell*, who for a while kept silent, and spoke not a word, and so did I, expecting the Governor's presence, but he did not come. But after a while *Mr. Nowell* bade the Executioner do his Office, then I desired to speak a few words, but *Mr. Nowell* answered, it is not now a time to speak, whereupon I took leave, and said, *Men, Brethren, Fathers, and Country-men, I beseech you to give me leave to speak a few words, and the rather because here are many Spectators to see me punished, and I am to seal with my Blood, if God give me strength, that which I hold and practice in reference to the Word of God, and the testimony of Jesus; that which I have to say in brief is this, Although I confess I am no Disputant, yet seeing I am to seal what I hold with my Blood, I am ready to defend it by the Word, and to dispute that point with any that shall come forth to withstand it.*

Mr. Nowell answered me, now was no time to dispute, then said I, then I desire to give an account of the Faith and Order I hold, and this I desired three times, but in comes *Mr. Flint*, and says to the Executioner, Fellow, do your Office, for this Fellow would but make a long Speech to delude the people; . . .

The Whipping of Obadiah Holmes—John Clarke

And as the man began to lay the strokes upon my back, I said to the people, though my Flesh should fail, and my Spirit should fail, yet God would not fail; so it pleased the Lord to come in, and so to fill my heart and tongue as a vessel full, and with an audible voice I broke forth, praying to the Lord not to lay this Sin to their charge, and telling the people, That now I found he did not fail me, and therefore now I should trust him forever who failed me not; for in truth, as the strokes fell upon me, I had such a spiritual manifestation of God's presence, as the like thereto I never had, nor felt, nor can with fleshly tongue express, and the outward pain was so removed from me, that indeed I am not able to declare it to you, it was so easy to me, that I could well bear it, . . . when he had loosed me from the Post, having joyfulness in my heart, and cheerfulness in my countenance, as the Spectators observed, I told the Magistrates, you have struck me as with Roses. . . .

And now being advised to make my escape by night, because it was reported that there were Warrants forth for me, I departed; and the next day after, while I was on my Journey, the Constable came to search at the house where I lodged, so I escaped their hands, and was by the good hand of my heavenly Father brought home again to my near relations, my wife and eight children, the Brethren of our Town and *Providence* having taken pains to meet me 4 miles in the woods, where we rejoiced together in the Lord.

Source: John Clarke, *Ill Newes from New-England: or A Narrative of New-Englands Persecution, Wherein is Declared, That while old England is Becoming new, New-England is become Old* (London: n.p., 1652), 16–22.

35

The Power of the Association, 1749

Philadelphia Baptist Association

A T OUR ANNUAL ASSOCIATION, MET September 19th, 1749, an essay on the power and duty of an Association of churches was proposed, as above hinted, to the consideration of the Association; and the same, upon mature deliberation, was approved and subscribed by the whole house; and the contents of the same was ordered to be transcribed as the judgment of the Association, in order to be inserted in the Association book, to the end and purpose that it may appear what power and Association of churches has, and what duty is incumbent on an Association; and prevent the contempt with which some are ready to treat such an assembly, and also to prevent any further generation from claiming more power than they ought—lording over the churches.

Essay

That an Association is not a superior judicature, having such superior power over the churches concerned; but that each particular church has complete power and authority from Jesus Christ, to administer all gospel ordinances, provided they have a sufficiency of officers duly qualified, or that they are supplied by the officers of another sister church or churches, as baptism, and the Lord's supper &c;. and to receive in and cast out, and also to try and ordain their own officers, and to exercise every part of gospel discipline and church government, independent of any other church or assembly whatever.

And that several independent churches, where Providence gives them their situation convenient, may, and ought, for their mutual strength, counsel, and other valuable advantages, by their voluntary and free consent, to enter into an agreement and confederation, as is hinted in our printed Narrative of discipline. . . .

Such churches there must be agreeing in doctrine and practice, and independent in their authority and church power, before they can enter into a confederation, as aforesaid, and choose delegates or representatives, to associate together; and thus the several independent churches being the constituents, the association, council or assembly of their delegates, when assembled, is not to be deemed a superior judicature, as having a superintendency over the churches, but subservient to the churches, in what may concern all the churches in general, or any one church in particular; and, though no power can regularly rise above its fountain from where it rises, yet we are of the opinion, that an Association of delegates of associate churches have a very considerable power in their hands, respecting those churches in their confederation; for if the agreement of several distinct churches, in sound doctrine and regular practice is the first motive; ground, and foundation or basis of their confederation, then it must naturally follow, that a defection in doctrine or practice in any church, in such a confederation, or any party in any such church, is ground sufficient for an Association to withdraw from such a church or party so deviating or making defection, and to exclude such from them in some formal manner, and to advertise all the churches in the confederation thereof, in order that every church in the confederation, may withdraw from such in all acts of church communion, to the end they may be ashamed, and that all the churches may discountenance such, and bear testimony against the defection.

. . . A godly man may, and ought to withdraw, not only from the heathen, but from such as have the form of godliness, if they appear to want the power of it, 2 Tim. iii. 5, by the same parity of reason the saints, in what capacity so ever they may be considered, may withdraw from defective or disorderly churches or persons; but excommunicate they cannot, there being no institution to authorize them to do so. But in the capacity of a congregational church, dealing with her own members, an Association, then, of the delegates of associate churches, may exclude and withdraw from defective and unsound or disorderly churches or persons, in manner above said; and this will appear regular and justifiable by the light and law of nature, as is apparent in the conduct and practice of all regular civil and political corporations and confederations whatsoever; all of which have certain rules to exclude delinquents from their societies, as well as for others to accede thereunto.

And further, that an Association of the delegates of the confederate church may doctrinally declare any person or party in a church, who are defective in principles or disorderly in practice, to be censurable, when the affair comes under the cognizance, and without exceeding the bounds of their power and duty, to advise the church that such belongs unto, how to deal with such, according to the rule of gospel discipline; and also to strengthen such a church, and assist her, if need be, by sending able men of their own number to help the church in executing the power vested in her by the ordinances of Jesus Christ, and to stand by her, and to defend her against the insults of such offending persons or parties.

Source: A. D. Gillette, ed., *Minutes of the Philadelphia Baptist Association from A.D. 1707 to A.D. 1807* (Philadelphia: American Baptist Publication Society, 1851), 60–63.

9

The Birth of the Charleston Association, 1751

Ward Furman

T HE SETTLEMENT OF MR. [OLIVER] Hart in Charleston is an important event in the annals of these churches. His unexpected arrival while the church was destitute of a supply, and immediately after the death of the excellent man who had occasionally officiated for them, was believed to have been directed by a special providence in their favor. He undertook the pastoral office with much seriousness, and soon entered on an extensive field of usefulness. His ardent piety and philanthropy, his discriminating mind and persuasive address, soon raised him in high esteem of the public, and gave him a distinguished claim to the affections of his brethren. Between him and the Rev. Mr. Pelot actuated by the same principles and possessing very respectable talents, a cordial intimacy commenced. Mr. Hart had seen, in the Philadelphia Association, the happy consequences of union and stated intercourse among churches maintaining the same faith and order. To accomplish similar purposes, a union of the four Churches before mentioned was contemplated and agreed on. Accordingly on the 21st of Oct. 1751 Delegates from Ashley River and Welch Neck met those of Charleston in the said City. The Messengers from Euhaw were prevented from attending. It was agreed that an annual meeting thenceforward be held on Saturday preceding the 2nd Sabbath of Nov. to consist of the Ministers and messengers of the several Churches: that the two first days should be employed in public worship, and a Sermon introductory to business preached on the Monday following at 10 o'clock.

The object of the Union was declared to be the promotion of the Redeemer's kingdom, by the maintenance of love and fellowship, and by mutual consultations for the peace and welfare of the churches. The independency of the churches was asserted, and the powers of the Association restricted to those of a Council of Advice. It was agreed to meet again in Charleston, Nov. 1752. At that time the delegates from Euhaw attended, and the proceedings of the first meeting were ratified. The instrument of Union bears the following signatures: John Stephens, Oliver Hart, Francis Pelot, John Brown, Joshua Edwards, Ministers: James Fowler, William Screven, Richard Bedon, Charles Barker, Benjamin Parmenter, Thomas Harrison, Philip Douglas, and John Mikell, Messengers.

The Association thus formed, held its meetings for a number of years at the place of its organization, and hence took the name of the "Charlestown Association." Its deliberations were begun and ended with prayer. Letters from the Churches were read, and the names of the Delegates recorded. For the maintenance of order, and the dispatch of business, a Moderator and Clerk were annually chosen. Queries on points of theology, or particulars of discipline were occasionally presented, and answers furnished. A Circular Letter was annually addressed to the churches; containing exhortations and encouragements to duty, and adapted to existing circumstances. Mutual satisfaction and benefit were experienced. Several new churches at intervals were added to the confederacy; so that in a few years their number was multiplied.

Source: Wood Furman, comp., *A History of the Charleston Association of Baptist Churches in the State of South Carolina* (Charleston: From the Press of J. Hoff, 1811), 8–10.

10

BIRTH OF THE SANDY CREEK BAPTIST ASSOCIATION, 1758

David Benedict

I N THE YEAR 1758, THREE years after [Shubal] Stearns and his company settled at Sandy-creek, a few churches having been constituted, and these having a number of branches which were fast maturing for churches, Stearns conceived that an Association composed of delegates from them all, would have a tendency to forward the great object of their exertions. For this purpose he visited each church and congregation, and explaining to them his contemplated plan, induced them all to send delegates to his meeting-house in January, 1758, when an Association was formed, which was called *Sandy-creek*, and which continues to the present time; but it has experienced many vicissitudes of prosperity and adversity; and at one time, on account of exercising too much power over the churches, it became much embarrassed in its movements, and very near to extinction.

For twelve years, all the Separate Baptists in Virginia and the two Carolinas, continued in connection with this Association, which was generally held at no great distance from the place where it originated. All who could, traveled from its remote extremities, to attend its yearly sessions, which were conducted with great harmony, and afforded sufficient edification to induce them to undertake with cheerfulness these long and laborious journeys. By the means of these meetings, the gospel was carried into many new places, where the fame of the Baptists had previously spread; for great crowds attending from distant parts, mostly through curiosity, many became enamored with these extraordinary people, and petitioned the Association to send preachers into their neighborhoods. These petitions were readily granted, and the preachers as readily complied with the appointments. These people were so much engaged in their evangelical pursuits, that they had no time to spend in theological debates, nor were they very scrupulous about the mode of conducting their meetings. When assembled, their chief employment was preaching, exhortation, singing, and conversing about their various exertions in the Redeemer's service, the success which had attended them, and the new and prosperous scenes which were opening before them. These things so inflamed the hearts of the ministers, that they would leave the Association with a zeal and courage, which no common obstacles could impede.

"At our first Association, (says the MS. of James Read, who was present) we continued together three or four days. Great crowds of people attended, mostly through curiosity. The great power of God was among us. The preaching everyday seemed to be attended with God's blessing. We carried on our Association with sweet decorum and fellowship to the end. Then we took leave of one another, with many solemn charges from our reverend old father Shubal Stearns, to stand fast unto the end."

Source: David Benedict, *A General History of the Baptist Denomination in American and Other Parts of the World* (Boston: Lincoln and Edmands, 1813), 2:49–50.

11

A Body of Doctrinal and Practical Divinity, 1769

John Gill

CHAP. II

OF THE SPECIAL DECREES OF GOD, RELATING TO RATIONAL CREATURES, ANGELS, AND MEN; AND PARTICULARLY OF ELECTION.

T HE SPECIAL DECREES OF GOD respecting rational creatures, commonly go under the name of *predestination*; though this sometimes is taken in a large sense, to express every thing that God has predetermined; and so it takes in all that has been observed in the preceding chapter; which some call eternal providence, of which, temporary providence is the execution; for with God there is not only a provision of things future, but a provision for the certain bringing of them to pass; and the counsel and will of God is the source and spring of all things, and the rule and measure according to which he works, Eph. i. 11. but predestination is usually considered as consisting of two parts, and including the two branches of election and reprobation, both with respect to angels and men; for each of these have place in both. Angels; some of them are called *elect* angels, 2 Tim. v. 21, others are said to be *reserved in chains*, in the chains of God's purposes and providence, *unto* the *judgment* of the great day, 2 Pet. ii. 4. Men; some of them are vessels of mercy, afore-prepared for glory; others vessels of wrath, fitted for destruction; some are the *election*, or the elect persons, that obtain righteousness, life, and salvation; and others are the *rest* that are left in, and given up to blindness. Rom. ix. 22, 23. and xi. 7. Though sometimes predestination only respects that branch of it called election, and the predestinated signify only the elect; for who else are called, justified, and glorified, enjoy adoption and the heavenly inheritance? not, surely, the non-elect. Rom. viii. 29, 30. Eph. i. 5, 11. This branch of predestination, election, must be considered first; I shall begin with,

I. The election of angels; of this the scriptures speak but sparingly, and therefore the less need to be said concerning it: that there are some angels that are elect is certain, from the proof already given: there is a similarity between their election and the election of men; though in some things there appears a little difference. . . .

II. The election of men to grace and glory, is next to be considered; and it may be proper in the first place to take some notice of the election of Christ, as man and mediator; who is God's first and chief elect; and is, by way of eminency, called his elect; . . .

But what will now be chiefly attended to, and what the scriptures speak so largely of, is the election of men in Christ unto eternal life.

Some are of the opinion that this doctrine of election, admitting it to be true, should not be published, neither preached from the pulpit, nor handled in schools and academies, nor treated of in the writings of men; the reasons they give, are because it is a secret, and secret things belong to God: and because it tends to fill men's minds with doubts about their salvation, and to bring them into distress, and even into despair; and because some may make a bad use of it, to indulge themselves in a sinful course of life, and argue, that if they are elected they shall be saved, let them live as they may, and so it opens a door to all licentiousness: but these reasons are frivolous and groundless; the doctrine of election is no secret, it is clearly and fully revealed, and written as with a sunbeam in the sacred scriptures; . . .

I proceed then,

First, To observe the phrases by which it is expressed in scripture, whereby may be learned what is the true meaning of the words *election* and *elect*, as used in scripture with respect to this doctrine. It is expressed by being ordained to eternal life Acts xiii. 48. *As many as were ordained to eternal life, believed*; by which ordination is meant no other than the predestination, choice, and appointment of men to everlasting life and salvation by Jesus Christ; . . .

This act of God is also expressed by the names of persons being *written in heaven*, and in the *book of life*, called, *the Lamb's book of life*; . . . But the more common phrases used concerning it, are those of being *chosen* and *elected*; hence the objects of it are called God's *elect*, and the *election*; that is, persons elected, . . . Wherefore the election treated of is not,

1. An election of a nation to some external privileges, as the people of Israel, who were chosen of God to be a special people, . . . And so this nation of ours is selected and distinguished from many others, by various blessings of goodness, and particularly by having the means of grace; yet all the individuals of it cannot be thought to be the objects of election to special grace, and eternal glory.

2. Nor of an election to offices; . . . and though Christ chose twelve to be his apostles, one of them was a devil: so that though those were chosen to offices, and even to the highest offices in the church and state, yet not to eternal life.

3. Nor of an election of whole bodies and communities of men, under the character of churches, to the enjoyment of the means of grace: . . .

5. This is to be understood of the choice of certain persons by God, from all eternity, to grace and glory; it is an act by which men are chosen of God's good will and pleasure, before the world was, to holiness and happiness, to salvation by Christ, to partake of his glory, and to enjoy eternal life, as the free gift of God through him, . . .

Secondly, The next thing to be considered is, by whom election is made, and in whom it is made: it is made by God, and it is made in Christ. 1. It is made by God, as the efficient cause of it; God, who is a sovereign Being, who does and may do whatever he pleases in heaven and in earth, among angels and men; and has a right to do what he will with his own; as with his own things, temporal and spiritual blessings; so with his own creatures. Shall he be denied that which every man thinks he has a right unto and does? Do not kings choose their own ministers; masters their servants; and every man his own favorites, friends, and companions? And may not God choose whom he pleases to commune with him, both here and hereafter; or to grace and glory? . . . And this now being the act of God, it is forever; for whatever God does in a way of special grace, it is forever; it is unchangeable and irrevocable; men may choose some to be their favorites and friends for a while, and then alter their minds, and choose others in their room; but God never acts such a part, he is in one mind, and none can turn him; his purpose, according to election, or with respect to that, stands sure, firm, and unalterable—

2. This act is made in Christ, *according as he hath chosen us in him*, Eph. 1. 4. Election does not find men in Christ, but puts them there; it gives them a being in him, and union to him; which is the foundation of their open being in Christ at conversion, . . .

. . . the reasons why men are elected, are not because Christ has shed his blood, died for them, redeemed and saved them; but Christ has done all this for them because they are elect; . . . now it is not Christ's laying down his life for them that makes them sheep, and elect; they are so previous to that; but because they are sheep, and chosen ones in Christ, and given him by his Father, therefore he laid down his life for them. . . .

Source: John Gill, *A Body of Doctrinal and Practical Divinity* (London: n.p., 1769).

12

AN APPEAL TO THE PUBLIC FOR RELIGIOUS LIBERTY, 1773

Isaac Backus

Introduction

I NASMUCH AS THERE APPEARS TO us a real need of such an appeal, we would previously offer a few thoughts concerning the general nature of liberty and government, and then show wherein it appears to us that our religious rights are encroached upon in this land.

It is supposed by multitudes that in submitting to government we give up some part of our liberty, because they imagine that there is something in their nature incompatible with each other. But the word of truth plainly shows, that man first lost his freedom by breaking over the rules of government and that those who now speak great *swelling words* about *liberty*, while they *despise government*, are themselves *servants of corruption*. What a dangerous error, yea, what a root of all evil then must it be, for men to imagine that there is anything in the nature of true government that interferes with true and full liberty! . . .

. . . And those who do not *know the truth* and have not been *made free* thereby, yet have never been able in any country to subsist long without some sort of government, neither could any of them ever make out to establish any proper government without calling in the help of the Deity. However absurd their notions have been, yet they have found human sight and power to be so short and weak, and able to do so little toward watching over the conduct, and guarding the rights of individuals, that they have been forced to appeal to heaven by oaths, and to invoke assistance from them to avenge the cause of the injured upon the guilty. Hence it is so far from being necessary for any man to give up any part of his real liberty in order to submit to government, that all nations have found it necessary to submit to some government in order to enjoy any liberty and security at all. . . .

Having offered these few thoughts upon the general nature of government and liberty, it is needful to observe, that God has appointed two kinds of government in the world which are distinct in their nature and ought never to be confounded together, one of which is called civil the other ecclesiastical government. And though we shall not attempt a full explanation of them yet some essential points of difference between them are necessary to be mentioned in order truly to open our grievances.

SECTION I

Some essential points of differences between civil and ecclesiastical government

1. The forming of the constitution and appointment of the particular orders and offices of civil government is left to human discretion, and our submission thereto is required under the name of their being the *ordinances of men* for the Lord's sake, 1 *Pet.* ii, 13, 14. Whereas in ecclesiastical affairs we are most solemnly warned not to be *subject to ordinances after the doctrines and commandments of men*, Col. ii, 20, 22. And it is evident that He who is the only worthy object of worship has always claimed it as his sole prerogative to determine by express laws what his worship shall be, who shall minister in it, and how they shall be supported. . . .

2. That as the putting any men into civil office is of men, of the people of the world, so officers have truly no more authority than the people give them. And how came the people of the world by any ecclesiastical power? They arm the magistrate with the *sword* that he may be a minister of God *to them for good* and might execute wrath upon *evil doers* for this cause they pay them *tribute*; upon which the apostle proceeds to name those divine commandments which are comprehended in love to our neighbor, and which work *no ill to him.* Surely the inspired writer had not forgotten the first and great command of love to God; but as this chapter treats the most fully of the nature and end of civil government of any in the New Testament, does it not clearly show that the crimes which fall within the magistrates' jurisdiction to punish are only such as work ill to our neighbor? *Rom.* xiii, 1–10, while church government respects our behavior toward God as well as man.

3. All acts of executive power in the civil state are to be performed in the name of the king or state they belong to, while all our religious acts

are to be done in the *name of the Lord Jesus and so are to be performed heartily as to the Lord and not unto men.* . . . And it is often pleaded that magistrates ought to do their duty in religious as well as civil affairs. That is readily granted but what is their duty therein? Surely it is *to bow to the name of Jesus* and to serve him with holy reverence. And if they do the contrary they may expect to *perish from the way, Phil.* ii, 10; *Psal.* ii, 10–12. But where is the officer that will dare to come in the name of the Lord to demand, and forcibly to take, a tax which was imposed by the civil state! . . .

4. In all civil governments some are appointed to judge for others and have power to compel others to submit to their judgment, but our Lord has most plainly forbidden us either to assume or submit to any such thing in religion, *Matt.* xxiii, 1–9; *Luke* xxii, 25–27. . . . And it appears to us that the true difference and exact limits between ecclesiastical and civil government is this, That the church is armed with *light and truth* to pull down the strongholds of iniquity and to gain souls to Christ and into his Church to be governed by his rules therein, and again to exclude such from their communion, who will not be so governed, while the state is armed with the *sword* to guard the peace and the civil rights of all persons and societies and to punish those who violate the same. And where these two kinds of government, and the weapons which belong to them are well distinguished and improved according to the true nature and end of their institution, the effects are happy, and they do not at all interfere with each other. But where they have been confounded together no tongue nor pen can fully describe the mischiefs that have ensued of which the Holy Ghost gave early and plain warnings. . . .

SECTION II

A brief view of how civil and ecclesiastical affairs are blended together among us to the depriving of many of God's people of that liberty of conscience which he has given them

We are not insensible that an open appearance against any part of the conduct of men in power is commonly attended with difficulty and danger. We have found any way wherein with clearness we could have avoided the present attempt, we would gladly have taken it. . . . And things appear so to us at present that we cannot see how we can fully obey this command without refusing any active compliance with some laws about religious affairs that are laid upon us. And as those who are interested against us, often accuse us of complaining unreasonably, we are brought under a necessity of laying open particular facts which otherwise we would gladly have concealed. . . .

1. Our legislature claims a power to compel every town and parish within their jurisdiction to set up and maintain a pedobaptist worship among them although it is well known, that infant baptism is never expressed in the Bible, only is upheld by men's reasonings that are chiefly drawn from Abraham's covenant which the Holy Ghost calls *The covenant of circumcision, Acts* vii. 8. And as circumcision was one of the handwriting of ordinances which Christ has *blotted out* where did any state ever get any right to compel their subjects to set up a worship upon this covenant?

2. Our ascended Lord gives *gifts* unto men in a sovereign way as seems good unto him, and he requires *Every man, as he has received the gift, even so to minister the same*; and he reproved his apostles when they forbid one who was improving his gift because he did not follow them, 1 *Pet.* iv, 10, 11; *Luke* ix, 49. But the Massachusetts legislature, while they claim a power to compel each parish to settle a minister, have also determined that he must be one, who has either an academical degree, or a testimonial in his favor from a majority of the ministers in the county where the parish lies. . . .

3. Though the Lord has *ordained that they which preach the Gospel shall live of the Gospel* or by the *free communications to them* which his Gospel will produce, 1 *Cor.* ix, 13, 14; *Gal.* vi, 6, 7. Yet the ministers of our land have chosen to *live by the law.* And as a reason therefore, one of their most noted writers, instead of producing any truth of God, recites the tradition of a man who said, "Ministers of the Gospel would have a poor time of it, if they must rely on a *free contribution of the people* for their maintenance." . . .

Now who can hear Christ declare that his kingdom is *not of this world*, and yet believe that this blending of church and state together can be pleasing to him? . . .

How essentially and how greatly does this constitution differ, and from the institutions established in God's word, both in their nature and effects?

1. In their *nature.* Here you find that every religious minister in that constitution, is called the king's minister, because he is settled by direction of the king's laws and the tax for such a minister's support is raised in the king's name and is called the king's dues. Whereas no man in the Jewish church might approach the minister at the holy altar but such as

were *called of God as was Aaron*. The means of their support were such things as God required his people to *offer and consecrate to Him*, . . .

2. The *effects* of the constitution of our country are such that as it makes the majority of the people the test of orthodoxy, so it emboldens them to usurp God's judgment seat, and (according to Dr. [Cotton] Mather's own account which we have often seen verified) they daringly give out their sentence that for *a few* to profess a persuasion different from the *majority*, it must be from bad motives, and that, they *know in their conscience* that they do not act by the universal law of equity, if they plead to be exempted from paying the *money* which the *majority* demand of them! And though in *our charter* the king grants to all Protestants *equal liberty of conscience*, yet for above thirty years after it was received the Congregationalists made no laws to favor the consciences of any men in this affair of taxes but their own sect. . . .

These evils cleaved so close to the first fathers of Massachusetts as to move them to imprison, whip, and banish men only for denying infant baptism and refusing to join in worship that was supported by violent methods. Yet they were so much blinded as to declare that there was this *vast difference* between these proceedings and the coercive measures which were taken against themselves in England, viz., We compel men to "God's institutions," they in England compelled to "men's inventions." . . .

Many try to vindicate their way by that promise that kings shall become nursing fathers and queens nursing mothers to God's people. But as the character carries in its very nature an *impartial care and tenderness for all their children*, we appeal to every conscience whether it does not condemn the way of setting up one party to the injury of another. Our Lord tells us plainly that *few* find the narrow way while *many* go in the *broad way*. Yet the scheme we complain of has given the *many* such power over the *few* . . . the *many* are *prepared* with such instruments of *war against them* as to seize their goods or cast their bodies into prison where they may starve and die for all that the constitution has provided for them. In cases of common debts the law has provided several ways of relief, as it has not in the case before us, for here the assessors plead that they are *obliged* to tax all according to law, and the collector has the same plea for the gathering of it. And the minister says, I agreed with the society for such a sum, and it is not my business to release any. So that we have had instances of serious Christians who must have died in prison for ministers' rates if Christianity and humanity had not moved people to provide them that relief which neither those ministers nor the law that upholds them have done. . . .

SECTION III

A brief account of what the Baptists have suffered under this constitution and of their reasons for refusing any active compliance with it

Many are ready to say, the Baptists are exempted from ministerial taxes, therefore, why do they complain? Answer. We would be far from forgetting or undervaluing our privileges, but are willing thankfully to acknowledge, that our honored rulers do protect our societies, so as not to allow them to be interrupted in their worship; and as the taking cognizance of marriage belongs to them, we take it as a favor that they grant our ministers power to administer it, so that we may have marriage solemnized among ourselves. Many other liberties we also enjoy under the government that is set over us, for which we desire to be thankful, both to the author, and to the instruments of them. Yet if our opponents could once put themselves into our place, we do not doubt but they would think it was high time, to seek for more full liberty than we have hitherto enjoyed. . . .

Our charter, as before observed, gives us equal religious liberty with other Christians. Yet, the pedobaptists being the greatest party, they soon made a perpetual law to support their own way, but did nothing of that nature to exempt our denomination from it, for thirty-six years. . . .

In civil states the power of the whole collective body is vested in a few hands, that they may with better advantage defend themselves against injuries from abroad, and correct abuses at home, for which end a few have a right to judge for the whole society; but in religion each one has an equal right to judge for himself; for we must all *appear* before the judgment seat of Christ, that *everyone* may receive the things *done in his body*, according to that *he has done* (not what any earthly representative has done for him) 2 *Cor.* v, 10. And we freely confess that we can find no more warrant from divine truth, for any people on earth to constitute any men their representatives, to make laws to impose religious taxes, than they have to appoint Peter or the Virgin Mary to represent them before the divine throne above. We are therefore brought to a stop about paying so much regard to such laws, as to give in annual certificates to the other denomination, as we have formerly done.

1. Because the very nature of such a practice implies an acknowledgement, that the civil power has a right to set one religious sect up

above another, else why need we give certificates to them any more than they to us? . . .

2. By the foregoing address to our legislature, and their committees report thereon, it is evident, that they claim a right to tax us from the *civil obligation*, as being the representatives of the people. . . . How came the kingdoms of this world to have a right to govern in Christ's kingdom which is *not of this world!*

3. That constitution not only emboldens people to *judge the liberty of other men's consciences*, and has carried them so far as to tell our general assembly, that they conceived it their *duty they owed to God* and their country, not to be dispensed with. . . . And only because our brethren in Bellingham, left that clause about the *conscience* out of their certificates last year, a number of their society who live at Mendon were taxed, and lately suffered the spoiling of their goods to uphold pedobaptist worship.

5. The custom which they want us to countenance is very hurtful to civil society. By the law of Christ *every man*, is not only allowed, but also required, to judge for himself, concerning the circumstantials as well as the essentials, of religion, and to act according to the *full persuasion of his own mind*, . . .

CONCLUSION

And now our dear countrymen, we beseech you seriously to consider these things. The great importance of a general union through this country, in order to the preservation of our liberties, has often been pleaded for with propriety. But how can such a union be expected so long as that dearest of all rights, equal liberty of conscience is not allowed? How can anyone reasonably expect that *he* who has the hearts of kings in his hand, will turn the heart of our earthly sovereign to hear the pleas for liberty, of those who will not hear the cries of their fellow subjects, under their oppressions? . . .

Suffer us a little to expostulate with our fathers and brethren, who inhabit the land to which our ancestors fled for religious liberty. You have lately been accused with being disorderly and rebellious, by men in power, who profess a great regard for order and the public good. Why don't you believe them, and rest easy under their administration? You tell us that you cannot, because you are taxed where you are not represented. Is it not really so with us? You do not deny the right of the British parliament to impose taxes within her own realm; only to complain that she extends her taxing power beyond her proper limits. Have we not as good a right as to say you do the *same thing*? So that wherein you judge others you condemn yourselves? . . .

. . . And as the present contest between Great Britain and America, is not so much about the greatness of taxes already laid, as about a submission to their taxing power. So (though what we have already suffered is far from being a trifle, yet) our greatest difficulty at present concerns the submitting to a taxing power in ecclesiastical affairs. . . .

Thus we have laid down before the public a brief view of our sentiments concerning liberty of conscience, and a little sketch of our sufferings on that account. If any can show us that we have made any mistakes, either about principles or facts, we would lie open to conviction. We hope none will violate the forecited article of faith so much, as to require us to yield a blind obedience to them, or to expect that spoiling of goods or imprisonment can move us to *betray* the cause of true liberty. . . .

Source: Isaac Backus, *An Appeal to the Public for Religious Liberty* (Boston: John Boyle in Marlborough Street, 1773).

13

BLACK BAPTISTS

George Lisle: Pioneer Black
Baptist Preacher ca. 1779

THE LIST [OF PIONEER PREACHERS] is a long and bril-
liant one. In the antebellum days it includes names which are immortal in our archives. George Lisle, a Negro, was the first American
Baptist foreign missionary, preceding William Carey, the renowned
European missionary, by at least fifteen years. Lisle, though handicapped
by the chains of human slavery and hampered by the law-enforced ignorance, incurring the penalties of being a Negro, rose above all these
degrading circumstances and became the chief human factor in the salvation of Jamaica, the most beautiful island in the Caribbean Sea. . . .
To Lisle belongs the honor of possibly being the first ordained Negro
Baptist preacher in the New World. He preached in Georgia during the
Revolutionary War, and his ministry was greatly blessed by a number of
converts whom he baptized in the Savannah River. At the close of the
war he went to Jamaica as the indentured servant of Col. Kirkland, an
English officer. On getting settled in his new home on the island, Lisle
was so deeply impressed with the sad conditions of superstitions and ignorance in which he found the Negroes of Kingston, that he determined
to do something to alleviate this state of affairs. He preached first at the
race tracks and on the street, but later, hired a room at his own expense
and organized a little Baptist church consisting of four persons.

Others joined him in forming a church which grew until in less than
eight years he had baptized 500 persons.

In 1789 he built a chapel, in spite of the relentless storm of persecution which he encountered, during which time he was imprisoned, placed

in the stocks and finally tried for his life, for preaching "sedition." From 1805 to 1814, a law forbidding all preaching to slaves was strictly carried out. One man was hung for preaching and baptizing—but their labor bore fruit when in 1814, Baptists in England were moved by letters of appeal from Lisle and others, to send missionaries. They found the people ready to greet them and cooperate in their work, because of the pioneer mission work established by George Lisle, 35 years before. . . .

Personal Letter of George Lisle
(Page 122 N.B.C. Minutes, 1915)

The first Baptist church was organized in 1784, in Kingston. A personal letter written to Dr. [John] Rippen, of London, in 1791, will show more fully the character, work and struggle of this man.

"I cannot tell what my age is, as I have no account of the time of my birth, but I suppose I am about 40 years old. I have a wife and four children. My wife was baptized by me in Savannah, and I have every satisfaction in life from her. She is much the same age as myself. My eldest son is 19 years old, my next son is 17, and the third, 14, and the last child, a girl of 11 years. They are all members of the church. My occupation is a farmer, but as the seasons of this part of the country are uncertain, I keep a team of horses and wagons for the carrying of goods from one place to another, which I attend myself, with the assistance of my sons, and by this way of life have gained the good will of the public, who recommended me to the business and to some very principal work for the government. I have a few good books, some good old authors and sermons, and one large Bible that was given to me by a gentleman. A good many of our members can read, and are all desirous to learn. They will be very thankful for a few books to read on Sundays and other days.

"There is no Baptist church in this country but ours. We have purchased a piece of land at the east end of Kingston, containing three acres, for the sum of $775, and on it we have begun a meeting house, 57 feet in length by 37 feet in breadth. We have raised the brick wall eight feet high from the foundation, and intend to have a gallery. . . . The chief part of our congregation are slaves, and their owners allow them, in common, but three or four bits a week to feed themselves, and out of so small a sum we cannot expect anything that can be of service from them; if we did, it would soon bring scandal upon religion. The free people in our society are poor, but they are willing, both free and slaves, to do what they can. As for my part, I am too much entangled with the affairs of the world to go on, as I would, with my design in supporting the cause. This has, I acknowledged, been a great hindrance to the gospel in one way; but I have endeavored to set a good example of good industry before the inhabitants of the land, it has given general satisfaction in another way. And, reverend sir, we think the Lord has put the power of the Baptist societies in England to help and assist us in completing this building, which we look upon to be the greatest undertaking in this country for the bringing of souls from darkness into the light of the gospel. And as the Lord had put it in your heart to inquire after us, we place all of our confidence in you to make our circumstances known to the several Baptist churches in England, and we look upon you as our father, friend and brother. Within the brick walls we have a shelter in which we worship until our building can be accomplished.

"Your letter was read in the church two or three times, and did create a great deal of love and warmness throughout the congregation, and we shouted for joy and comfort to think that the Lord has been so gracious as to satisfy us in this country, with the same kind of religion of our beloved brethren in the old country, according to the Scriptures, and that such a worthy—of London could write so loving a letter to such poor worms as we are. And I beg leave to say that the whole congregation sang out they would, through the assistance of God, remember you in their prayers. They all together give their Christian love to you and all the worthy professors of Jesus Christ in your church at London, and beg the prayers of your churches in general and of our congregation wherever it pleases you to make known our circumstances. I remain, with the utmost love, reverend sir, your unworthy fellow laborer, servant and brother in Christ.

George Lisle

Source: Lewis G. Jordan, *Negro Baptist History, U.S.A.* (Nashville: Sunday School Publishing Board, NBC, n.d. [1930], 46–48. Copyright © 1930, Townsend Press, a division of the Sunday School Publishing Board of the National Baptist Convention, USA, Inc., Nashville, Tennessee. Reprinted by permission.

A General History of the Baptist Denomination in America, David Benedict, ca. 1792

CHAP. XIII.

An Account of four Baptist Churches of Africans in Georgia, and of two in the West Indies; together with some general Observations respecting the Circumstances of the African Slaves in the Southern and Western States.

A MYSTERIOUS Providence has permitted a large portion of the sable sons of Africa to be transported from their native country to this western world, and here to be reduced to a state of absolute and perpetual slavery; but He who can bring good out of evil, has overruled this calamity for their spiritual advantage; and thousands of these poor, enslaved, and benighted people, we have very satisfactory reason to believe, have found gospel liberty in the midst of their temporal bondage, and are preparing to reign forever in the kingdom of God.

There are multitudes of African communicants, in all the Baptist churches in the southern and western States; and in Georgia there are four churches, wholly composed of them. Some brief sketches of their history will now be given.

First Coloured Baptist Church in Savannah.

The origin of this church, according to Rippon's Register and Holcombe's Repository, was in the following manner. About the beginning of the American War, George Leile, sometimes called George Sharp, but more commonly known among his brethren and friends by the name of brother George, began to preach at Brampton and Yamacraw, near the city of Savannah. . . . When the country was evacuated by the British, George, with many others, removed from Georgia to Kingston, in the island of Jamaica. . . .

Previous to George's departure for Jamaica, he came up to the city of Savannah from Tylee-river, where departing vessels frequently lay ready for sea, and baptized Andrew Bryan and Hannah his wife, and two other black women, whose name were Kate and Hagar. These were the last labors of George Leile in this quarter. About nine months after his departure, Andrew began to exhort his black brethren and friends, and a few whites who assembled to hear him. Edward Davis, Esq. permitted him and his hearers to erect a rough wooden building on his land at Yamacraw, in the suburbs of Savannah. Of this building they were, in a short time, very artfully dispossessed. It appears that these poor, defenseless slaves met with much opposition from the rude and merciless white people, who, under various pretences, interrupted their worship, and otherwise treated them in a barbarous manner. Andrew Bryan, and his brother Samson, who was converted about a year after him, were twice imprisoned, and they, with about fifty others, without much ceremony were severely whipped. Andrew was inhumanly cut, and bled abundantly; but while under their lashes, he held up his hands and told his persecutors, that he rejoiced not only to be whipped, but *would freely suffer death for the cause of Jesus Christ*. The Chief Justice, Henry Osbourne, James Habersham, and David Montague, Esquires, were their examinants, who released them. Jonathan Bryan, Esq. the kind master of Andrew and Samson, interceded for his own servants and the rest of the sufferers, and was much grieved at their punishment. The design of these unrighteous proceedings against these poor innocent people, was to stop their religious meetings. Their enemies pretended, that under a pretense of religion, they were plotting mischief and insurrections. But by *well doing* they at length silenced and shamed their persecutors, and acquired a number of very respectable and influential advocates and patrons, who not only rescued them from the power of their enemies, but declared that such treatment as they had received would be condemned even among barbarians. Chief Justice Osbourne then gave them liberty to continue their worship any time between sun-rising and sun-set; and the benevolent Jonathan Bryan told the magistrates that he would give them the liberty of his *own house or barn*, at a place called Brampton, about three miles from Savannah, and that they should set up meetings at their master's barn, where they had little or no interruption for about two years. Such was the beginning of the first African church in Savannah, which, after having been the mother of two others, now contains about fifteen hundred members. . . .

Towards the close of the year 1792, they began to build a place of worship in the suburbs of the city of Savannah, which, by the assistance of a number of benevolent gentleman of different denominations, was finished in due time, and is 42 feet by 49. The plan of building this house, it seems, was projected by Messrs. Jonathan Clark, Ebenezer Hills, and others. The corporation of the city of Savannah gave them a lot for the purpose.

This colored church, as it is generally called, (for no white person belongs to it) is now a large and respectable establishment. Many of its members are free, and are possessed of some estate. It was one of the three churches which formed the Savannah-river Association; and by its returns to that body in 1812, it contained about fifteen hundred members, many of whom belong to the plantations in the neighborhood of Savannah, and some are a number of miles out in the country. But their masters give them liberty every Sabbath to meet with their brethren, and the poor creatures, with peculiar delight, go up to their Jerusalem to worship.

Andrew Bryan, the pastor of this church, is now an old man, and is spoken of by all who know him in terms of peculiar respect. He was born at a place called Goose-Creek, about 16 miles from Charleston, (S.C.) in what year is not known. He was a slave when he began to preach; but his kind master indulged him with uncommon liberties. After his death, he purchased his freedom from one of his heirs. . . .

Since writing the above, I have been informed by Mr. Johnson of Savannah, that this venerable man finished his course in October 1812. He was supposed to have been about 90 years of age. . . .

Although he was a slave when he began to preach, yet he left an estate worth about three thousand dollars. He is succeeded in the pastoral office by his nephew Andrew Marshall, who is now working his time out, (as they call it) and is said to be a man of promising parts.

Second African Baptist Church in Savannah.

This church was formed in 1802, and now consists of upwards of three hundred members. This church has also a comfortable meeting-house in Savannah, 67 feet by 30. It is under the pastoral care of a very respectable black preacher, whose name is Henry Cunningham. He, like Andrew Bryan, was originally a slave, but is now free, having worked his time out.

The African Church on the Great Ogechee River, commonly called the Great Ogechee Coloured Church.

This body, like the last mentioned, originated from the African church in Savannah, under the care of Andrew Bryan; and was constituted in 1803. But it has not been so prosperous as the two others, and has diminished rather than increased.

African Church in Augusta.

This church appears to have been raised up by the laborers of Jesse Peter, a black preacher of very respectable talents, and an amiable character. It was constituted in 1793, by elders Abraham Marshall and David Tinsley.

Jesse Peter, sometimes called Jesse Golfin, on account of his master's name, continued as the pastor of this church a number of years, and was very successful in his ministry. I find his character thus given by Mr. Abraham Marshall, in 1793, in Rippon's Register, Vol. I. p. 545: "He is a servant of Mr. Golfin, who lived twelve miles below Augusta, and who, to his praise be it spoken, treats him with respect. His countenance is grave, his voice charming, his delivery good; nor is he a novice in the mysteries of the kingdom."

Mr. Peter died about 1806. Their present pastor is Caesar M'Cridy, under whose ministry the church appears to flourish and prosper. They have a meeting-house at Springfield, in the upper-end of the city of Augusta.

This church was once upwards of five hundred in number; but it is now reduced, by various means, to a little less than four hundred, who walk together in harmony and love.

This church has belonged to the Georgia Association from its beginning. Abraham Marshall, the friend of black people, lives but a short distance from it; and to his fatherly care they are much indebted for many of their comforts.

There are multitudes of black people in all the churches in the southern States; but I know of no church of the Baptist denomination which is wholly composed of them, except those whose history has been related.

Their white brethren generally do not encourage them to form churches by themselves. Such are their circumstances, their mode of life, and their want of knowledge to regulate church affairs, that it is altogether best, in the present state of things, that they should be connected with their white brethren, who are capable of guiding and instructing them.

Source: David Benedict, *A General History of the Baptist Denomination in America* (Boston: Manning and Loring, 1813), 2:189–94.

Negro Work for the Negro, Elias C. Morris, 1911

BROTHER PRESIDENT, LADIES AND GENTLEMEN:

Having had the honor of attending the first meeting of the Baptist World Alliance, and having enjoyed the privilege of making a few remarks in that meeting, I deem it extraordinary to be given a place on the program at this time, and beg to assure you that I fully appreciate the distinction that this appointment gives.

I recognize that I am speaking to the representatives of an irresistible army of Christians—those who are in line with the direct successors of the apostles of Jesus Christ and who, upon the doctrines of Jesus Christ, are as firm as Gibraltar. To be in the presence of such representatives is sufficient to give renewed inspiration and courage to any speaker.

You will pardon reference to that fact that while I appear to you as a Baptist, yet I come as the representative of a denomination of Christian people commonly known in the United States as Negro Baptists, whose principal missionary organization is the National Baptist Convention. While these are not different in doctrine or practice, they are separate and distinct from the white Baptists in many things. But we are proud of the fact that we represent one-third of all the Baptists in the world, having a certified membership of two million two hundred and sixty-two thousand communicants.

I am asked to speak upon "The Negro Work for the Negro." This theme as indicated is in plain accord with the polity of American Baptists as well as with my own ideas as to the most effective way to direct religious efforts among any people. It is not to be understood, however, that there are or should be any color or racial lines drawn in the kingdom of grace, but rather it is my purpose to give emphasis to the fact that in undertaking any great work the matter of adaptability must be taken into account in the employment of factors, if success is to abundantly follow the effort. . . .

Let me localize my subject for a brief moment. For a number of years following the close of the Civil War in this country, the great heart of the Christian people North and South went out to the emancipated, and many devout white Christians came to the Negro people to do missionary and educational work among them. Their effort met with signal success. But as the Negro people became educated, it developed that they preferred teachers and preachers from among their own race; hence, the strength of the race was turned towards educating teachers and preachers, so as to supply their schools and churches. The Negroes felt, and rightly so, I think, that their ministers and teachers should associate with them, should eat and drink in their humble homes, and do by contact, by social example much that could not be done by anyone in the schoolroom or pulpit alone. Owing to the wide race distinctions, this could not become a rule with the white ministers and teachers, and the most that they could do without sacrificing their social standing among their own people, was to preach, teach, and baptize the Negroes. The Negroes, as a rule, were opposed to the social intermingling of the races, preferring to maintain their peculiar racial identity. Hence, the demand for Negro churches and Negro preachers became imperative.

In the matter of separation in the church life of the people on this continent, the blacks have been the beneficiaries to a very large extent. This has enabled them in the forty-five years of their freedom to establish more than one hundred high schools and colleges, twenty-seven thousand church houses with a valuation of forty million dollars. They have also twenty-five thousand ordained ministers, and more than ten thousand well-educated men and women who are teaching in schools and preaching in churches, while others are successfully following the professions of law and medicine and all other vocations. Then, again, the Negroes have enrolled fully fifty per cent of the entire race in this country in Christian churches. This, in my opinion, is a showing which cannot be made by any other race in so short a time, and is due largely to the fact that the Negro people regard their ministers as their God-appointed leaders, and, as a rule, accept their teaching without question.

But in speaking of the Negro work for the Negro, we are including a larger range of thought and territory than that which applies to the Negroes of the United States, and we hope to make it plain that the Negroes of the United States are the logical Christian leaders of the black people of the world.

In the beginning of the Negroes' life as freemen in the United States, a wise Providence directed that the race should make as the base of its future the principles of Christianity, taking as a guide, that Scripture which says, "Seek ye first the kingdom of God and His righteousness, and all these things shall be added unto you." They believed then and believe now that whatever else is necessary to complete a well-rounded Christian civilization must follow in its time. That their choice was wise will be seen by making comparison with other emancipated people who were emancipated during the past century. . . .

But, my friends, I would have you know that it is a condition which warrants what I have here said. For I firmly believe that the time will come when there will be "neither Jew nor Greek, bond nor free," white nor black, European nor American, Asiatic or African in the kingdom of God, but all will be one in Christ Jesus.

But until that time shall come, we should work along, recognizing the metes and bounds set by an All-Wise Creator, who will, in His own time and way level the hills and mountains: and raise up the valleys, until this division of labor and distribution of tasks shall unite to promote the oneness of Christ and His cause the world over. . . .

Source: Elias C. Morris, "The Negro Work for the Negro," *The Baptist World Alliance, Second Congress, Philadelphia, June 19–25, 1911, Record of Proceedings* (Philadelphia: Harper & Brothers, 1911), 286–90.

14

THE RIGHTS OF CONSCIENCE INALIENABLE, 1791

John Leland

S UPPOSE A MAN TO REMOVE to a desolate island, and take a peaceable possession of it, without injuring any, so that he should be the honest inheritor of the isle. So long as he is alone, he is the absolute monarch of the place, and his own will is his law, which law is as often altered or repealed as his will changes. In process of time, from this man's loins ten sons are grown to manhood, and possess property. So long as they are all good men, each one can be as absolute, free, and sovereign as his father: but one of the ten turns vagrant, by robbing the rest. This villain is equal to, if not an over-match for any one of the nine: not one of them durst engage him in single combat. Reason and safety both dictate to the nine the necessity of a confederation, to unite their strength together to repel or destroy the plundering knave. Upon entering into confederation, some compact or agreement would be stipulated by which each would be bound to do his equal part in fatigue and expense. It would be necessary for these nine to meet at stated times to consult means of safety and happiness. A shady tree, or small cabin, would answer their purpose, and, in case of disagreement, four must give up to five.

In this state of things, their government would be perfectly democratic, every citizen being a legislator.

In a course of years, from these nine there arises nine thousand: their government can be no longer democratic—prudence would forbid it. Each tribe, or district, must then choose their representative, who, for the term that he is chosen, has the whole political power of his constituents. These representatives, meeting in assembly, would have power to make laws binding on their constituents, and while their time was spent in making laws for the community, each one of the community must advance a little of his money as a compensation therefore. Should these representatives differ in judgment, the minor must be subject to the major, as in the case above.

From this simple parable, the following things are demonstrated: First, the law was not made for a righteous man, but for the disobedient. Second, that righteous men have to part with a little of their liberty and property to preserve the rest. Third, that all power is vested in, and consequently derived from the people. Fourth, that the law should rule over rulers, and not rulers over the law. Fifth, that government is founded on a compact. Sixth, every law made by legislators, inconsistent with the compact, modernly called a constitution, is usurping in the legislators, and not binding on the people. Seventh, that whenever government is found inadequate to preserve the liberty and property of the people, they have an indubitable right to alter it so as to answer those purposes. Eighth, that legislators, in their legislative capacity, cannot alter the constitution, for they are hired servants of the people to act within the limits of the constitution.

From these general observations, I shall pass on to examine a question which has been the strife and contention of ages. The question is, *"Are the rights of conscience alienable, or inalienable?"*

The word *conscience*, signifies *common science*, a court of judicature which the Almighty has erected in every human breast: a *censor morum* over all his conduct. Conscience will ever judge right, when it is rightly informed, and speak the truth when it understands it. But to advert to the question, "Does a man, upon entering into social compact, surrender his conscience to that society, to be controlled by the laws thereof; or can he, in justice, assist in making laws to bind his children's consciences before they are born?" I judge not, for the following reasons:

First. Every man must give an account of himself to God, and therefore every man ought to be at liberty to serve God in a way that he can best reconcile to his conscience. If government can answer for individuals at the day of judgment, let men be controlled by it in religious matters; otherwise, let men be free.

Second. It would be sinful for a man to surrender that to man, which is to be kept sacred for God. . . . How painful then must it be to an honest heart, to be bound to observe the principles of his former belief, after he is convinced of their imbecility? And this ever has, and ever will be the case, while the rights of conscience are considered alienable.

Third. But supposing it was right for a man to bind his *own conscience*, yet surely it is very iniquitous to bind the consciences of his children—to make fetters for them before they are born is very cruel. . . .

Fourth. Finally, religion is a matter between God and individuals: the religious opinions of men are not the objects of civil government, or in any way under its control.

The state of Rhode Island has stood above one hundred and sixty years without any religious establishment. The state of New York never had any. New Jersey claims the same. Pennsylvania has also stood from its first settlement until now upon a liberal foundation; and if agriculture, the mechanical arts and commerce, have not flourished in these states, equal to any of the others, I judge wrong.

It may further be observed, that all the states now in union, saving two or three in New England, have no legal force used about religion, in directing its course, or supporting its preachers. And, moreover, the federal government is forbidden by the constitution, to make any laws, establishing any kind of religion. If religion cannot stand therefore, without the aid of law, it is likely to fall soon, in our nation, except in Connecticut and Massachusetts.

The evils of such an establishment are many.

First. Uninspired, fallible men make their own opinions tests of orthodoxy, and use their own systems, as Pocrustes used his iron bedstead, to stretch and measure the consciences of all others by. Where no toleration is granted to non-conformists, either ignorance and superstition prevail, or persecution rages; . . .

Second. Such establishments not only wean and alienate the affections of one from another, on account of the different usage they receive in their religious sentiments, but are also very impolitic, especially in new countries; for what encouragement can strangers have to migrate with their arts and wealth into a state, where they cannot enjoy their religious sentiments without exposing themselves to the law? . . .

Third. These establishments metamorphose the church into a creature, and religion into a principle of state, which has a natural tendency to make men conclude that *Bible religion* is nothing but a *trick of state*; . . .

Fourth. There are no two kingdoms and states that establish the same creed and formalities of faith, which alone proves their debility. In one kingdom a man is condemned for not believing a doctrine that he would be condemned for believing in another kingdom. Both of these establishments cannot be right, but both of them can be and surely are, wrong. . . .

If these, and many more evils, attend such establishments, what were, and still are the causes that ever there should be a state establishment of religion in any empire kingdom, or state?

The causes are many—some of which follow:

First. The love of importance is a general evil. . . .

Second. An over-fondness for a particular system or sect. . . .

Third. To produce uniformity in religion. . . .

Is uniformity of sentiments, in matter of religion, essential to the happiness of civil government? Not at all. Government has no more to do with the religious opinions of men, than it has with the principles of mathematics. Let every man speak freely without fear, maintain the principles that he believes, worship according to his own faith, either one God, three Gods, no God, or twenty Gods; and let government protect him in so doing, i.e., see that he meets with no personal abuse, or loss of property, for his religious opinions. . . .

Fourth. The common objection, "that the ignorant part of the community are not capacitated to judge for themselves," supports the Popish hierarchy, and all Protestant as well as Turkish and Pagan establishments in idea.

But is this idea just? Has God chosen many of the wise and learned? Has he not hid the mystery of gospel truth from them, and revealed it unto babes? Does the world by wisdom know God? . . .

Fifth. The groundwork of these establishments of religion is, *clerical influence*. Rulers, being persuaded by the clergy that an establishment of religion by human laws, would promote the knowledge of the gospel, quell religious disputes, prevent heresy, produce uniformity, and finally be advantageous to the state; establish such creeds as are framed by the clergy; and this they often do more readily, when they are flattered by the clergy; that if they thus defend the truth, they will become nursing fathers to the church, and merit something considerable for themselves.

What stimulates the clergy to recommend this mode of reasoning is:

First. Ignorance, not being able to confute error by fair argument.

Second. Indolence, not being willing to spend any time to confute the heretical.

Third. But chiefly covetousness, to get money, for it may be observed that in all these establishments, settled salaries for the clergy, recoverable by law, are sure to be interwoven; and was not this the case, I am well convinced that there would not be many, if any religious establishments in the Christian world.

Source: L. F. Greene, ed., *The Writings of the Late Elder John Leland* (New York: G. W. Wood, 1845), 179–86.

15

AN ENQUIRY, 1792
William Carey

Introduction

A S OUR BLESSED LORD HAS required us to pray that his kingdom may come, and his will be done on earth as it is in heaven, it becomes us not only to express our desires of that event by words, but to use every lawful method to spread the knowledge of his name. In order to do this, it is necessary that we should become, in some measure, *acquainted with the religious state of the world*; and as this is an object we should be prompted to pursue, not only the gospel of our Redeemer, but even by the feelings of humanity, so an inclination to conscientious activity therein would form one of the strongest proofs that we are the subjects of grace, and partakers of that spirit of universal benevolence and genuine philanthropy, which appear so eminent in the character of God himself. . . .

In order that the subject may be taken into more serious consideration, I shall enquire, whether the commission given by our Lord to his disciples is not still binding on us,—take a short view of former undertakings,—give some account of the present state of the world,—consider the practicability of doing something more than is done,—and the duty of Christians in general in this matter.

Section I

An Enquiry Whether the Commission Given by Our Lord to His Disciples Be Not Still Binding on Us

Our Lord Jesus Christ, a little before his departure, commissioned his apostles to "GO, and teach all nations;" or, as another evangelist expresses it, "Go into all the world, and preach the gospel to every crea-ture." This commission was as extensive as possible, and laid them un-der obligation to disperse themselves into every country of the habitable globe, and preach to all the inhabitants, without exception or limitation. They accordingly went forth in obedience to the command, and the pow-er of God evidently wrought with them.

Many attempts of the same kind have been attended with various success; but the work has not been taken up, or prosecuted of late years (except by a few individuals) with that zeal and perseverance with which the primitive Christians went about it. It seems as if many thought the commission was sufficiently put in execution by what the apostles and others have done; that we have enough to do to attend to the salvation of our own countrymen; and that, if God intends the salvation of the hea-then, he will some way or other bring them to the gospel, or the gospel to them. It is thus that multitudes sit at ease, and give themselves no con-cern about the far greater part of their fellow sinners, who to this day are lost in ignorance and idolatry. . . . To the consideration of such persons I would offer the following observations.

First, if the command of Christ to teach all nations is restricted to the apostles, or those under the immediate inspiration of the Holy Ghost, then that of baptizing should be so too; and every denomination of Christians, except the Quakers, do wrong in baptizing with water at all.

Secondly, If the command of Christ to teach all nations is confined to the apostles, then all such ordinary ministers who have endeavored to carry the gospel to the heathens, have acted without a warrant, and run before they were sent. . . .

Thirdly, If the command of Christ to teach all nations extends only to the apostles, then, doubtless, the promise of the divine preference in this work must be so limited; but this is worded in such a manner as expressly precludes such an idea. Lo, I am with you always, to the end of the world. . . .

It has been said that we ought not to force our way, but to wait for the openings, and leadings of Providence; but it might with equal pro-priety be answered in this case, neither ought we to neglect embracing those openings in Providence which daily present themselves to us. What openings of Providence do we wait for? We can neither expect to be transported into the heathen world without ordinary means, nor to be endowed with the gift of tongues, etc., when we arrive there. These would not be providential interpositions, but miraculous ones. Where a command exists nothing can be necessary to render it binding but a removal of those obstacles which render obedience impossible, and these are removed already. Natural impossibility can never be pleaded so long as facts exist to prove the contrary.

It has been objected that there are multitudes in our own nation, and within our immediate spheres of action, who are as ignorant as the South Sea savages, and that therefore we have work enough at home, without going into other countries. That there are thousands in our own land as far from God as possible, I readily grant, . . . Our own countrymen have the means of grace, and may attend on the Word preached if they choose it. They have the means of knowing the truth, . . . but with them the case is widely different, who have no Bible, no written language, (which many of them have not) no ministers, no good civil government, nor any of those advantages which we have. Pity therefore, humanity, and much more Christianity, call loudly for every possible exertion to introduce the gospel amongst them. . . .

Section V

An Enquiry into the Duty of Christians in General, and What Means Ought to Be Used, in Order to Promote This Work

If the prophecies concerning the increase of Christ's kingdom are true, and if what has been advanced, concerning the commission given by him to his disciples are obligatory on us, are just, it must be inferred that all Christians ought heartily to concur with God in promoting his glorious designs, for he that is joined to the Lord is one Spirit.

One of the first, and most important of those duties which are incumbent upon us, is fervent and united prayer. However, the influence of the Holy Spirit may be set at nought, and run down by many, it will be found upon trial, that all means which we can use, without it, will be ineffectual. If a temple is raised for God in the heathen world, it will not be by might, nor by power, nor by the authority of the magistrate, or the eloquence of the orator; but by my Spirit, says the Lord of Hosts. We must therefore be in real earnest in supplicating his blessings upon our labors. . . .

With respect to our own immediate connections, we have within these few years been favored with some tokens for good, granted in answer to prayer which should encourage us to persist, and increase in that important duty. I trust our monthly prayer-meetings for the success of the gospel have not been in vain. It is true a want of importunity too generally attends our prayers; yet unimportunate, and feeble as they have been, it is to be believed that God has heard, and in a measure answered them. The churches that have engaged in the practice have in general since that time been evidently on the increase; some controversies which have long perplexed and divided the church, are more clearly stated than ever; there are calls to preach the gospel in many places where it has not been usually published; yes, a glorious door is opened, and is likely to be opened wider and wider, by the spread of civil and religious liberty, accompanied also by a diminution of the spirit of popery; a noble effort has been made to abolish the inhuman slave trade, and though at present it has not been so successful as might be wished, yet it is to be hoped it will be persevered in, till it is accomplished. . . .

We must not be contented however with praying, without exerting ourselves in the use of means for the obtaining of those things we pray for. . . .

Suppose a company of serious Christians, ministers and private persons, were to form themselves into a society, and make a number of rules respecting the regulation of the plan, and the persons who are to be employed as missionaries, the means of defraying the expense, etc. This society must consist of persons whose hearts are in the work, men of serious religion, and possessing a spirit of perseverance; there must be a determination not to admit any person who is not of this description, or to retain him longer than he answers to it.

From such a society a committee might be appointed whose business it should be to procure all the information they could upon the subject, to receive contributions, to enquire into the characters, tempers, abilities and religious views of the missionaries, and also to provide them with necessaries for their undertakings. . . .

If there is any reason for me to hope that I shall have any influence upon any of my brethren, and fellow Christians, probably it may be more especially amongst them of my own denomination. I would therefore propose that such a society and committee should be formed amongst the particular Baptist denomination.

I do not mean by this, in any way to confine it to one denomination of Christians. I wish with all my heart that everyone who loves our Lord Jesus Christ in sincerity, would in some way or other engage in it. But in the present divided state of Christendom, it would be more likely for good to be done by each denomination engaging separately in the work, than if they were to embark in it conjointly. . . .

In respect to contributions for defraying the expenses, money will doubtless be wanting; and suppose the rich were to embark a portion of that wealth over which God has made them stewards, in this important undertaking, perhaps there are few ways that would turn to a better account at last.

Nor ought it to be confined to the rich; if persons in more moderate circumstances were to devote a portion, suppose a tenth, of their annual increase to the Lord, it would not only correspond with the practice of the Israelites, who lived under the Mosaic economy, but the patriarchs Abraham, Isaac, and Jacob, before that dispensation commenced. Many of our most eminent forefathers amongst the Puritans followed that practice; and if that were but attended to now, there would not only be enough to support the ministry of the gospel at home, and to encourage village preaching in our respective neighborhoods, but to defray the expenses of carrying the gospel into the heathen world.

If congregations were to open subscriptions of one penny, or more per week, according to their circumstances, and deposit it as a fund for the propagation of the gospel, much might be raised in this way. . . .

Many persons have of late left off the use of West India sugar on account of the iniquitous manner in which it is obtained. Those families who have done so, and have not substituted anything else in its place, have not only cleansed their hands of blood, but have made a saving to their families, some of sixpence, and some of a shilling a week. If this, or a part of this were appropriated to the uses before-mentioned, it would abundantly suffice. We have only to keep the end in view, and have our hearts thoroughly engaged in the pursuit of it, and means will not be very difficult.

Source: William Carey, *An Enquiry into the Obligations of Christians to use means for the Conversion of the Heathens* (Leicester: n.p., 1792).

16

THE "WALL OF SEPARATION"

*Danbury Baptist Association (Connecticut)
to President Jefferson, October 7, 1801*

Sir,

A MONG THE MANY MILLION IN America and Europe
who rejoice in your election to office, we embrace the first opportunity which we have enjoyed in our collective capacity since your inaugu-
ration, to express our great satisfaction, in your appointment to the chief
magistracy in the United States: And though our mode of expression
may be less courtly and pompous than what many others clothe their ad-
dresses with, we beg you sir, to believe, that none are more sincere.

Our sentiments are uniformly on the side of religious liberty—that
religion is at all times and places a matter between God and individuals—that no man ought to suffer in name, person, or effects on account
of his religious opinions—that the legitimate power of civil government
extends no further than to punish the man who works ill to his neighbor.
But, sir, our constitution of government is not specific. Our ancient charter, together with the laws made coincident therewith, were adopted as
the basis of our government at the time of our revolution; and such had
been our laws and usages, and such still are; that religion is considered as
the first object of legislation; and therefore what religious privileges we
enjoy (as a minor part of the state) we enjoy as favors granted, and not
as inalienable rights; and these favors we receive at the expense of such
degrading acknowledgements, as are inconsistent with the rights of freemen. It is not to be wondered at therefore, if those, who seek after power
and gain under the pretense of government and religion should reproach
their fellow man—should reproach their Chief magistrate, as an enemy
of religion, law and good order because he will not, dare not assume the
prerogative of Jehovah and make laws to govern the kingdom of Christ.

74

Sir, we are sensible that the president of the United States, is not the national legislator, and also sensible that the national government cannot destroy the laws of each state; but our hopes are strong that the sentiments of our beloved president, which have had such genial effect already, like the radiant beams of the sun, will shine and prevail through all these states and all the world till hierarchy and tyranny are destroyed from the earth. Sir when we reflect on your past services, and see a glow of philanthropy and good will shining forth in a course of more than thirty years we have reason to believe that America's God has raised you up to fill the chair of state out of that goodwill which he bears to the millions which you preside over. May God strengthen you for the arduous task which providence and the voice of the people have called you to sustain and support you and your administration against all the predetermined opposition of those who wish to rise to wealth and importance on the poverty and subjection of the people.

And may the Lord preserve you safe from every evil and bring you at last to his heavenly kingdom through Jesus Christ our Glorious Mediator.

President Jefferson to Danbury Baptist Association, January 1, 1802

Gentlemen:

The affectionate sentiments of esteem and approbation which you are so good as to express towards me on behalf of the Danbury Baptist Association, give me the highest satisfaction. My duties dictate a faithful and zealous pursuit of the interests of my constituents, and in proportion as they are persuaded of my fidelity to those duties, the discharge of them becomes more and more pleasing.

Believing with you that religion is a matter which lies solely between Man and his God, that he owes account to none other for his faith or his worship, that the legitimate powers of government reach actions only, and not opinions, I contemplate with sovereign reverence that act of the whole American people which declared that their legislature should "make no law respecting an establishment of religion, or prohibiting the free exercise," thus building a wall of separation between Church and State. Adhering to this expression of the supreme will of the nation in behalf of the rights of conscience, I shall see with sincere satisfaction the progress of those sentiments which tend to restore to man all natural rights, convinced he had no natural right in opposition to his social duties.

I reciprocate your kind prayers for the protection & blessing of the common father and creator of man, and tender you for yourselves & your religious association, assurances of my high respect & esteem.

Source: Thomas Jefferson Papers, Library of Congress, Washington, D.C.

17

FORMATION OF THE ENGLISH BAPTIST UNION, 1813

The Baptist Magazine

FOR SEVERAL YEARS PAST IT has been thought desirable, that a more general Union of the Baptist Churches than has hitherto, (at least, for the last 130 years) existed in this country, should be promoted. Our readers will recollect that several papers, tending to bring about this measure, have appeared in our Magazine during the past year, and we now cordially congratulate the friends of the Measure, that a basis has been laid for a general and beneficial Union of our churches.

As our work is designed to be a register of passing events in the denomination, we shall give the history of this Subject somewhat in detail. The Society of Associated ministers in London, consisting of the pastors of 17 churches, and other ministering brethren, being desirous of bringing about this object, which they had been requested by ministers in the country to undertake, appointed a Committee of seven persons to arrange the plan. They accordingly appointed a meeting to be held at Dr. [John] Rippon's Vestry, Carter Lane, at 8 o'clock on Thursday the 25th of June, and invited all the Baptist Ministers and Messengers of the churches to attend and take into consideration the proposed measure. . . .

Dr. Rippon being called to the chair, the meeting was opened with prayer, by Dr. Ryland.

After which the Chairman, having congratulated his Brethren who formed this pleasing and respectable Assembly, proceeded to observe, that for many years a Union Meeting of the representatives of the Particular or Calvinistic Baptist Churches in Town and Country had appeared to be an object of considerable importance—that of late the consideration of the subject had been resumed; and as it had been asked, What business would probably engage the attention of such an Assembly? He suggested, it had been thought,—

That one of the first and most important duties of it would no doubt be solemn Prayer to the God of all grace for the eminent out-pouring of his Holy Spirit on the Churches, and the whole world . . . That at such meetings our Missions in the East Indies would necessarily present a signal object of regard; when we should be able to recommend Auxiliary Societies, or Annual Collections for its support, in the far greater part of our Congregations.

That the yearly Accounts of the state of religion transmitted from the Associated Churches, and others, would create an endless variety of claims, either on our sympathy, our gratitude, or our benevolence; and, some of them, on the united exertions of the whole body.

That our Academies, the larger and smaller, would have their demands on our attention. How can they be more effectually supported? Can any other assistance be given to such whose views are towards the ministry?

That here suitable methods might be proposed by which the talents and influence of the most valuable members of every church might be brought into action, for the good of the whole.

That it would be natural to consult on the best methods of Catechizing, and to recommend the same to our families and churches.

That such an Assembly might deliberate on the most effectual means of supporting, all through the kingdom, aged respectable ministers—and on the provision which might be made for the education of the children of our Ministers deceased, as among the United Brethren, and other denominations of Christians.

That such an assembly would afford the best opportunities to concert plans for the encouragement and support of Village preaching—of Sunday Schools—and for the establishment of Penny, and also of Mite Societies, resembling those of our Brethren in various parts of America.

That here an opportunity would be given of recommending interesting publications, and of selecting, and disseminating through the country, such small tracts, and pamphlets, as the general state of religion, and of our own denomination might require.

That the Brethren assembled from the various districts would be able to advise where it is proper that New Meeting-houses should be erected; and of determining that, henceforward, no Case for building, enlarging, or repairing any place of worship, shall be countenanced, unless it has, previously to such erection or alteration, obtained, in writing, the direction, encouragement, and recommendation of the principal Ministers of their own district.

The Chairman then took a rapid glance at the state of the Baptist Churches in foreign parts; and closed with remarking that what he had been saying presented but a few articles, out of a vast multitude, which would press themselves on the consideration of such an Assembly, in which whatever relates to the real interests of the denomination at home and abroad, would engage the general attention. . . .

Source: *The Baptist Magazine* 4 (1812): 356–58.

18

ADDRESS AT THE FORMATION OF THE TRIENNIAL CONVENTION, 1814

Richard Furman

B ELOVED BRETHREN AND FRIENDS,
    In what manner and to what extent it has pleased the blessed God, of late, to direct the attention of many among us, to the interests of the Redeemer's Kingdom, some of you are already sensible, and others will learn from the preceding pages. Under the smiles of a propitious Providence, a Convention has assembled in Philadelphia, consisting of delegates from parts of our union, various and remote, to devise a plan, and enter into measures, for combining the efforts of our whole denomination, in behalf of the millions upon whom the light of evangelic truth has never shone. The result of their serious and affectionate consultations, you have an opportunity of perusing. . . .

    Within the last few years, it has pleased the good spirit of our God to awaken in his churches a serious concern for the diffusion of the Savior's cause. Numerous, and in some instances large associations of Christians have been formed for the purpose: considerable sums of money have been collected; bibles and religious tracts are extensively and gratuitously circulating, and the hope which thousands cherish that the glory of the latter days is at hand, is as operative as it is joyous. The blessing which has succeeded the efforts of our denomination in India, demands our gratitude. In a few years, the word of life will probably be translated into all the languages of the East. The change of sentiment relative to the subject of baptism that has lately occurred in the minds of two respectable characters, who were sent out as Missionaries by another denomination of our Christian brethren, appears to have been of the Lord and designed as a means of exciting the attention of our churches to foreign Missions. . . . The brevity of life, the value of immortal souls, the obligations under which divine mercy has laid us, our past inactivity, . . . and the incalculable blessings that may follow our endeavors, form a body of motive which we hope will kindle in many of our youth an ardent desire to enter on Missionary services, and in you the holy resolution to minister of your abundance to all who shall go forth in the name of the Lord.

But, while we call your attention to the spread of evangelic truth, we would impress on your minds that many other and most important advantages may arise to the interests of Christ among us from our acting as societies and on the more extended scale of a Convention, in delightful union. . . . Is it not a fact that our churches are ignorant of each other to a lamentable degree? But for the labors of one or two individuals, it is probable that whole Associations might have assembled in different parts of our Union without being known or knowing that others existed. . . .

The efforts of the present convention have been directed chiefly to the establishment of a foreign Mission; but, it is expected that when the general concert of their brethren and sufficient contributions to a common fund shall furnish them with proper instruction and adequate means, the promotion of the interests of the churches at home will enter into the deliberations of future meetings.

It is deeply to be regretted that no more attention is paid to the improvement of the minds of pious youth who are called to the gospel ministry. While this is neglected the cause of God must suffer. . . . Other denominations are directing their attention with signal ardor to the instruction of their youth for this purpose. . . . While we avow our belief that a refined or liberal education is not an indispensable qualification for ministerial service, let us never lose sight of its real importance, but labor to help our young men by our contributions, by the origination of education Societies, and if possible, by a general theological seminary, where some at least may obtain all the advantage which learning and mature studies can afford, ...

Source: *Proceedings of the Baptist Convention for Missionary Purposes* (Philadelphia: n.p., 1814), 38–43.

19

TREATISE ON SLAVERY, 1822
Richard Furman

Exposition of the Views of the Baptists Relative To The Coloured Population Of The United States in a Communication to the Governor of South Carolina

Charleston, 24th December 1822

Sir,

WHEN I HAD, LATELY, THE honor of delivering to your Excellency an Address, from the Baptist Convention in this State, requesting that a Day of Public Humiliation and Thanksgiving might be appointed . . . I took the liberty to suggest, that I had a further communication to make on behalf of the Convention, in which their sentiments would be disclosed respecting the . . . lawfulness of holding slaves—the subject being considered in a moral and religious point of view. . . .

On the lawfulness of holding slaves, considering it in a moral and religious view, the Convention think it their duty to exhibit their sentiments, . . . because they consider it their duty to God, the peace of the State, the satisfaction of scrupulous consciences, and the welfare of the slaves themselves, as intimately connected with a right view of the subject. The rather, because certain writers on politics, morals and religion, and some of them highly respectable, have advanced positions, and inculcated sentiments, very unfriendly to the principle and practice of holding slaves; . . . These sentiments, the Convention, on whose behalf I address your Excellency, cannot think just, or well founded; for the right of holding slaves is clearly established in the Holy Scriptures, both by precept and example. In the Old Testament, the Israelites were directed to purchase their bond-men and bond-maids of the Heathen nations; except they were of the Canaanites, for these were to be destroyed. . . .

In the New Testament, the Gospel History, or representation of facts, presents us with a view correspondent with that, which is furnished by other authentic ancient histories of the state of the world at the commencement of Christianity. The [empires] were full of slaves. Many of these with their masters, were converted to the Christian Faith, and received, together with them into the Christian Church, while it was yet under the ministry of the inspired Apostles. In things purely spiritual, they appear to have enjoyed equal privileges; but their relationship, as masters and slaves, were not dissolved. . . .

Had the holding of slaves been a moral evil, it cannot be supposed, that the inspired Apostles, who feared not the faces of men, and were ready to lay down their lives in the cause of their God, would have tolerated it. . . . If they had done so on a principle of accommodation, in cases where the masters remained heathen, to avoid offences and civil commotion; yet, surely, where both master and servant were Christian, as in the case before us, they would have enforced the law of Christ, and required, that the master should liberate his slave in the first instance. But, instead of this, they let the relationship remain untouched, as being lawful and right, and insist on the relative duties.

In proving this subject justifiable by Scriptural authority, its morality is also proved; for the Divine Law never sanctions immoral actions. . . .

[Slaves] become a part of his [the master's] family . . . and the care of ordering it, and of providing for its welfare, devolves on him. The children, the aged, the sick, the disabled, and the unruly, as well as those, who are capable of service and orderly, are the objects of his care: The labor of these is applied to the benefit of those, and to their own support, as well as to that of the master. Thus, what is effected, and often at a great public expense, in a free community, by taxes, benevolent institutions, bettering houses, and penitentiaries, lies here on the master, to be performed by him, whatever contingencies may happen; and often occasions much expense, care and trouble, from which the servants are free. Cruelty is certainly, inadmissible; but servitude may be consistent with such degrees of happiness as men usually attain in this imperfect state of things.

If the above representation of the Scriptural doctrine, and the manner of obtaining slaves from Africa is just; and if also purchasing them has been the means of saving human life, which there is great reason to believe it has; then, however the slave trade, in present circumstances, is justly censurable, yet might motives of humanity and even piety have been originally brought into operation in the purchase of slaves, when sold in the circumstances we have described. If, also, by their own confession, which has been made in manifold instances, their condition, when they have come into the hands of humane masters here, has been greatly bettered by the change; if it is, ordinarily, really better, as many assert, than that of thousands of the poorer classes in countries reputed civilized and free; and, if, in addition to all other considerations, the translation from their native country to this has been the means of their mental and religious improvement, and so of obtaining salvation, as many of themselves have joyfully and thankfully confessed—then may the just and humane master, who rules his slaves and provides for them, according to Christian principles, rest satisfied, that he is not, in holding them, chargeable with moral evil, nor with acting, in this respect, contrary to the genius of Christianity.—It appears to be equally clear, that those, who by reasoning on abstract principles, are induced to favor the scheme of general emancipation, and who ascribe their sentiments to Christianity, should be particularly careful . . . that they do not by a perversion of the Scriptural doctrine . . . not only invade the domestic and religious peace and rights of our Citizens, but, also by an intemperate zeal, prevent indirectly, the religious improvement of the people they design . . . to benefit; and, perhaps, become . . . the means of producing in our country, scenes of anarchy and blood; and all this in a vain attempt to bring about a state of things, which, if arrived at, would not probably better the state of that people; which is thought, by men of observation to be generally true of the Negroes in the Northern States, who have been liberated. . . .

. . . It is, therefore, firmly believed, that general emancipation to the Negroes in this country, would not, in present circumstances, be for their own happiness, as a body; while it would be extremely injurious to the community at large in various ways. . . . If a man has obtained slaves by purchase, or inheritance, and the holding of them as such is justifiable by the law of God; why should he be required to liberate them . . . ?

Should, however, a time arrive, when the Africans in our country might be found qualified to enjoy freedom; and, when they might obtain it in a manner consistent with the interest and peace of the community at large, the Convention would be happy in seeing them free: . . . But there seems to be just reason to conclude that a considerable part of the human race, whether they bear openly the character of slaves or are reputed free men, will continue in such circumstances . . . while the world continues. . . .

And here I am brought to a part of the general subject, which, I confess to your Excellency, the Convention . . . wish it may be seriously considered by all our Citizens: This is the religious interests of the Negroes. For though they are slaves, they are also men; and are with ourselves accountable creatures; having immortal souls, and being destined to future eternal award. Their religious interests claim a regard from their masters of the most serious nature; and it is indispensable. Nor can the community at large, in a right estimate of their duty and happiness, be indifferent on this subject. . . .

The Convention is particularly unhappy in considering, that an idea of the Bible's teaching the doctrine of emancipation as necessary, and tending to make servants insubordinate to proper authority, has obtained access to any mind; . . . the idea is an erroneous one; . . . the influence of a right acquaintance with that Holy Book tends directly and powerfully, by promoting the fear and love of God, together with just and peaceful sentiments toward men, to produce one of the best securities to the public, for the internal and domestic peace of the state.

It is also a pleasing consideration, . . . that in the late projected scheme for producing an insurrection among us, there were very few of those who were, as members attached to regular churches, . . . who appear to have taken a part in the wicked plot, . . . It is true, that a considerable number of those who were found guilty and executed, laid claim to a religious character; yet several of these were grossly immoral, and, in general, they were members of an irregular body, which called itself the *African Church*, and had intimate connection and intercourse with a similar body of men in a Northern City, among whom the supposed right to emancipation is strenuously advocated.

The result of this inquiry and reasoning, on the subject of slavery, brings us, sir, if I mistake not, very regularly to the following conclusions:—That the holding of slaves is justifiable by the doctrine and example contained in Holy writ; and is, therefore consistent with Christian uprightness, both in sentiment and conduct. That, all things considered, the Citizens of America have in general obtained the African slaves, . . . on principles, which can be justified; . . . That slavery, when tempered with humanity and justice, is a state of tolerable happiness; equal, if not superior, to that which many poor enjoy in countries reputed free. That a master has a scriptural right to govern his slaves so as to keep them in subjection; to demand and receive from them a reasonable service; and to correct them for the neglect of duty, for their vices and transgressions; but that to impose on them unreasonable, rigorous services, or to inflict on them cruel punishment, he has neither a scriptural nor a moral right. . . . That it is the positive duty of servants to reverence their master, to be obedient, industrious, faithful to him, and careful of his interests; and without being so, they can neither be the faithful servants of God, nor be held as regular members of the Christian Church. . . . That masters having the disposal of the persons, time and labor of their servants, and being the heads of families, are bound, on principles of moral and religious duty, to give these servants religious instruction; or at least, to afford them opportunities, under proper regulations to obtain it: And to grant religious privileges to those, who desire them, and furnish proper evidence of their sincerity and uprightness: Due care being at the same time taken, that they receive their instructions from right sources, . . . It is, also, believed to be a just conclusion, that the interest and security of the state would be promoted, by allowing, under proper regulations, considerable religious privileges, to such of this class, as know how to estimate them aright, and have given suitable evidence of their own good principles, uprightness and fidelity; . . . All which is, with deference, submitted to the consideration of your Excellency.

With high respect, I remain, personally, and on behalf of the
Convention,
Sir, your very obedient and humble servant,
RICHARD FURMAN
President of the Baptist State Convention

Source: Richard Furman, *Exposition of the Views of the Baptists Relative to the Coloured Population of the United States* (Charleston, SC: A. E. Miller, 1823).

20

PRIMITIVISM AND THE
ANTIMISSION MOVEMENT
Views on the Two Seeds, Daniel Parker, 1826

M UCH HAS BEEN SAID UPON the doctrine of Election and Non-Elect. If we could correctly understand the light afforded us, in this part of the curse levied on the serpent, for what he had done, it per-haps would afford us as much information as any part of Divine Writ. . . . I shall first show a distinction in the natural existence of these two seeds; and secondly, the two covenants by which they are distinguished.

First. The natural existence of these seeds appears first in our text [Genesis 3:15]—yet they are sources from whence they sprung. The seed of the woman was no doubt Christ in the prime or true sense of the word. Yet, as Christ and his church are one, He the head and the church the body, we shall find the seed to be the members of the body.

A Trinity appears in the one only true and living God. . . . thus as the Father, Word and Holy Ghost are all one, and in one, so was the man, seed, and the woman: God the Father, Christ the Seed, and the Holy Ghost the instrument of their spiritual existence. So as we bore the image of our natural father, from our natural birth, we shall bare the image of our Heavenly Father by this spiritual birth. . . .

We shall now return to man in his first formation. When Adam stood with his wife and seed in him, I cannot believe that there stood any in him but the church of Christ—therefore all that stood and fell in Adam, were the elect of God, chosen in Christ before the world began. Some of my reasons are these, (weigh them well), there are two settled points with me. First, that God never created a set of beings, neither directly nor indirectly, that he suffered to be taken from him, and made the subjects of his eternal wrath and indignation; (think how would this be consistent with the Divine Creator?). Second, that God, as God, in no case possess-es more love and mercy than power and wisdom. If he does, oh, think, the pain and distress the great I AM must feel and bear, to see the objects of his love and mercy to sink to woe and misery for the want of power and wisdom in himself to save (where would be the glory now?).

As there is a third point equally settled in my mind, which is that the Universalian doctrine is false, and that the unbelievers, dying in their sins, will sink to eternal woe—it now devolves on me to show from what source the Non-elect has sprung. So at it we go.

I shall first take another view of Adam; for as he bore the name, and was the head and sovereign, not only of his own seed and wife, but of all creation which was put under him, and they all were effected by his standing, or falling. So he was the figure of Christ, which was to come, who was the head of all principalities and powers, and all things were to be affected by his standing or falling in the work of redemption. As there can be no living head without a body, there can be no Christ without a church; and Christ was from everlasting to everlasting, ere the earth was, by and for whom the world was made. And as there can be no shadow without a substance, I view Adam with the seed and woman in him, the complete figure of the Lord Jesus Christ, with the church in him, before all worlds was: therefore, while he was in the world, he could look to his Father to glorify him, with the same glory he had with the Father before the world was.

Thus when the church was beguiled and had sinned, Christ was not deceived, but his love, relationship, and union to, and with her, was such that he could not be glorified without his bride, therefore he resolves to die with her, or that she should live with him; for it was impossible to separate them—his love was stronger than death. He takes upon himself, not the nature of angels, but the seed of Abraham, marries her human nature, owns the debt of his bride. . . . He bore our sins in his own body on the tree; dies for her sins: rises again for her justification, redeems her from the curse of the law, and brings life and immortality to light through the Gospel; washes her spiritual seed with his own blood, and fits them for eternal glory with himself. . . . This law required nothing to be done by Adam to preserve his standing, or making him any better—it was a law of prohibitions, (though a finite being) was able to perform. The act of doing became the sin. Thus we see where the spirit and principle of doing came from. The serpent distilled it into the woman, and set her to doing that which God had forbid, with a spirit of pride and unbelief, with a view of making herself something more than her God had made her; thus the spirit and principle of the works of the law for justification became instilled in the human heart, and has been at war with the sovereignty of God from that day to this. . . .

This brings us to the text—here God, as a curse to the Serpent for what he had done, lays the foundation of war between the Serpent and the woman, and the Serpent's seed the woman's seed. The woman here is certainly a figure of the church of Christ. The enmity of the Serpent against the church has plainly appeared through the persecutions in the different ages of the world while she standing opposed to the works of darkness, has proved her enmity to the Serpent. And the woman's seed here spoken of, I think was Christ and his elect in him, which was created in Adam, and by ordinary generation God designed should be brought into a natural existence in the world. And as Christ and his people are one, wherever I find one of this seed, distinguished in their natural birth, I shall feel authorized to notice it as the seed of the woman. The Serpent's seed here spoken of, I believe to be the Non-elect, which were not created in Adam, the original stock, but were brought into the world as the product of sin, by way of sin, by way of a curse on the woman, who by means of sin, was made susceptible of the seed of the Serpent, through the means of her husband, who had partook with her in the transgression, and thereby became the medium through which the Serpent's seed was, and is communicated to the woman, and she became the mother of this seed, which is evidently the curse God laid upon her, when, "Unto the woman he said, I will greatly multiply thy sorrow and thy conception, in sorrow shalt though bring forth children, and thy desire shall be to thy husband, and he shall rule over thee." . . .

. . . It is evident that there are that two seeds, the one of the Serpent, the other of the woman; and they appear plain in Cain and Abel, and their offsprings. The Serpent's seed is first spoken of, and Cain first appears, although Eve owns him as a man from the Lord, yet she does not claim him her seed; . . . Eve claims Abel as her seed, and can say at the birth of Seth, that God had appointed her another seed, instead of Abel, whom Cain slew.

Thus the enmity between the two seeds appears, and the wickedness on the part of the Serpent's seed, when Cain slew Abel. . . .

I am apprized that unbelieving critics will try to believe (notwithstanding what I have said on the subject) that agreeable to my views the Devil has created a great set of beings; this is not my view; for if the Devil had the power of creating, he would be almighty. There is a great difference between creating and begetting. A man may beget, but he cannot create. Which is most reasonable to believe, that Satan had power to beget a principle and nature in man (which is admitted on all sides) or to believe that he, by permission, possessed power to beget material existence through or by the beings God had made, and in whom he had begot his own principle and nature. . . .

Another point of inquiry arises, did the Serpent's seed, or Non-Elect, stand or fall in Adam? I answer, No, the elect of God only was created, stood, and fell in Adam, partook of the serpentine nature, and were by nature the children of wrath, even as others; and therefore the original sin is in, or entailed on them. . . . Although they did not receive it by the fall of man, yet they received this wicked nature immediately from the same corrupt source, which had involved the elect of God; thus in the nature of the two seeds no difference appears; for Satan had wholly captivated the elect, and engraved his image in their hearts.

And though Satan's seed had not fell in Adam, with the elect, under the curse of the divine law, yet they were sin in the abstract, flowing from the fountain of corruption. . . .

Come, my reader, let us reason together a moment. You may think my doctrine wretched—but think again, is it scripturally and experimentally reasonable to believe, but that there are sinners lost? Are these lost sinners the creatures of God by creation? Is it not more reasonable to believe they sprung from Satan, than from the Divine Being? As I think you believe with me, that God never created any one for destruction, is it not more to the glory and honor of God, to believe that he will punish Satan in his own seed, than in beings, which he himself had made, and Satan had got possession of? Does God possess more love and mercy than wisdom and power? Does he, as God, want to save more than he will or can save? How can these things be, and he be a God of infinite power and wisdom? . . .

. . . For although God did not create the Serpent's seed, or non-elect, in Adam, yet he had given man the power of begetting, and the woman of conceiving; and Satan, by sin, through the man, begets his seed in the woman, while God, for sin by the woman, multiplies her conception; and thus the Serpent's seed comes through the original stock, and yet God was not their creator in the original stock.

Source: Daniel Parker, *Views on the Two Seeds, taken from Genesis 3d chapter, and part of 15th verse* (Vandalia, Ill.: Robert Blackwell, 1826).

The Black Rock Address, 1832

Minutes of the Proceedings and Resolutions, Drafted by the Particular Baptists, convened at Black Rock, Maryland, September 28, 1832. A meeting of Particular Baptists of the Old School convened agreeable to a previous appointment at the Black Rock meeting-house, Baltimore, Md., on Friday, 28th September, 1832. Resolved, That a committee of seven brethren, viz: Trott, Healy, Poteet, Barton and Beebe, together with the Moderator and Clerk, be appointed to prepare an Address expressive of the views of this meeting, touching the object for which it was convened. The committee appointed to prepare an Address, submitted the following, which was unanimously adopted. To the Particular Baptist Churches of the "Old School" in the United States.

BRETHREN:—It constitutes a new era in the history of the Baptists, when those who would follow the Lord fully, and who therefore manifest a solicitude to be, in all things pertaining to religion, conformed to the Pattern showed in the mount, are by Baptists charged with antinomianism, inertness, stupidity, &c., for refusing to go beyond the word of God; but such is the case with us.

We will notice several of the claims of the principal of these modern inventions, and state some of our objections to them for your candid consideration.

We commence with the Tract Societies. These claim to be extensively useful. Tracts claim their thousands converted. They claim the prerogative of carrying the news of salvation into holes and corners, . . . and they claim each to contain gospel enough, should it go where the Bible has never come, to lead a soul to the knowledge of Christ. . . .

If we were to admit that tracts may have occasionally been made instrumental by the Holy Ghost for imparting instruction or comfort to inquiring minds, it would by no means imply that tracts are an instituted means of salvation . . . we cannot admit the propriety of uniting with or upon the plans of the existing Tract Societies, even laying aside the idea of their being attempted to be palmed upon us as religious institutions. . . . They [those who join societies] thus become accustomed to receive everything as good which comes under the name of religion, whether it be according to the word of God or not; and are trained to the habit of letting others judge for them in matters of religion, and are therefore fast preparing to become the dupes of priestcraft. Can any conscientious follower of the Lamb submit to such plans? If others can, we cannot.

Sunday Schools come next under consideration. These assume the same high stand as do Tract Societies. They claim the honor of converting their tens of thousands; of leading the tender minds of children to the knowledge of Jesus; of being as properly the instituted means of bringing children to the knowledge of salvation, as is the preaching of the gospel that of bringing adults to the same knowledge, &c. Such arrogant pretensions we feel bound to oppose. First, because these as well as the pretensions of the Tract Societies are grounded upon the notion that conversion or regeneration is produced by impressions made upon the natural mind by means of religious sentiments instilled into it; and if the Holy Ghost is allowed to be at all concerned in the thing, it is in a way which implies his being somehow blended with the instruction, or necessarily attendant upon it; all of which we know to be wrong.

Secondly, because such schools were never established by the apostles, nor commanded by Christ. . . .

Thirdly. We have exemplified in the case of the Pharisees, the evil consequences of instructing children in the letter of the Scripture, under the notion that this instruction constitutes a saving acquaintance with the word of God. We see in that instance that it only made hypocrites of the Jews; and . . . we cannot believe it will have any better effect on the children in our day.

We pass to the consideration of the Bible Society . . . The idea of giving the Bible, without note or comment, to those who are unable to procure it for themselves, is in itself considered, calculated to meet the approbation of all who know the importance of the sacred Scriptures. But under this auspicious guise, we see reared in the case of the American Bible Society, an institution as foreign from anything which the gospel of Christ calls for, as are the kingdoms of this world from the kingdom of Christ. . . . We see united in this combination all parties in politics, and all sects in religion; and the distinctive differences of the one, and the sectarian barriers of the other, in part thrown aside to form the union. At the head of this vast body we see placed a few leading characters, who have in their hands the management of its enormous printing establishment, and its immense funds, and the control of its powerful influence, . . .

We will now call your attention to the subject of Missions. Previous to stating our objections to the mission plans, we will meet some of the false charges brought against us relative to this subject, by a simple and unequivocal declaration, that we do regard as of the first importance the command given of Christ, . . . to "Go into all the world, and preach the gospel to every creature," . . . We also believe it to be the duty of individuals and churches to contribute according to their abilities, for the support, not only of their pastors, but also of those who go preaching the gospel of Christ among the destitute. But we at the same time contend, that we have no right to depart from the order which the Master himself has seen fit to lay down, relative to the ministration of the word. We therefore cannot fellowship the plans for spreading the gospel, generally adopted at this day, under the name of Missions; because we consider those plans throughout a subversion of the order marked out in the New Testament. . . .

Brethren, we cheerfully acknowledge that there have been some honorable exceptions to the character we have here drawn of the modern missionary, and some societies have existed under the name of Mission Societies which were in some important points exceptions from the above drawn sketch; but on a general scale we believe we have given a correct view of the mission plans and operations, and of the effects which have resulted from them, and our hearts really sicken at this state of things. . . .

Colleges and Theological Schools next claim our attention. In speaking of colleges, we wish to be distinctly understood that it is not to colleges, or collegial education, as such, that we have any objection. We would cheerfully afford our own children such an education, did circumstances warrant the measure. But we object, in the first place, to sectarian colleges, as such. The idea of a Baptist College, and of a Presbyterian College, &c., necessarily implies that our distinct views of church government, of gospel doctrine and gospel ordinances, are connected with human sciences, a principle which we cannot admit: . . . In the second place, we object to the notion of attaching professorships of divinity to colleges; because this evidently implies that the revelation which God has made of himself is a human science on a footing with mathematics, philosophy, law, &c. . . . Thirdly. We decidedly object to persons, after professing to have been called of the Lord to preach his gospel, going to a college or academy to fit themselves for that service.—1st. Because we believe that Christ possesses perfect knowledge of his own purposes, and of the proper instruments by which to accomplish them. . . . 2nd. Because we believe that the Lord calls no man to preach his gospel, till he has made him experientially acquainted with that gospel, and endowed him with the proper measure of gifts suiting the field he designs him to occupy. . . .

We now pass to the last item which we think it necessary particularly to notice, viz: four-days or protracted meetings. . . . Therefore, whenever circumstances call a congregation together from day to day, as at an association or the like, we would embrace the opportunity of preaching the gospel to them from time to time . . . but to the principles and plans of protracted meetings, distinguishingly so called, we do decidedly object. The principle of these meetings we cannot fellowship. Regeneration, we believe, is exclusively the work of the Holy Ghost, performed by his divine power, at his own sovereign pleasure, according to the provisions of the everlasting covenant; but these meetings are got up either for the purpose of inducing the Holy Spirit to regenerate multitudes who would otherwise not be converted, or to convert them themselves by the machinery of these meetings, . . .

Brethren, we have thus laid before you some of our objections to the popular schemes in religion, and the reasons why we cannot fellowship them. Ponder these things well. Weigh them in the balances of the sanctuary; and then say if they are not such as justify us in standing aloof from those plans of men, and those would-be religious societies, which are bound together, not by the fellowship of the gospel, but by certain money payments. If you cannot for yourselves meet the reproach by separating yourselves from those things which the word of God does not warrant, still allow us the privilege to obey God rather than man.

Source: B. L. Beebe, ed., *The Feast of Fat Things* (Middletown, NY: G. Beebe's Son, n.d.), 3–30.

21

REPORT AND WARNING ABOUT CAMPBELLISM, 1830

Franklin Baptist Association (Kentucky)

TO THE CHURCHES COMPOSING THE Franklin Association.

Dear Brethren:

You will learn from our Minutes, the results of this called session of our association. Before Alexander Campbell visited Kentucky, you were in harmony and peace; you heard but the one gospel, and knew only the one Lord, one faith and one baptism. Your church constitutions were regarded, and their principles expounded and enforced, by those who occupied your pulpits. Thus you were respected by other denominations, as a religious community. . . . Have not these happy days gone by? In place of preaching, you now may hear your church covenants ridiculed, your faith, as registered upon your church books, denounced, and yourselves traduced; while the more heedless and unstable, abjure the faith, and join with the wicked, in scenes of strife, schism and tumult. The fell spirit of discord stalks in open day through families, neighborhoods and churches. If you would protect yourselves as churches, make no compromise with error; mark them who cause divisions; divest yourselves of the last vestige of Campbellism.

As an Association we shall esteem it our duty to drop correspondence with any and every Association, or Church, where this heresy is tolerated. Those who say they are not Campbellites, and yet countenance and circulate his little pamphlets, are insincere: they are to be avoided. . . .

. . . And that you may know the full extent of our objections, we herewith send you several articles gathered from his Christian Baptist, and Millennial Harbinger with a reference to the pamphlet and to the page, where you can read and judge, whether they are, or are not, the reformation tenets.

It may be said that these scraps are garbled from many volumes. Verily, they are but scraps; but each scrap embodies an opinion easily understood; so that this may, with some propriety, be called a Confession of Opinions. We are not obliged to re-publish his pamphlets. Were we, however, to do it, the nature and bearing of these opinions would not be changed.

THE THIRTY-NINE ARTICLES!!
or
A new edition of old errors, extracted from Alexander Campbell's Christian
Baptist and Millenial Harbinger.

1. "That there has been no preaching of the gospel since the days of the apostles."

2. "That the people have been preached to from texts of scripture until they have been literally preached out of their senses." . . .

5. "That all the faith that men can have in Christ, is historical . . ."

8. "That baptism, which is synonymous with immersion, and for which every such believer is a proper subject, actually washes away sin, and is regeneration. . . ."

9. "That in the moral fitness of things in the evangelical economy, baptism or immersion is made the first act of a Christian's life, or rather the regenerating act itself; in which the person is properly born again—born of water and spirit—without which, into the kingdom of heaven he cannot enter." . . . C[hristian]. B[aptist]. vol. 5, p. 223. . . .

12. "That by the mere act of a believing immersion into the name of the Father, Son, and Holy Spirit, we are born again, have all our sins remitted, receive the Holy Spirit, and are filled with joy and peace." C. B. vol. 5, p. 213. "Query. Is a believer in Christ not actually in a pardoned state, before he is baptized? Answer. Is not a man clean before he is washed!! . . . And, blessed be God! He has not drawn a mere artificial line between the plantations of nature and of grace. No man has any proof that he is pardoned until he is baptized . . ." Ch. Bap. vol. 6, p. 188.

13. "That Christian immersion is the gospel in water. The Lord's supper is the gospel in bread and wine." C. B. vol. 5, p. 158. As water saved Noah, so baptism saves us. . . ." C. B. vol. 7, p. 125. . . .

16. "All the sons of men cannot show that there is any other faith, but the belief of facts either written in the form of history or orally delivered. Angels, men, or demons, cannot define anything under the term faith,

but the belief of facts or of history; except they change it into confidence. . . ." C. B. 6 vol. p. 186. . . .

18. "Millions have been tantalized by a mock gospel, which places
them as the fable places Tautalus, standing in a stream parched with
thirst, and the water running to his chin, and so circumstanced that he
could not taste it. There is a sleight of hand, or religious legerdemain, in
getting around the matter. To call anything grace, or favor, or gospel, not
adapted to man, as it finds him, is the climax of misnomers. To bring the
cup of salvation to the lips of a dying sinner, and then tell him for his soul
he cannot taste it, without some sovereign aid beyond human control, is
to mock his misery and to torment him more and more." C. B. 6 vol. p.
187. . . .

26. "I have not spent, perhaps, an hour in ten years in thinking about
the Trinity. It is no term of mine. It is a word which belongs not to the
bible, in any translation of it I ever saw. I teach nothing, I say nothing
about it, save that it is not a scriptural term, and consequently, can have
no scriptural ideas attached to it." C. B. 7 vol. p. 208. . . .

28. "Come, Holy Spirit, Heavenly Dove,
    With all thy quick'ning powers!
    Kindle a flame of sacred love
    In these cold hearts of ours."

"In the singing of this hymn, which is very ingeniously adapted to
your sermon and prayer, you have unfortunately fallen into two errors.
First—you are singing to the Holy Spirit, as you prayed to it, without example from any of the old saints, either in the Old or New Testament; and
without the possibility of ever receiving an answer to your prayer. The
second error into which you have fallen, is this: you acknowledge your
church to be the church of Christ; and if the church of Christ, its members of course have the spirit of Christ."—Ch. Bap. vol. VII, p. 129. . . .

32. "THE BELIEF OF ONE FACT, and that upon the best evidence
in the word, is all that is requisite as far as faith goes, to salvation. The
belief of this one FACT, and submission to ONE INSTITUTION expressive of it, is all that is required of Heaven to admission into the church.
The one fact is, that Jesus, the Nazarene, is the Messiah. The evidence
upon which it is to be believed, is, the testimony of twelve men, confirmed by prophecy, miracles, and spiritual gifts. The one institution is,
baptism into the name of the Father, and of the Son, and of the Holy
Spirit. Every such person is a Christian, in the fullest sense of the word."
C. B. vol. 1, p. 221.

33. "Revivals. Enthusiasm flourishes, blooms, under the popular systems. This man was regenerated when asleep by a vision of the night. That man heard a voice in the woods, saying, 'Thy sins are forgiven thee.' A third saw his Savior descending to the tops of the trees at noon day. A thousand form a band, and set up all night to take heaven by surprise. Ten thousand are waiting for a power from on high, to descend upon their souls; they frequent meetings for the purpose of obtaining this power." C. B. 1 vol. p. 187. . . .

35. Some look for another call, a more powerful call than the written Gospel presents. They talk of an inward call, of hearing the voice of God in their souls. This special call is either a lie or it makes the general call a lie. This is where the system ends. The voice of God, and the only voice of God, which you will hear, till he calls you home, is his written Gospel." Mil. Har. No. 3, p. 126–7. . . .

38. "In the natural order of the evangelical economy, the items stand thus:—1st, Faith; 2d, Reformation; 3d, Immersion; 4th, Remission of sins; 5th, Holy Spirit; 6th, Eternal Life." C. B. 6 vol. p. 66. "There are three Kingdoms; the Kingdom of Law, the Kingdom of Favor, and the Kingdom of Glory; each has a different constitution, different subject's privileges, and terms of admission. The blood of Abraham brought a man into the Kingdom of Law, and gave him an inheritance in Canaan. Being born, not of blood, but through water and the spirit of God, brings a person into the Kingdom of Favor; which is righteousness, peace, joy, and a holy spirit, with a future inheritance in prospect. But if the justified draw back, or the washed return to the mire, or if faith dies and brings forth no fruits, into the Kingdom of Glory he cannot enter. Hence good works through faith, or springing from faith in Jesus, give a right to enter into the holy city." C. B. 6 vol. 255. . . .

39. Vol. 5, p. 122. "There is no democracy nor aristocracy in the governmental arrangements of the church of Jesus Christ. The citizens are all volunteers when they enlist under the banners of the Great King, and as soon as they place themselves in the ranks, they are bound to implicit obedience in all the institutes and laws of their sovereign. So that there is no putting the question to vote, whether they shall obey any particular law or injunction. Their Rulers or Bishops have to give an account of their administration, and have only to see that the laws are known and obeyed."

[Truly, this is not democracy; nor is it a moderate aristocracy. What is it, short of Episcopacy or Papacy!]

BRETHREN: Can you read this, and say or think that it is not, even now, high time to "march out of Babylon?" Doubtless you cannot hesitate. In February, 1825, Mr. Campbell denounced reformation. "The very name, (he said), has become as offensive as the term "Revolution" in France." He is now in a paroxism about Reformation. In all the extravagance of unbridled fanaticism, he fancies that he has already introduced the Millenium, as far as his tenets, have prevailed. The Millenium, he dreams, has bursted in upon South Benson, Versailles, Clear Creek, David's Fork, and Shawnee Run. Who besides himself, and those who have sold their birth right—who have commuted their heads and hearts for reformation pottage, can indulge in a conceit so silly and ridiculous. From such frenzy and quackery, and above all from such a Millenium, may a kind Providence deliver us. Amen.

Source: *Minutes*, Franklin Association of Baptists, Frankfort, Kentucky, July 1830.

22

THE GEORGIA TEST CASE AND THE ALABAMA RESOLUTIONS

The Georgia Test Case, American Baptist Home Mission Society, 1844

T HE EXECUTIVE BOARD OF THE American Baptist Home Mission Society, having examined the application of the Executive Committee of the Georgia Baptist Convention for the appointment of Eld. James E. Reeve, feel it their duty to state that, in addition to the information required of applicants this communication contains a statement that Mr. Reeve is a slaveholder, and that fact is offered as a reason for his appointment, in the following terms: "We wish his appointment so much the more, as it will stop the mouth of gainsayers. I will explain. There are good brethren among us, who, notwithstanding the transactions of our Society at Philadelphia, are hard to believe that you will appoint a slaveholder as a Missionary, even when the funds are supplied by those who wish such an appointment." The application, therefore, is an unusual one.

We disclaim attributing to our Georgia brethren a design to *disturb the deliberations of the Board* by introducing the subject of slavery through the medium of their application, but such, evidently, is its tendency. In the opinion of several members of the Board, the application seeks the appointment, not in the usual manner, merely of a Missionary, but of a slaveholder, and is designed as a test whether the Board will appoint a slaveholder as a Missionary, . . .

The appointment of Missionaries, constitutionally eligible, and recommended according to our established rules, without the introduction of extraneous considerations calculated to disturb our deliberations, this Board are during the period of their appointment, sacredly bound in equity and justice, to make, to the extent of their pecuniary ability—keeping in view a fair distribution throughout the field, of the funds, committed to their trust. But when an application is made for the appointment of a slaveholder, or an abolitionist, or an anti-slavery man, as such, or for appropriations to fields where the design of the applicant is apparently to test the action of the Board in respect to the subjects of slavery or anti-slavery, their official obligation either to act on the appointment or to entertain the application, ceases. Therefore,

Resolved, That in view of the preceding considerations it is not expedient to introduce the subjects of slavery or anti-slavery into our deliberations, nor to entertain applications in which they are introduced.

Resolved, That taking into consideration all the circumstances of the case, we deem ourselves not at liberty to entertain the application for the appointment of Rev. James E. Reeve.

Resolved, That the Corresponding Secretary transmit a copy of the foregoing views and resolutions to the Chairman of the Executive Committee of the Georgia Convention.

By order of the Executive Board.

BENJAMIN M. HILL, Cor. Sec'y.

Source: From *Minutes of the Meetings of the American Baptist Home Mission Society and of Its Executive Committee*, 7 Oct. 1844 book 2, 303.

The Alabama Resolution, Baptist General Convention (Alabama), 1844

Marion, Perry Co., Alabama, Nov. 25, 1844. Eld. Daniel Sharp, President of the Board of Managers of the Baptist General Convention.

Dear Brother:—Agreeably to the appointment of "The Baptist State Convention of Alabama," we transmit to you the following preamble and resolutions, and request you to lay them before the Board. We shall wait your reply.

Preamble and Resolutions

Whereas, The holding property in African negro slaves has for some years excited discussion, as a question of morals, between different portions of the Baptist denomination united in benevolent enterprise; and by a large portion of our brethren is now imputed to the slaveholders in these Southern and South-western States, as a sin, at once grievous, palpable, and disqualifying:—

1. *Resolved*, By the Convention of the Baptist denomination in the State of Alabama, that when one party to a voluntary compact among Christian brethren is not willing to acknowledge the entire social equality with the other, as to all the privileges and benefits of the union, nor even to refrain from impeachment and annoyance, united efforts between

such parties, even in the sacred cause of Christian benevolence, cease to be agreeable, useful, or proper.

2. *Resolved*, That our duty at this crisis requires us to demand from the proper authorities in all those bodies to whose funds we have contributed, or with whom we have in any way been connected, the distinct, explicit, avowal that slaveholders are eligible, and entitled, equally with non-slaveholders, to all the privileges and immunities of their several unions; and especially to receive any agency, mission, or other appointment, which may run within the scope of their operation or duties. . . .

5. *Resolved*, also, That the Treasurer of this body be, and he is hereby instructed, not to pay any money intended to be applied without the limits of this State, except at the written order of the President of this Convention, with the concurrence of the Board of officers before mentioned; and this body, profoundly sensible of the vast issues dependent on the principles herein advanced, will await, in prayerful expectation, the responses of our non-slaveholding brethren. . . .

Reply of the Acting Board, American Baptist Home Mission Society, 1844

Dear Sir:—We have received from you a copy of a Preamble and Resolutions which were passed by the "Baptist State Convention of Alabama." And as there is a "demand" for distinct and explicit answers from our Board to the inquiries and propositions which you have been pleased to make, we have given to them our deliberate and candid attention.

Before proceeding to answer them, allow us to express our profound regret that they were addressed to us. They were not necessary. We have never, as a Board, either done, or omitted to do, any thing which requires the explanation and avowals that your resolutions "demanded." They also place us in the new and trying position of being compelled to answer hypothetical questions, and to discuss principles, or of seeming to be evasive and timid, and not daring to give you the information and satisfaction which you desire. . . .

We need not say that slaveholders, as well as non-slaveholders, are unquestionably entitled to all the privileges and immunities which the Constitution of the Baptist General Convention permits and grants to its members. We would not deprive either of any of the immunities of the mutual contract. In regard, however, to any agency, mission, or other appointment, no slaveholder or non-slaveholder, however large his subscription to Foreign Missions, or those of the church with which he is connected, is on that account entitled to be appointed to any agency or a mission. The appointing power, for wise and good reasons, has been confided to the "Acting Board," they holding themselves accountable to the Convention for the discreet and faithful discharge of this trust.

Should you say, "the above remarks are not sufficiently explicit, we wish distinctly to know whether the Board would or would not appoint a slaveholder as a Missionary;"—before directly replying, we would say, that in the thirty years in which the Board has existed no slaveholder, to our knowledge, has applied to be a Missionary. And as we send out no domestics or servants, such an event as a Missionary taking slaves with him, were it morally right, could not, in accordance with all our past arrangements or present plans, possibly occur. If, however, any one should offer himself as a Missionary, having slaves, and should insist on retaining them as his property, we could not appoint him. One thing is certain; we can never be a party to any arrangement which would imply approbation of slavery. . . .

In regard to our Board, there is no point on which we are more unanimously agreed than that of the independence of churches. We disclaim all and every pretension to interfere with the discipline of any church. We disfellowship no one. Nevertheless, were a person to offer himself as a candidate for Missionary service, although commended by his church as in good standing, we should feel it our duty to open our eyes on any facts to the disadvantage of his moral and religious character, which might come under our observation. And while we should not feel that it was our province to excommunicate or discipline a candidate of doubtful character, yet we should be unworthy of our trust, if we did not, although he were a member of a church, reject his application. . . .

We have, with all frankness, but with entire kindness and respect, defined our position. If our brethren in Alabama, with this exposition of our principles and feelings, can co-operate with us, we shall be happy to receive their aid. If they can not, painful to us as will be their withdrawal, yet we shall submit to it as neither sought nor caused by us.

There are sentiments avowed in this communication, which, although held temperately and kindly, and with all due esteem and Christian regard for the brethren addressed, are nevertheless, dearer to us than any pecuniary aid whatever.

We remain yours, truly,
In behalf of the Board,
DAN. SHARP, President.

BARON STOW, Rec. Sec'y.
Ray. JESSE HARTWELL, President Alabama Baptist State Convention.

Source: *The Baptist Missionary Magazine*, August, 1845, Vol. XXV, 220 ff.

23

Southern and Northern Perspectives on the 1845 Schism

A Southern Perspective, Religious Herald (Virginia), 1845

W E LAST WEEK STATED THAT the Board of the Baptist Triennial Convention, after mature deliberation, had decided that they could not, and would not appoint a slaveholder, a missionary. A decision so adverse to the rights of the Southern portion of the Baptist church it could not fail to attract immediate attention, and decided action. As soon, therefore, as suitable notice could be given, the Board of the Virginia Baptist Foreign Missionary Society, met at the Second Baptist Church in this city, and the result of their deliberations our readers will perceive from the accompanying documents.

We have no doubt but that their course will be approved by the great body of the Southern and South Western Baptists. We have for some time felt apprehensive, that union could not be much longer maintained. The altered tone of the Baptist periodicals in New England, and in some of the Western states, since the meeting of the Convention in April; their constant and unremitted denunciations of slaveholders—the frequent annunciation that the Board was becoming daily more pro-slavery; the passage of antislavery resolutions at the annual meeting of the Boston and Salem associations gave strong premonitory symptoms of the existence of a feverish excitement, which would probably at a distant period, exhibit itself in some overt act which would compel the South to withdraw. . . .

At the last meeting the Convention decided that they had no control over slavery or anti-slavery——that these questions should have no bearing on their acts as a missionary body. Acting on this principle, slaveholders as well as anti-slavery members, were placed on the Board. If the Convention had not been willing to recognize the equality of their Southern brethren; to admit them to all offices, agencies, and appointments, as readily as non slaveholders, that would surely have been the proper time to have laid down the rule of future action. But they, voluntarily and freely elected, several slaveholders as members of the Board, selected to conduct its operations until the next annual meeting.

In this course they but carried out the principle strictly adhered to from the first organization of the Society. . . . Several of the delegates, and members of the first Board, were slaveholders. . . . Without the co-operation of Southern Baptists, it would probably not have been formed; at least its ability to do good must have been seriously curtailed. Slaveholders, then, formed an essential part of the social compact. . . .

The course of the Convention has been uniform and decided on the subject. There has been no exhibition of doubt or hesitation. On every suitable occasion, the right of the South to a full participation of all the offices and privileges in the gift of the Society, was fully and freely admitted. Slavery was declared to be a subject over which it had no cognizance—which it would not entertain nor discuss.

If the Convention was thus precise and guarded in its action on this subject, it certainly intended that the Board to which the direction of its business was entrusted during the interim betwixt one meeting and another, should be equally cautious. It had laid down the principle and it had a right to expect that it should be a rule of action to the Board. The Board surely had no right to adopt a course which the society had disclaimed. . . . If any one thing was clearly laid down as a part of its policy, a maxim from which it would not depart, at its last meeting, it was that the subject of slavery and slaveholding, as connected with the rights of southern members, should not be entertained. The Board, therefore, had no right to impose a test which the Convention by its uniform course had rejected . . . no authority was given to the Board, or could be intended to be conferred upon it, to nullify the acts of their principal by saying—you have appointed slaveholders to office, you have recognized their equality, but we will not give them our sanction—we will not appoint them missionaries.

But it seems they wished to show their disapprobation of slavery. . . . If an alteration was deemed expedient it was the province of the Convention to change the existing relation, not theirs. They were allowed to entertain their own views, elsewhere, but not in the Convention, and of course not in the Board. . . . As agents they ought to have said to the Alabama brethren—this is a question we must leave to the Convention—they have decided that no difference shall be made, betwixt the friends and opponents of slavery, . . .

At each session of the Convention a Board of Managers is chosen, consisting of eighteen vice presidents, and forty managers, besides the officers, scattered throughout the different states of the Union which send delegates to the Convention. A portion of these members living in and around Boston, are termed the Acting Board. Now, all these members have a right to meet with the Acting Board, and to participate in its proceedings. In any difficult case, they can be called on to attend, and afford to the Acting Board the aid of their counsel. Seventeen of these members reside in the slaveholding states, and a majority of them would probably have been opposed to the decision of the Board. Why, on such a momentous question, were not the other members consulted? . . .

There was a portion of the Baptists in the New England states, who were not willing to join the Free Baptist Foreign Missionary Society, believing that they could influence the Board to do some act which would cause a rupture with the South. The [Christian] Reflector, their organ, was constantly boasting, that the Board was becoming more pro-slavery. It confidently asserted that no slaveholder would be appointed as a missionary. It was asserted as a fact that the Home Secretary, Dr. Pattison, was corresponding with Jesse Bushyhead, one of its missionaries, and a slaveholder, to induce him to resign. His death occurring removed this difficulty. These intimations probably induced the Alabama Convention to propose the enquiry to the Board. To secure apparently the good will of this fraction of the Baptist church, the Board have decided to disfranchise the South. . . .

Of 707,942 Baptists in the United States in 1844, by the returns in the Baptist Almanack, 391,211, considerably over one half are in the slaveholding states. If according to an admitted principle, the majority ought to govern, the opinions of that majority ought to have been ascertained and respected by the Board. . . .

A Southern Convention had been suggested some months ago, by the Editor of the Christian Index. We have no doubt that it will be generally approved, and we trust unite in harmonious co-operation with the South. The time and place are simply suggested, and may be altered if deemed expedient. Under present circumstances, we deem further cooperation no longer expedient, nor desirable. To be consistent, the Board must reject slaveholding agents, and slaveholding members of the Board. . . .

TO THE BAPTIST CHURCHES OF VIRGINIA. Dear Brethren: Accompanying this communication you will find a letter addressed by the Board of the Baptist Triennial Convention to the Rev. Jesse Hartwell, President of the Alabama State Convention, in reply to a preamble and resolutions recently adopted by this body. . . . But the letter of the Board has dissipated all misconception on this subject. From it we learn that no slaveholder, under any circumstances, would be appointed by the Board as a missionary, or even as an agent, (this is plainly implied,) to collect funds from slaveholding churches. Concerning this unexpected resolution of the Board, we wish to speak with candor and courtesy, but we must also speak with frankness and firmness. It is an outrage on our rights. This will clearly appear for the following considerations:—

1. The decision of the Board is unconstitutional. The Triennial Convention was formed and, from its organization, it has been sustained by slaveholders and non slave-holders. They have met and acted in the Convention itself, and in its Board, on terms of perfect social and religious equality. No man, who is at all acquainted with the history of the Convention, can entertain any doubt that the Southern Baptists would have indignantly refused to co-operate with it on any terms implying their inferiority. . . .

2. The decision of the Board is a manifest violation of the compromise resolution adopted at the last meeting of the Convention. This is the resolution—"Resolved, That in cooperating together as members of this Convention in the work of Foreign Missions, we disclaim all sanction, either expressed or implied, whether of slavery or of anti slavery; but, as individuals, we are perfectly free both to express and to promote, elsewhere our own views on these subjects in a Christian manner and spirit." . . .

. . . The Convention resolved that the views of slavery or of anti-slavery should be no bar to harmonious effort;

3. The decision of the Board is inconsistent with admissions made by the letter under consideration. . . .

4. The decision of the Board is unjust to the Southern supporters of the Convention. From the organization of the Convention to the present time, the Baptists of the South have contributed cheerfully, and in some cases, liberally, to its treasury. But, can any man believe they would have made these contributions, had they known, or even suspected, that the Board would have refused to appoint a slaveholder, under any circumstances, as a missionary or agent? . . .

5. The decision of the Board, supposing it was not intended to produce division, is as unwise as it is unjust.

A slaveholder would not be likely to apply for an appointment as a missionary to the East—and certainly he would not think of carrying slaves with him on such a mission. But suppose a slaveholder should desire an appointment as a missionary among the Indians,—he might be eminently qualified for the office; intelligent, pious, humane to his slaves, held in high estimation by his brethren; such a minister in a word, as has heretofore been cheerfully admitted into Northern pulpits; his slaves might earnestly desire to accompany him, and there might be no law to prevent it, and no prejudice against slavery in the proposed field of his labor to diminish his usefulness; and yet, under the decision of the Board, he would be ineligible to the appointment. . . .

In view, brethren, of these considerations, we feel that we have been injured by the decision of the Board. For their conscientious opinions on the subject of slavery, we censure them not. If they are unwilling to co-operate with slaveholding Christians in the Missionary enterprise, we have no right to complain. We have cherished a sincere sympathy with them in their delicate and embarrassing situation.—We have vindicated their conduct and their motives. We have cherished no unfavorable suspicions against them. But we are disappointed, and pained at their decision—a decision which tramples alike on the constitution and the rights of Southern members.

And now brethren, in this exigency, what shall we do? To remain united with the Board is impossible. Self respect forbids it. All hope that the Board will revoke their decision is vain. They have acted, so we learn from the *Christian Reflector*, deliberately and unanimously. They have examined the ground, and taken their position.

In view of the considerations above presented, the Board of the Virginia Foreign Mission Society has adopted the following resolutions:

1. Resolved, That this Board have seen with sincere pain the decision of the Board of the Baptist Triennial Convention, contained in a recent letter addressed to Rev. Jesse Hartwell, of Ala. and that we deem the decision unconstitutional, and in violation of the rights of the Southern members of the Convention; and that all farther connection with the Board, on the part of such members is inexpedient and improper.

2. Resolved, That the Treasurer of this Board be required to deposit in one of the Savings banks of the city, any funds which may be in his hands or which may come into them, to be disposed of as the Society, at its annual meeting, may direct.

3. Resolved, That this Board are of opinion, that in the present exigency, it is important that those brethren who are aggrieved by the recent decision of the Board in Boston, should hold a Convention to confer on the best means of promoting the Foreign Mission cause, and other interests of the Baptist denomination in the South.

4. Resolved, That in the judgment of this Board, Augusta, Geo., is a suitable place for holding such a Convention; and that Thursday before the 2nd Lord's day in May next is a suitable time.

5. Resolved, That while we are willing to meet our Southern brethren in Augusta, or any other place which may be selected, we should heartily welcome them in the city of Richmond—and should it be deemed proper to hold it in this city, the Thursday before the 4th Lord's day in June next will be a suitable time.

On motion,

Resolved, That churches and associations of the State be recommended to appoint delegates to the proposed Convention.

Resolved, That churches and all associations of the State be published under the direction of brethren Taylor, Jeter, Walker, and Smith.

J. B. TAYLOR, Pres't Board.
C. WALTHALL, Sec'y.

Source: *The Religious Herald* (VA), March 13, 1845, 2–3.

A Northern Perspective, American Baptist Home Mission Society, 1883

In 1832, the great anti-slavery contest in England culminates in the introduction and passage of a bill for the abolition of slavery, throughout the wide domains of Great Britain, after 1834. The effect of this in America is to strengthen the hands of those who for years had been agitating the abolition of slavery here. . . .

In 1844, at the annual meeting of the Society, in Philadelphia, the subject is introduced for the first time in the form of a resolution by Rev. S. Adlam, of Me., to the effect that slaveholding should not debar a minister from appointment as a missionary of the Society. He explains that his resolution is put in a negative form purposely, but he and others who are opposed to the appointment of slaveholding missionaries, want an unequivocal answer to the question. Rev. Richard Fuller, of S.C., offers an amendment to the effect that, as the constitution of the Society allows auxiliary Societies the right of appointment and designation of funds, any action concerning slavery or anti-slavery is unconstitutional, as well as unwise; that the Society is only an agency to receive and disburse funds committed to it according to the wishes of contributors, and should not meddle with this matter. The subject is warmly discussed

Friday forenoon, Monday afternoon and Tuesday forenoon, when the amendment of Dr. Fuller prevails by a vote of 123 to 61. Immediately, Rev. J. S. Maginnis, of N.Y., moves the appointment of a committee consisting of three from the North, three from the South, and three from the West, together with the chairman, "to take into consideration the subject of an amicable dissolution of this Society, or to report such alterations in the constitution as will admit of the co-operation of brethren who cherish conflicting views on the subject of slavery." . . .

At Providence, in 1845, the majority report of the committee, appointed the year before, is adverse to any alteration of the constitution or plan of operation. A counter report is brought in by Dr. [Nathaniel] Colver. . . . It is evident that separation is inevitable. The special committee submit the following report:

"As the existing Society was planted at the North, has its Executive Board there, and there received a character of incorporation, which it seems desirable to preserve, and as a separation seems to many minds inevitable, owing to the strong views of Churches and individuals against the appointment of slaveholders to serve the Society, and as such views prevail principally at the North, therefore in case of such separation, we recommend the adoption of the following resolutions:

1st. *Resolved*, Should such separation among the former friends and patrons of the Society be deemed necessary, that the existing charter be retained by the Northern and other Churches, which may be willing to act together upon the basis of restriction against the appointment of slaveholders.

2d. *Resolved*, That the Executive Board be instructed, in such case, to adjust, upon amicable, honorable and liberal principles, whatever claims may be presented by brethren who shall feel, upon the separation, unable further to co-operate with the Society, or disposed to form a separate organization at the South.

After much discussion, the report is adopted. The Society takes no action on the appointment of slaveholders, or in any other respect which can be used as a reason for separation; but leaves the responsibility of separation with those who choose to take the step; it being well understood, however, that it will doubtless come, and provision being made for the contingency. Hence the separation takes place, not as the result of positive action by the Society, but by the logic of events.

Southern brethren withdrew and organized the Southern Baptist Convention in 1845. Though an attempt is made in 1846 to engraft upon the constitution some antislavery restrictions, yet in the circumstances, this is felt to be unnecessary. In 1849 Dr. Colver secures the appointment of a committee to investigate representations "that this Society is in some way fraternally connected with American slavery." This committee consists of Drs. Nathaniel Colver, John Peck, and Edward Lathrop, after full examination, present a detailed report, the conclusion of which is:

"That in so far as your committee are able to ascertain there is no relation or action of the Society which involves directly or indirectly the countenance and fellowship of slavery."

So ends the controversy.

Source: "Labors of Baptists for the Negro in America, Before 1862," in *Baptist Home Missions in North America, 1832–82*, Henry L. Morehouse, ed. (New York: Baptist Home Mission Society, 1883), 393–95.

24

Address Explaining Why the Southern Baptist Convention Was Organized, 1845

William B. Johnson

THE SOUTHERN BAPTIST CONVENTION
To the Brethren in the United States;
to the congregations connected with
the respective Churches; and
to all candid men.

A PAINFUL DIVISION HAS TAKEN place in the missionary operations of the American Baptists. We would explain the origin, the principles and the objects of that division, or the peculiar circumstances in which the organization of the Southern Baptist Convention became necessary.

Let not the extent of this disunion be exaggerated. At the present time it involves only the Foreign and Domestic Missions of the denomination. Northern and Southern Baptists are still brethren. They differ in no article of the faith. They are guided by the same principles of gospel order. Fanatical attempts have indeed been made, in some quarters, to exclude us of the South from Christian fellowship. We do not retort these attempts; and believe their extent to be comparatively limited. Our Christian fellowship is not, as we feel, a matter to be obtruded on by anyone. We abide by that of our God, his dear Son, and all his baptized followers. The few ultra Northern brethren to whom we allude, must take what course they please. Their conduct has not influenced us in the movement. We do not regard the rupture as extending to foundational principles, nor can we think that the great body of Northern brethren will so regard it. Disunion has proceeded, however, deplorably far. The first part of our duty is to show that its entire origin is with others. This is its history.

I. The General Convention of the Baptist denomination of the United States was composed of brethren from every part of the American Republic. Its Constitution knows no difference between slaveholders and non-slaveholders. Nor during the period of its existence, for the last thirty years, has it, in practice, known anything of this distinction. Both parties have contributed steadily and largely (if never adequately) to those funds which are the basis of its constituency, both have yielded its office-bearers of all grades; its missionaries and translators of God's word; its men of toils many, and of prayers not unavailing, abroad and at home. The honored dead of both of these classes have walked in closest sympathy with each other; anticipating in the Board-room and in the Monthly Concert, that higher, but not holier union now in their case consummated. Throughout the entire management of its early affairs, the whole struggle with its early difficulties, there was no breach of discord between them. Its Richard Furman and its Wm. Staughton, its Jesse Mercer, and its Thomas Baldwin, led on the sacramental host shoulder to shoulder, and heart to heart. Their rivalry being only in earnest efforts for a common cause, their entire aversions and enmities were directed with all the strength of their souls, against the common foe. And to the last, did they not cherish the strong belief that they left no other enmities or aversions; no other rivalry to their successors?

In particular, a special rule of the Constitution defines who may be missionaries, viz: "Such persons only as are in full communion with some church in our denomination; and who furnish satisfactory evidence of genuine piety, good talents, and fervent zeal for the Redeemer's cause." Now, while under this rule the slaveholder has been in his turn, employed as a missionary, it is not alleged that any other persons than those above described, have been appointed. Moreover, the important post of a superintendent of the education of native missionaries has been assigned, with universal approbation, to the pastor of one of our largest slaveholding churches.

But an evil hour has arrived. Even our humble efforts in the conquest of the world to God, excited the accuser of our brethren to cast discord among us; and in the last two Triennial Conventions, slavery and anti-slavery men began to draw off on different sides. How did the nobler spirits on each side endeavor to meet this? They proposed and carried almost unanimously, the following explicit resolution:

"Resolved, That in cooperating together, as members of this Convention, in the work of foreign missions, we disclaim all sanction, either expressed or implied, whether of slavery or anti-slavery; but as individuals, we are free to express and to promote, elsewhere, our views on these subjects, in a Christian manner and spirit."

Our successors will find it difficult to believe that so important and plain a declaration had become, before the close of the first year of the triennial period, a perfect nullity. In December last, the acting Board of the Convention, at Boston, adopted a new qualification for missionaries, a new special rule, viz: that "If anyone who shall offer himself for a missionary, having slaves, should insist on retaining them as his property, they could not appoint him." "One thing is certain," they continue, "we could never be a party to any arrangement which implies approbation of slavery."

We pray our brethren and all candid men to mark the date of this novel rule—the close of the first six months of their three years power, a date at which the compromise resolution could scarcely have reached our remoter mission stations. If usurpation had been intended, could it have been more fitly timed? A usurpation of ecclesiastical power that was quite foreign to our polity. Such power was assumed at a period when the aggrieved "thousands of Israel" had, as it now appears, no practical remedy. Its obvious tendency was, either our final subjugation to that power, or a serious interruption of the flow of Southern benevolence. The latter was the far more probable evil; and the Boston Board knew this well. They were from various quarters apprised of it. We, on the other hand, did not move in the matter of a new organization until three liberal States had refused to send northward any more contributions. Our leaders had chosen new rules. Thus came war within our gates: while the means of war on the common enemy was daily diminishing.

By this decision, the Board had placed itself in direct opposition to the Constitution of the Convention. The only reason given for this extraordinary and unconstitutional dictum being—that "The appointing power for wise and good purposes, is confided to the acting Board." On such a slight show of authority, this Board undertook to declare that to be a disqualification in one who should offer himself for a missionary, which the Convention had said, shall not be a disqualification. It had also expressly given its sanction to anti-slavery opinions, and impliedly fixed its condemnation on slavery, although the Convention had said that "neither" should be done. And further, it forbade those who shall apply for a missionary appointment to "express and promote elsewhere" their views on the subject of slavery in a right "manner and spirit" when the Convention declared they "were free" to do so. These brethren, thus acted upon a sentiment they have failed to prove—That slavery is, in all circumstances sinful. Whereas their own solemn resolution in the last Convention, (theirs as much as ours) left us free to promote slavery. Was not this leaving us free, and *"in a Christian spirit and manner"* to promote that which in their hearts, and according to the present showing of their conduct, they regard as a sin?

Enough, perhaps, has been said of the origin of the movement. Were we asked to characterize the conduct of our Northern brethren in one short phrase, we should adopt that of the Apostle. It was "FORBIDDING US *to speak* UNTO THE GENTILES." Did this deny us no privilege? Did it obstruct us, lay a kind of Romish interdict upon us in the discharge of an imperative duty; a duty to which the church has been, after the lapses of the ages, awakened universally and successfully; a duty the very object, and only object, of our long cherished connection and confederation?

And this would seem the place to state that our Northern brethren were dealt with as brethren to the last moment. Several of our churches cherished the hope that by means of remonstrance and expostulation, through the last Annual Meeting of the Board of Managers, at Providence, the Acting Board might be brought to feel the grievous wrong they have inflicted. The Managing Board was therefore affectionately and respectfully addressed on the subject, and was entreated to revise and reverse the obnoxious interdict. Alas! The results were—contemptuous silence as to the application made; and a deliberate resolve, expressing sympathy with the Acting Board, and a determination to sustain them. . . .

By order of the Convention.
William B. Johnson, D. D.
Augusta. Ga., 12th May, 1845.

Source: *Annual*, SBC, 1845, 17–20.

25

Old Landmarkism: What Is It?

J. R. Graves, 1880

From the Preface

M Y THOUGHTS WERE FIRST AWAKENED to the subject discussed in this little book in 1832, upon witnessing the immersion of my mother and sister by a Pedobaptist minister, and the plunging of another subject face forward as he knelt in the water, and the pouring water upon another while kneeling in the water, the sprinkling it upon another in the same position, and the sprinkling upon several others while standing on the banks of the stream, and yet others out of a pitcher in the meeting-house. Those different acts for "*one baptism*" made an indelible impression, and the more so because the administrator seemed to be in ill humor when he immersed, and *dipped his hand in water and laid it upon the heads of the candidates he immersed while he repeated the formula*! The questions started were: "If he did not believe in immersion, was the act at his hands valid? If 'what is not of faith is sin,' could his sin be an act acceptable to God?"

Twenty-two years after, that mother applied to the 2d Church in Nashville, of which I was pastor, for membership upon her immersion, which brought the whole matter up afresh as a practical question for serious examination. Being quite young and this my first pastorate, I referred the whole matter and responsibility to Dr. [Robert Boyle Crawford] Howell, then pastor of the 1st Church, telling him that I was in serious doubt about the validity of her baptism. He promptly decided it all sufficient and according to the *usage* of the denomination. From this time I commenced the careful study of the question, "Can an unbaptized man administer baptism?" Reason said, No; and I found no example of it in the New Testament after a church had been organized. Soon the question with me assumed a proper form: "Has any organization, save a scriptural church,

116

the right to authorize anyone, baptized or unbaptized, to administer church ordinances?" I decided this, by God's Word, in the negative; and subsequently this additional question came up: "Are immersions administered by the authority of a scriptural church with an *unscriptural design* valid?" Such immersions I also decided, by the clear light of the Scriptures, to be null and void; and thus I instructed my church, which, from that day to this, has never been troubled about unscriptural baptisms.

Shortly after I had the pleasure of seeing that mother and sister observe the ordinance as first delivered.

In 1846 I took charge of "The Tennessee Baptist," and soon commenced agitating the question of the validity of alien immersions, and the propriety of Baptists recognizing, by any act, ecclesiastical or ministerial, Pedobaptist societies or preachers as churches and ministers of Christ. This agitation gave rise to the convention, which met at Cotton Grove, W[est]. T[ennessee]., June 24, 1851, of all Baptists willing to accept and practice the teachings of Christ and his apostles in these matters. In that convention these questions were discussed, and the decisions of that meeting embodied in the famous "Cotton Grove Resolutions," which attracted the attention of Baptists throughout the whole South. As a matter of history, I copy them from the minutes, which were offered in the form of "queries."

"Rev. J. R. Graves offered the following queries:

"1st. Can Baptists, consistently with their principles or the Scriptures, recognize those societies not organized according to the pattern of the Jerusalem Church, but possessing different *governments*, different *officers*, a different class of *members*, different *ordinances*, *doctrines* and *practices*, as churches of Christ?

"2d. Ought they to be called gospel churches, or churches in a religious sense?

"3d. Can we consistently recognize the ministers of such irregular and unscriptural bodies as gospel ministers?

"4th. Is it not virtually recognizing them as official ministers to invite them into our pulpits, *or by any other act that would or could be* construed into such a recognition?

"5th. Can we consistently address as brethren those professing Christianity, who not only have not the doctrine of Christ and walk not according to his commandments, but are arrayed in direct and bitter opposition to them?"

These queries were unanimously answered in the negative, and the Baptists of Tennessee generally, and multitudes all over the South, indorsed the decision.

The name of Old Landmarkers came in this way. In 1854 J[ames]. M[adison]. Pendleton, of Kentucky, wrote an essay upon this question at my special request, viz: "Ought Baptists to recognize Pedobaptist preachers as gospel ministers?" which I brought out in tract form, and gave it the title, "An Old Landmark Reset." This calm discussion, which had an immense circulation in the South, was reviewed by many of the leading writers, North and South, and they, by way of reproach, called all Baptists "Old Landmarkers" who accepted his conclusions, and the impression was sought to be made that Brother Pendleton and myself were aiming at dividing the denomination and starting a new sect.

From this brief history it will be seen that *we*, who only deem ourselves "strict Baptists," are not responsible for the name, but our opposers. But that we have no reason to be ashamed of it will be seen by everyone who will read this little book. Why should *we* object to the name "Old Landmarkers," when those ancient Anabaptists, whom we alone represent in this age, were content to be called Cathari and Puritans, which terms mean the same thing as Old Landmarkers?

I put forth this publication now, thirty years after inaugurating the reform, to correct the manifold misrepresentations of those who oppose what *they* are pleased to call our principles and teachings, and to place before the Baptists of America what "Old Landmarkism" really is. Many believe that simple opposition to inviting ministers into our pulpits is the whole of it, when the title to the tract indicated that *that* was only *one* of the landmarks of our fathers. Others have been influenced to believe that we hold to "apostolic succession;" others, that we hold that baptism is essential to salvation, but its efficacy is ineffectual unless we can *prove* the unbroken connection of the administrator with some apostle; and yet others, that we hold that any flaw in the qualification of the present administrator, or any previous one in the line of his succession, however remote, invalidates all his baptisms and ministerial acts, as marriages, etc., past, present, and future, and necessitates the re-baptisms and re-marriages of all he has ever immersed or married. It is certainly due to those who bear the name to be vindicated from these hurtful misrepresentations. I think it is no act of presumption in me to assume to know what *I* meant by the Old Landmarks, since I was the first man in Tennessee, and the first *editor* on this continent, who publicly advocated the policy of *strictly* and consistently *carrying out in our practice those principles which all true Baptists, in all ages, have professed to believe.* Be this as it may, one thing is certainly true, no man in this century has suffered, or is now suffering, more than myself "in the house of my friends," for a rigid maintenance of them.

In 1846 pulpit affiliations, union meetings, receiving the immersions of Pedobaptists and Campbellites, and inviting Pedobaptists, as "evangelical ministers," to seats in our associations and conventions, even the Southern Baptist, had become, with but few exceptions, general throughout the South. At the North not only all these customs, but inviting Pedobaptist preachers to assist in the *ordinations*, and *installations*, and recognitions of Baptist ministers, was quite as common. I have noticed that in some of these meetings Universalist, if not Unitarian, ministers affiliated, and delegates were appointed by Baptist associations to meet Pedobaptist associations and Methodist conferences.

At this writing, January, 1880—and I record it with profound gratitude—there is only one Baptist paper in the South, of the sixteen weeklies, that approve of alien immersion and pulpit affiliation ("The *Religious Herald*"), while already two papers in the Northern States avow and advocate Landmark principles and practice. I do not believe that there is one association *in the whole South* that would today indorse an alien immersion as scriptural or valid, and it is a rare thing to see a Pedobaptist or Campbellite in our pulpits, and they are no longer invited to seats in our associations and conventions anywhere in the South.

Landmark Reasons for Refusing
Communion to Non-Baptists

The inconsistencies and evils of intercommunion among Baptists.
"Truth is never contradictory or inconsistent with itself."—*Tombes.*

Baptist churches, with all their rights, have no right to be *inconsistent*, nor to favor a practice unwarranted by the word of God, and productive of *evils*. Under the inflexible law of "usage," which compels the pastor to invite "all members of sister churches present to the Lord's Supper, the following *inconsistencies* and *evils*, exceedingly prejudicial to our denominational influence and growth, are practiced and fostered.

1. Baptist churches that practice intercommunion have practically no communion of their own. They have church members, church conferences, church discipline, but no church communion; and, therefore, no scripturally observed Lord's Supper and, therefore, none at all, as I have shown in Chapter VII. The communion of such churches is *denominational* and not *church* communion.

2. Baptist churches that practice intercommunion have no guardianship over the Lord's Supper, which is divinely enjoined upon them to exercise. They have control of their own members to exclude them from the table if unworthy, . . . but they can not protect the table from such so long as they do not limit it to their membership. . . .

4. There are multitudes—I rejoice to say nearly all our Southern churches outside the cities—who will not receive persons immersed by Catholics or Campbellites, Protestants or Mormons, because they do not regard them as baptized at all; yet by their open denominational invitations they receive all such—and there are many of them in the churches—to their table, as duly qualified. . . .

Consistency.—If each Baptist church had its own communion, with its own members, independent of all others, then each church could receive into membership or exclude from membership, whoever it pleases, and no other church or communion be injured by it. On the one hand, the church excluding a person would have no power to prevent his uniting with another church made up of members no better than himself; and, on the other hand, the church receiving the excluded person would not, in so doing, restore him to the communion from which he had been cast out.

The Evils of Denominational Communion

1. It opens the *door* to the table to all the ministerial impostors that pervade the land. . . . These impostors hold "revival meetings" until all their borrowed sermons are exhausted, and make it a point to do all the baptizing, and have the weakness of some other ministers to keep a record of the number of their baptisms. It is needless to say that the church is often divided by their influence, and left in confusion and disgrace when they are exposed. . . .

The remedy is, let no strange traveling preacher be admitted to the table as a participant, nor into our pulpits, until the church has written back and learned that he is in all respects worthy.

2. *Denominational communion* never has been sustained, and never can be, but at the expense of peace. . . .

3. It has encouraged tens of thousands of Baptists, on moving away from the churches to which they belong, to go without transferring their membership to a church where they were going, as they could have the church privileges—preaching and COMMUNION—without uniting with, and bearing the church's burdens. . . . If Baptists could have no

such privileges without membership, they would keep their membership with them and enjoy it. . . .

6. We annually lose thousands and tens of thousands of worthy persons who would have united with us, but for what they understand as our unwarranted close-communion. Our practice can never be satisfactorily explained to them as consistent, so long as we practice a partial, and not a general, open communion. Our denominational growth is very materially retarded by our present inconsistent practice of intercommunion. If we practiced strict church communion, these, and all Christians, could understand the matter at once; and no one would presume to blame us for not inviting members of *other* denominations to our table, when we refuse, from principle, to invite members of other Baptist churches—our own brethren.

7. It is freely admitted by reliable brethren who enjoy the widest outlook over the denomination in America, that for the last few decades of years the general drift has been, and now is, setting towards "open communion"—it is boasted of as a "broadening liberalism." There are numbers in all our churches—and the number is increasing, especially in our fashionable city and wealthy town churches—who are impatient of the present restrictions imposed upon the table; because, not being able to divide a principle, they are not able to see the consistency of inviting members of sister churches, and rejecting those whom we admit to be *evangelical* churches, as though all evangelical churches are not our sister; nor can they divine why Pedobaptist ministers are authorized to preach the gospel and to *immerse*; are invited to occupy our pulpits, and even to serve our churches as supply pastors for a season—all their ministrations recognized as valid, and yet they are debarred from our table. They work for us, and we refuse to allow them to eat. The only ground upon which we can successfully meet and counteract the liberalizing influences, which are gently bearing the Baptists of America into the slough of open communion, is strict local church communion, and the firm and energetic setting forth of the "Old Baptist Landmarks" advocated in this little book. . . .

Landmark Views on Kingdom and Church Continuity

Landmark Baptists very generally believe that for the Word of the Living God to stand, and for the veracity of Jesus Christ to vindicate itself, the kingdom which he set up "in the days of John the Baptist," has had an unbroken continuity until now. I say kingdom, instead of succession of churches, for the sake of perspicacity. Those who oppose "church succession" confuse the unthinking, by representing our position to be, that the identical organization which Christ established—the First Church of Judea—has had a continued existence until today; or, that the identical churches planted by the apostles, or, at least, *some one* of them, has continued until now, and that Baptist ministers are successors of the apostles; in a word, that our position is the old Romish and Episcopal doctrine of apostolic succession. I have, for full a quarter of a century, by pen and voice, vehemently protested against *these* misrepresentations, as Baptists have, for twice as many more, against the charge of teaching that no one can be I saved without immersion, and quite as vainly; for those who oppose us seem determined to misrepresent, and will not be corrected. We repudiate the doctrine of apostolic succession; we do not believe *they* ever had a successor, and, therefore, no one today is preaching under the apostolic commission any more than under that which Christ first gave to John the Baptist. They are our opposers who, in fact, hold to apostolic succession; for the majority do believe that, if ministers, they are preaching by the authority contained in that commission! So much for this charge.

Nor have I, or any Landmarker known to me, ever advocated the succession of any particular church or churches; but my position is that Christ, in the very "days of John the Baptist" did establish a visible kingdom on earth, and that this *kingdom* has never yet been "broken in pieces," or given to another class of subjects—has never for a day "been moved," or ceased from the earth, and never will until Christ returns personally to reign over it; that the organization he first set up, which John called "the Bride," and which Christ called his church, constituted that visible kingdom, and today all his *true* churches on earth constitute it; and, therefore, if his *kingdom* has stood unchanged, and will to the end, he must always have had true and uncorrupted churches, since his kingdom cannot exist without true churches.

The sense in which any existing Baptist church is the successor of the First Church of Judea—the model and pattern of all—is the same as that existing between any regular Masonic Lodge and the first Lodge that was ever instituted. Ten thousand local Lodges may have existed and passed away, but this fact in nowise affects the continuity of Masonry. From the day it was organized as symbolic Masonry, it has stood; and though it may have decayed in some places, it has flourished in others, and never has had but *one beginning*. Thus it has been with that institution called the Kingdom of Christ; it has had a continuous existence, or the words of Christ have failed; and therefore, there has been no need of originating it, *de novo*, and no unbaptized man ever had any authority to originate baptism, or a church, *de novo.* I understand that Christ's declaration (Matt. 16:18), and Paul's statement (Heb. 12:28), are emphatic commentaries upon the prophecy of Daniel (2:44).

We do not admit that it devolves upon us more than upon every other lover of Jesus to prove, by incontestable historical facts, that this kingdom of the Messiah has stood from the day it was set up by him, unbroken and unmoved; to question it, is to doubt his sure word of promise. To deny it, is to impeach his veracity, and to leave the world without a Bible or a Christ. We dare not do this. We believe that his kingdom has stood unchanged, as firmly as we believe in the divinity of the Son of God, and, when we are forced to surrender the one faith, we can easily give up the other. If Christ has not kept his promise concerning his *church*, how can I trust him concerning *my salvation*? If he has not the power to save his *church*, he certainly has not the power to save me. For Christians to admit that Christ has not preserved his kingdom unbroken, unmoved, unchanged, and uncorrupted, is to surrender the whole ground to infidelity. I deny that a man is a believer in the Bible who denies this.

Nor do we admit the claims of the "Liberals" upon us, to prove the continuous existence of the church, of which we are a member, or which baptized us, in order to prove our doctrine of church succession, and that we have been scripturally baptized or ordained. As well might the Infidel call upon me to prove every link of my descent from Adam, before I am allowed to claim an interest in the redemptive work of Christ, which was confined to the family of Adam! We point to the Word of God, and, until the Infidel can destroy *its* authenticity, our hope is unshaken. In like manner, we point the "Liberal" Baptist to the words of Christ, and will he say *they are not sufficient*? When the Infidel can prove, by incontestable historical facts, that his kingdom has been broken and removed one year, one day, or one *hour* from the earth, then we surrender our Bible with our position. . . .

I have no space to devote to the historical argument to *prove* the continuity of the kingdom of Christ, but assure the reader that, in our opinion, it is irrefragable. All that any candid man could desire—and it is from Catholic and Protestant sources—frankly admitting that churches, substantially like the Baptists of this age have existed, and suffered the bitterest persecution from the earliest ages until now; and, indeed, they have been the only religious organizations that have stood since the days of the apostles, and are older than the Roman Catholic Church itself.

Source: J. R. Graves, *Old Landmarkism: What Is It?* (Texarkana, Tex.; Baptist Sunday School Committee, 1928), ix–xv, 113–19, 121–27. Permission granted by the Baptist Sunday School Committee and Bogard Press.

26

A LETTER FROM CHINA
Lottie Moon, 1887

I N A FORMER LETTER I called attention to the work of Southern
Methodist women, endeavoring to use it as an incentive to stir up the
women of our Southern Baptist churches to greater zeal in the cause
of missions. I have lately been reading the minutes of the ninth annual
meeting of the Woman's Board of Missions, M[ethodist]. E[piscopal].,
South, and find that in the year ending in June, they raised over sixty-six
thousand dollars. Their work in China alone involved the expenditure of
more than thirty-four thousand dollars, besides which they have missions
in Mexico, Brazil, and the Indian Territory. They have nine workers in
China, with four more under appointment and two others recommended
by the committee for appointment. I notice that when a candidate is appointed, straight way some conference society pledges her support in
whole or in part. One young lady is to be sent out by means of the liberal offer of a Nashville gentleman, to contribute six hundred dollars for
traveling expenses. A gentleman in Kansas gave five thousand dollars to
build a church in Shanghai in connection with woman's work there.

The efficient officers of this Methodist Woman's organization do
their work without pay. Traveling and office expenses are allowed the
President of the Board of Missions. This money is to be used at her discretion in visiting conference societies that are not able to pay her expenses. Office expenses alone are allowed the Corresponding Secretary
and her assistant, and also to the Treasurer. A sum is appropriated for
publications, postage, and mite boxes. The expenses for all purposes
are less than seventeen hundred dollars. In a word, Southern Methodist
women, in one year, have contributed to missions, clear of all expenses,
nearly sixty-five thousand dollars! Doesn't this put us Baptist women to
shame? For one, I confess I am heartily ashamed.

In the matter of appointments to mission work, extreme care is taken in the selection of candidates, and, judging by the high character and efficient work of Southern Methodist women in China, this care is not exercised in vain. Candidates are sent up by the societies of their respective conferences. There is a standing committee for the examination of candidates. Above this is a committee on missionary candidates appointed at the annual meeting. There is also an educational committee, whose duty it is to ascertain if the applicant comes up to the required standard in education. When the candidate has satisfactorily passed these various examining committees the case comes before the Board, and the applicant, if accepted, is recommended to the Bishop for appointment.

I am convinced that one of the chief reasons our Southern Baptist women do so little is the lack of organization. Why should we not learn from these noble Methodist women, and instead of the paltry offerings we make, do something that will prove that we are really in earnest in claiming to be followers of him who, "though he was rich, for our sake became poor?" How do these Methodist women raise so much money? By prayer and self-denial. Note the resolution "unanimously approved" by the meeting above:

"Resolved, That this Board recommend to the Woman's Missionary Society to observe the week preceding Christmas as a week of prayer and self-denial." "In preparation for this,

"Resolved, That we agree to pray every evening for six months, dating from June 25, 1887, for the outpouring of the Holy Spirit on the Woman's Missionary Society and its work at home and in the foreign fields."

Its "work at home," be it noted, is to arouse an interest and collect money for the foreign field, as also the Indian Territory.

Need it be said why the week before Christmas is chosen? Is not "the festive season, when families and friends exchange gifts in memory of The Gift laid on the altar of the world for the redemption of the human race, the most appropriate time to consecrate a portion from abounding riches and scant poverty to send forth the good tidings of great joy into all the earth?"

In seeking organization we do not need to adopt plans or methods unsuitable to the views, or repugnant to the tastes of our brethren. . . . Power of appointment and of disbursing funds should be left, as heretofore, in the hands of the Foreign Mission Board. Separate organization is undesirable, and would do harm; but organization in subordination to the Board is the imperative need of the hour.

Some years ago the Southern Methodist Mission in China had run down to the lowest water-mark; the rising of the tide seems to have begun with the enlisting of the women of the church in the cause of missions. The previously unexampled increase in missionary zeal and activity in the Northern Presbyterian church is attributed to the same reason—the thorough awakening of the women of the church upon the subject of missions. In like manner, until the women of our Southern Baptist churches are thoroughly aroused, we shall continue to go in our present "hand to mouth" system. We shall continue to see mission stations so poorly manned that missionaries break down from overwork, loneliness, and isolation; we shall continue to see promising fields unentered and old stations languishing and we shall continue to see other denominations no richer and no better educated than ours, outstripping us in the race. I wonder how many of us really believe that "it is more blessed to give than to receive." A woman who accepts that statement of our Lord Jesus Christ as a fact, and not as "impracticable idealism," will make giving a principle of her life. She will lay aside sacredly not less than one-tenth of her income or her earnings as the Lord's money, which she would no more dare to touch for personal use than she would steal. How many there are among our women, alas! alas! Who imagines that because "Jesus paid it all," they need pay nothing, forgetting that the prime object of their salvation was that they should follow in the footsteps of Jesus Christ in bringing back a lost world to God, and so aid in bringing the answer to the petition our Lord taught his disciples. "Thy kingdom come."

L. MOON.
Tungchow, Sept. 15, 1887.

Source: *Foreign Mission Journal*, December 1887, 10.

27

ANOTHER WORD CONCERNING THE DOWN-GRADE

Charles Haddon Spurgeon, 1887

N O LOVER OF THE GOSPEL can conceal from himself the fact that the days are evil. We are willing to make a large discount from our apprehensions on the score of natural timidity, the caution of age, and the weakness produced by pain; but yet our solemn conviction is that things are much worse in many churches than they seem to be, and are rapidly tending downward. Read those newspapers which represent the Broad School of Dissent, and ask yourself, How much farther could they go? What doctrine remains to be abandoned? What other truth to be the object of contempt? A new religion has been initiated, which is no more Christianity than chalk is cheese; and this religion, being destitute of moral honesty, palms itself off as the old faith with slight improvements, and on this plea usurps pulpits which were erected for gospel preaching. The Atonement is scorned the inspiration of Scripture is derided, the Holy Spirit is degraded into an influence, the punishment of sin is turned into fiction, and the resurrection into a myth, and yet these enemies of our faith expect us to call them brethren, and maintain a confederacy with them!

At the back of doctrinal falsehood comes a natural decline of spiritual life, evidenced by a taste for questionable amusements, and a weariness of devotional meetings. At a certain meeting of ministers and church-officers, one after another doubted the value of prayer-meetings; all confessed that they had a very small attendance, and several acknowledged without the slightest compunction that they had quite given them up. What means this? Are churches in a right condition when they have only one meeting for prayer in a week, and that a mere skeleton? Churches which have prayer-meetings several times on the Lord's-day, and very frequently during the week, yet feel their need of more prayer; but what can be said of those who very seldom practice united supplication? Are there few conversions? Do the congregations dwindle? Who wonders that this is the case when the spirit of prayer has departed?

As for questionable amusements—time was when a Nonconformist minister who was known to attend the play-house would soon have found himself without a church. And justly so; for no man can long possess the confidence, even of the most worldly, who is known to be a haunter of theatres. Yet at the present time it is matter of notoriety that preachers of no mean repute defend the play-house, and do so because they have been seen there. Is it any wonder that church members forget their vows of consecration, and run with the unholy in the ways of frivolity, when they hear that persons are tolerated in the pastorate who do the same? We doubt not that, for writing these lines we shall incur the charge of prudery and bigotry, and this will but prove how low are the tone and spirit of the churches in many places. The fact is, that many would like to unite church and stage, cards and prayer, dancing and sacraments. If we are powerless to stem this torrent, we can at least warn men of its existence, and entreat them to keep out of it. When the old faith is gone, and enthusiasm for the gospel is extinct, it is no wonder that people seek something else in the way of delight. Lacking bread, they feed on ashes; rejecting the way of the Lord, they run greedily in the path of folly. . . .

Alas! Many are returning to the poisoned cups which drugged that declining generation, when it surrendered itself to Unitarian lethargy. Too many ministers are toying with the deadly cobra of "another gospel," in the form of "modern thought." As a consequence, their congregations are thinning: the more spiritual of their members join the "Brethren," or some other company of "believers unattached;" while the more wealthy, and show-loving, with some of unquestionable devoutness, go off to the Church of England. . . .

The case is mournful. Certain ministers are making infidels. Avowed atheists are not a tenth as dangerous as those preachers who scatter doubt and stab faith. A plain man told us the other day that two ministers had derided him because he thought we should pray for rain. A gracious woman bemoaned in my presence that a precious promise in Isaiah which had comforted her had been declared by her minister to be uninspired. It is a common thing to hear working-men excuse their wickedness by the statement that there is no hell, "the parson says so." But we need not prolong our mention of painful facts. Germany was made unbelieving by her preachers, and England is following in her track. Attendance at places of worship is declining, and reverence for holy things is vanishing; and we solemnly believe this to be largely attributable to the skepticism which has flashed from the pulpit and spread among the people. Possibly the men who uttered the doubt never intended it to go so far; but none the less they have done the ill, and cannot undo it. Their own observation ought to teach them better. Have these advanced thinkers filled their own chapels? Have they, after all, prospered through discarding the old methods? Possibly, in a few cases genius and tact have carried these gentry over the destructive results of their ministry; but in many cases their pretty new theology has scattered their congregations. In meeting houses holding a thousand, or twelve hundred, or fifteen hundred, places one packed to the ceiling with ardent hearers, how small are the numbers now! We would mention instances, but we forbear. The places which the gospel filled the new nonsense has emptied, and will keep empty. . . .

The other day we were asked to mention the name of some person who might be suitable pastor for a vacant church, and the deacon who wrote said, "Let him be a converted man, and let him be one who believes what he preaches; for there are those around us who give us the idea that they have neither part nor lot in the matter." This remark is more commonly made than we like to remember, and there it is alas! Too much need for it. A student from a certain college preached to the congregation we sometimes visit such a sermon that the deacon said to him in the vestry, "Sir do you believe in the Holy Ghost?" The youth replied, "I suppose I do." To which the deacon answered, "I suppose you do *not*, or you would not have insulted us with such false doctrine." . . .

It now becomes a serious question how far those who abide by faith once delivered to the saints should fraternize with those who have turned aside to another gospel. Christian love has its claims, and divisions are to be shunned as grievous evils; but how far are we justified in being in confederacy with those who are departing from the truth? It is a difficult question to answer so as to keep the balance of duties. For the present it behooves believers to be cautious, lest they lend their support and countenance to the betrayers of the Lord. It is one thing to overlap all boundaries of denominational restriction for the truth's sake: this we hope all godly men will do more and more. It is quite another policy which would urge us to subordinate the maintenance of truth to denominational prosperity and unity. Numbers of easy-minded people wink at error so long as it is committed by a clever man and a good-natured brother, who has so many fine points about him. Let each believer judge for himself; but, for our part, we have put on a few fresh bolts to our door, and we have given orders to keep the chain up; for, under colour of begging the friend-ship of the servant, there are those who aim at robbing THE MASTER.

We fear it is hopeless ever to form a society which can keep out men base enough to profess one thing and believe another; but it might be pos-sible to make an informal alliance among all who hold the Christianity of their fathers. Little as they might be able to do, they could at least protest, and as far as possible free themselves of that complicity which will be involved in a conspiracy of silence. If for a while the evangelicals are doomed to go down, let them die fighting, and in the full assurance that their gospel will have a resurrection when the inventions of "modern thought" shall be burned up with fire unquenchable.

Source: *The Sword and Trowel*, August 1887.

28

THE BAPTIST WORLD ALLIANCE

Speech to the Baptist World Congress, John H. Shakespeare, 1905

I N ISSUING THE OFFICIAL REPORT of the proceedings of the first Baptist World Congress, it seems fitting to put on record an introductory statement as to the origin of the Congress, the method of organization adopted, and some general impressions of its value, influence and lessons.

The desire for a world gathering of Baptists has been expressed by several influential men within the last five years, but it was left to Dr. J. N. Prestridge, of Louisville, Kentucky, to give the necessary driving force to the suggestion. In an editorial in his paper, *The Baptist Argus*, two years ago, he pleaded for a meeting of the leading officers of the various Baptist Unions with a view to a Congress. Later, he appealed to Dr. [John] Clifford and myself. We favored the holding of the Congress itself at an early date. Dr. Prestridge obtained opinions from Baptists in different parts of the world, published them in his paper, and when it was found that the project would meet with universal acceptance, a resolution of invitation was adopted by the Baptist Union, assembled at Bristol, October, 1904, for the Congress to be held in London in July, 1905. A strong Baptist Union Committee was elected, representatives were added from the Committee of the Baptist Missionary Society, and the work of preparation began. Special Committees were formed to deal with the different sections of this great undertaking.

At this point a serious initial difficulty arose. It was clearly impossible, in the short time available, for me to carry through the details of the organization without assistance of a very high order, unless I could be entirely liberated from the regular secretarial work of the Baptist Union. The unanimous choice of the Committee fell upon the Rev. W. T. Whitley, M.A., LL.D., the pastor of Fishergate Church, Preston, as my assistant secretary, and on Mr. Harold Knott, M.A., as assistant organizing secretary. Dr. Whitley had the great advantage of being known in Australia and America by most of the leaders of the Baptist Societies in the two continents. His church freely liberated him for an average of three days a week, and during the last month for continuous service. His patience, courtesy, untiring industry and business-like method have been beyond praise. A pleasant episode during the preparation for the Congress was that he won the Jay Gould prize of £200 for the best work on the Douay Version of the Bible. Mr. Harold Knott was able generously to give his whole time to the work of the Congress. Trained by Dr. Maclaren, he has been recognized among Baptists for some years as one of their finest characters and ablest workers. For three years he labored as the secretary for Lancashire on behalf of the Twentieth Century Fund. Deeply imbued with the spirit of the Quakers, and disliking any recognition other than that of the Great Master, he might easily escape the tribute which is his due. As general secretary I have the happiness to record that, through a time of strain and tension, the harmony and good understanding between my assistant secretaries and myself have been absolute and complete.

The most important fact of the Congress is that it has been a World Congress in the sense that representatives came from almost every country upon earth. We scarcely expected that the representation would be so large or so varied. Of course, the largest contingent was from America. Canada, Germany and Sweden also contributed a great number of delegates. Considering the distance, Australia nobly supported the gathering. Never before had we realized the strength, determination and consecration of our brethren in the various countries of Europe. The Russian delegates, headed by Baron Uixkiull, who had suffered so much, and as had most of them, been imprisoned or fined, were undoubtedly the heroes of the Congress. One Baptist preacher came even from far Tiflis. The picturesque element was supplied by the Negro brethren, of whom about fifty were present, and who were cheered and seen everywhere. Indeed, the cordiality of their reception was so marked that one American was heard to say, "Would you rather be the governor of your State or a negro delegate in London?"

The tone of the Congress has been marked pre-eminently in two directions. First, it has been distinctly evangelical. It was not only that from the simpler negro delegates there was the unqualified declaration of loyalty to the Gospel and the Bible, but the Congress sermon preached by Dr. [Augustus Hopkins] Strong, one of the profoundest theologians of the United States of America, asserted with the utmost vehemence the essential doctrines of Christianity. From first to last there was no wavering note on any of the great realities of faith. The other note was that of optimism. The American host was naturally jubilant, but even from those countries where the Baptists are few in number, poor and, in some cases, persecuted, there was the same certainty that at the end of the day the Baptist propaganda would triumph, and that the Evangelical Church, under the pressure of sacramentarianism, would be led back to primitive doctrine and practice with regard to baptism.

Source: *The Baptist World Congress, London, July 11–19, 1905; Authorized Record of the Proceedings* (London: Baptist Union Publication Department, 1905), v–vi.

Address to the Baptist World Congress, John Clifford, 1911

THE BAPTIST WORLD ALLIANCE: ITS ORIGIN AND CHARACTER, MEANING AND WORK

Address from the Chair of the Baptist World Alliance, Delivered on Tuesday, June 20th, 1911, in Philadelphia, U.S.A
By John Clifford, M.A., LL.D., D.D.

Dear Brethren and Friends:

I cannot enter upon the duties of this office without first of all thanking you with all my heart for the honor you have conferred upon me. Frankly, I must say, it was one of the great surprises of my life when the Baptist World Congress held in London in 1905, elected me to the Presidency of this newly created Alliance. . . .

And now, my brethren, the one subject your President cannot escape from, on this, the first occasion of our meeting as an Alliance, is the ALLIANCE ITSELF, ITS CREATION AND CHARACTER, ITS MEANING AND WORK. . . .

The novelty of this organization is surprising, partly because it appears in a people delivered over, body and soul, to individualism, and in mortal terror of the slightest invasion of their personal and ecclesiastical independence; and yet to others, who have grasped the intrinsic catholicity of our fundamental principles, it is astonishing that we have been so long arriving at the present stage of our development.

For although this Alliance is a new creation; it is really the outward and visible sign of an inward and spiritual grace that has been working within us, with special energy and vitality, during the last ten or fifteen years; and witnesses to magnetic and cohesive forces operating, though latent, and powerful though silent. . . .

Deep in the soul of us has always dwelt the conviction that we are the possessors of a genuinely universal religion; although it has only found voice here and there. For the most part we have not known one another. . . .

But a new day has dawned. The barriers are broken down. The post and the press, the telegraph and the telephone, the rail and the steamboat unite us. . . . So our alliance is *possible*. Molded under different conditions, dwelling under different flags, trained in different cities and by different teachers with different methods, we come together rejoicing, that in the new nature, we have received through the grace of God, there is neither Greek nor Jew, Englishman nor American, black nor white, bond nor free, but that all are one in Christ. . . .

II.

What is new is that this is a *World* Alliance of Baptists. We have other unions; but they are restricted. This is all embracing. They unite two or three churches in a locality, a hundred in a county, or thousands in a nation; this represents all, and is really and not factitiously ecumenical.

It is not our immense numbers that creates this union; though we must have more than eight millions of registered members, and a host of adherents; nor is it by the authority of persons that we meet, as of a Pope claiming infallibility, or a body of Patriarchs compelling our appearance; nor is it again, in obedience to the mandate of a church, or the action of the machinery of the State. Our cohesiveness is due to our ideas. They bind us together. They are our driving and inspiring force. . . .

III.

But this organization is a World Alliance of *Baptists*, and that means that the catholic principles on which we base ourselves we derive straight from Jesus, are accepted on His authority, and involve in all who accept them total subjection of soul to his gracious and benignant rule. He is Lord of all, and He only is Lord of all. . . . Jesus Christ holds the first place and the last. His word is final. His rule is supreme.

(2) And now it follows upon that, that the ideas to which we give witness root themselves, first in the teaching of the New Testament, and secondly in the soul's experience of Christ. . . .

IV.

Another cord binding us together is an indissoluble spiritual union, and clothing this Alliance with a true catholicity is our unswerving maintenance of an exclusively regenerated church-membership. . . . On spiritual experience we build; not on creeds; but on "conversion," "a change of heart," the awakening of the soul to God in Christ. Regeneration by the Holy Ghost, a conscious possession of the mind and spirit of Jesus, a will surrendered to God, a life dedicated to His service. . . .

Therefore we preach "soul liberty," and contend against all comers that the spirit of man has the privilege of a direct conscious relation to God in Christ and through Christ. Nothing may come between the soul and God. . . . The soul must be free. . . .

V.

In speaking of the *work* of this Alliance it is important, at the outset, to recall the limitations imposed upon us by ecumenical character. From sheer necessity we are not competent to judge one another's local work with accuracy. We lack sufficient data. We miss the special point of view. We are too far apart and we have the enormous difficulty of the "personal equation." Britishers do not know the United States and yet some of them do not hesitate from passing sentence upon the American churches, stating their problems, and showing how they could be solved, even though they have only had the opportunity of playing flying visits to these climes; and they do it apparently unaware that their verdicts are no more than thinly disguised assertions of their own prejudges and presuppositions. Nor can Americans estimate the weight of the social pressure on Baptists in England, and the enormous resistance we have to overcome in following the light we see. You do not see the diminished returns in the till of the village shop, and the persecution in the village streets consequent upon State patronage and support of one particular church. To know that you must get into touch with our village churches as I have done for more than fifty years. . . .

Besides it avails nothing to make light of the fact that we do not think as Christendom thinks on the vital elements of Christianity. The great historic churches are against us: the Roman Catholic, the Eastern, the Anglican, and some other communions; and against us on subjects that go to the uttermost depths of the soul of the gospel of Christ; and therefore "Separation" is one of the inevitable conditions of faithfulness to our experience of the grace of God, to our interpretation of the claims of Jesus Christ, and to the principles He has given as the ground and sphere of our collective life. It cannot be helped. We accept the isolation, and all the penalties it involves. . . .

VI.

And now standing upon this eminence, let us ask what is the outlook for the Baptist people all over the earth? What is the position likely to be assigned to us in leading and shaping the religious life of mankind?

To answer that question we need ask first, towards what sea are the deeper currents of thought and action in modern civilization setting? What is the "Stream of tendency" amongst the progressive peoples? Is it with our principles or against them?

The reply is unequivocal and complete.

(1) Protestantism is to the fore. The races leading the life of the world are either distinctly Protestant, as in Britain and the Unites States or they are effectively using Protestant ideas as weapons against Roman Catholicism as in France and Spain. . . . Protestantism is one of the chief factors molding the coming generations of men.

(2) The leaven of teaching concerning the intervention of the magistrate in religious affairs cast by John Smith and Roger Williams into the three measures of human meal in Holland and England and America, has been doing its work. The United States has established forever the doctrine of the neutrality of the State towards all Christian societies. France has cut the concordat in twain, and State and Church are free of each other. Portugal is doing the same this year. Welsh Disestablishment is at the doors. And though England, as usual, lags behind, yet both within and without the Anglican Church the conviction that separation is just, gains strength, and all that is wanted is the opportunity to translate the conviction into legislative deed.

(3) In like manner the reflective forces of the age make against an exclusive and aggressive priestism. Indeed, it has received its sentence of death, and is only waiting for the executioner. It has to go. . . .

(4) Nor can prelacy stand against the divine right of the democracy. Although the cry of "Increase the Episcopate" is heard, yet the Bishops themselves admit that they must give the laity some share in the administration of the affairs of prelatical churches. The people cannot be excluded from churches or from nations. Their day has dawned; and it will go on to its full noon. Not churches, not parties, not nations merely, but the people are the legatees of the future; the inheritance is theirs. . . .

(5) But the most outstanding characteristics of our time is the amazing dominance of the idea of social service. The age is permeated with the obligation of brotherhood, the duty of self-sacrificing ministry, to the more needy members of the Commonwealth. We cannot escape it. Social problems are supreme. "The condition of the people" question is

everywhere surging to the front. Housing and health, temperance and purity, drill for the body, education for the mind; these and kindred phases of life are never out of sight. The churches have broadened out so as to embrace them. . . .

(6) All this movement is intensely moral. The illuminated and energized conscience is in it. It is ennobled by a high ethic. The spirit has "convinced the *world* of sin and righteousness and judgment;" and in the strength of that conviction, a concerted and comprehensive attack is being made by churches and States, by individuals and societies on the strongholds of injustice and misery, and a long stride is taken to that one far-off divine event towards which the whole creation moves.

VII.

Need I trace the parallel between those manifest tendencies of this New Century and the principles which our fathers set forth and which we maintain? Is it not obvious that the ideas and aims are ours, and that whatever becomes of us as churches, this, at least, is certain, that those ideas of ours are working mightily as the formative factors of the future? . . .

For in addition to our ruling ideas we have a freedom as to verbal forms of belief and of organized collective life, though we are so immovably fixed as to principles, that leave us wholly at liberty to adapt ourselves to the teaching of experience, and the changing needs of societies as continuously living organisms can and must. Biblical criticism does not disturb us, for we do not rest on it, but on personal experience of the grace of Christ. Modes of political government do not affect us; we can accept any, but we fare best under the most democratic; . . .

Let us then humbly accept our responsibility for leadership of the religion of the future and go forward to our place. Pioneers never get the best pay, but they do the best work; . . . Be ready to endure the cross and despise shame. Rise to the courage of your best moments. Push your convictions into deeds. Scorn bribes. Stand true. Be faithful to Christ and His holy gospel, and so help to lead the whole world into the light and glory of His redeeming love.

Source: John Clifford, "The Baptist World Alliance: Its Origin and Character, Meaning, and Work." Address before the Baptist World Alliance, Philadelphia, June 1911.

29

THE KINGDOM OF GOD, 1917

Walter Rauschenbusch

I F THEOLOGY IS TO OFFER an adequate doctrinal basis for the social gospel, it must not only make room for the doctrine of the Kingdom of God, but give it a central place and revise all other doctrines so that they will articulate organically with it.

This doctrine is itself the social gospel. Without it, the idea of redeeming the social order will be but an annex to the orthodox conception of the scheme of salvation. It will live like a Negro servant family in a detached cabin back of the white man's house in the South. If this doctrine gets the place which has always been its legitimate right, the practical proclamation and application of social morality will have a firm footing.

To those whose minds live in the social gospel, the Kingdom of God is a dear truth, the marrow of the gospel, just as the incarnation was to Athanasius, justification by faith alone to Luther, and the sovereignty of God to Jonathan Edwards. It was just as dear to Jesus. He too lived in it, and from it looked out on the world and the work he had to do.

Jesus always spoke of the Kingdom of God. Only two of his reported sayings contain the word "Church," and both passages are of questionable authenticity. It is safe to say that he never thought of founding the kind of institution which afterward claimed to be acting for him. . . .

But the Kingdom was merely a hope, the Church a present reality. The chief interest and affection flowed toward the Church. Soon, through a combination of causes, the name and idea of "the Kingdom" began to be displaced by the name and idea of "the Church" in the preaching, literature, and theological thought of the Church. Augustine completed this process in his *De Civitate Dei*. The Kingdom of God which has, through our human history opposed the Kingdom of sin, is today embodied in the Church. The millennium began when the Church was founded. This practically substituted the actual, not the ideal Church for the Kingdom of God. The beloved ideal of Jesus became a vague phrase which kept intruding from the New Testament. Like Cinderella in the kitchen, it saw the other great dogmas furbished up for the ball, but no prince of theology restored it to its rightful place. The Reformation, too, brought no renascence of the doctrine of the Kingdom, it had only eschatological value, or was defined in blurred phrases borrowed from the Church. The present revival of the Kingdom idea is due to the combined influence of the historical study of the Bible and of the social gospel.

When the doctrine of the Kingdom of God shriveled to an undeveloped and pathetic remnant in Christian thought, this loss was bound to have far-reaching consequences. We are told that the loss of a single tooth from the arch of the mouth in childhood may spot the symmetrical development of the skull and produce malformations affecting the mind and character. The atrophy of that idea which had occupied the chief place in the mind of Jesus, necessarily affected the conception of Christianity, the life of the Church, the progress of humanity, and the structure of theology. I shall briefly enumerate some of the consequences affecting theology. This list, however, is by no means complete.

1. Theology lost its contact with the synoptic thought of Jesus. Its problems were not at all the same which had occupied his mind. It lost his point of view and became to some extent incapable of understanding him. His ideas had to he rediscovered in our time. Traditional theology and the mind of Jesus Christ became incommensurable quantities. It claimed to regard his revelation and the substance of his thought as divine, and yet did not learn to think like him. The loss of the Kingdom is one key to this situation.

2. The distinctive ethical principles of Jesus were the direct outgrowth of his conception of the Kingdom of God. When the latter disappeared from theology, the former disappeared from ethics. Only persons having the substance of the Kingdom ideal in their minds, seem to be able to get relish out of the ethics of Jesus. Only those Church bodies which have been in opposition to organized society and have looked for a better city with its foundations in heaven, have taken the Sermon on the Mount seriously.

3. The Church is primarily a fellowship for worship; the Kingdom is a Fellowship of righteousness. When the latter was neglected in theology, the ethical force of Christ was weakened; when the former was emphasized in theology, the importance of worship was exaggerated. . . . Thus the religious energy and enthusiasm which might have saved man-

kind from its great sins, were used up in hearing and endowing masses, or in maintaining competitive Church organizations, while mankind is still stuck in the mud. . . .

4. When the Kingdom ceased to be the dominating religious reality, the Church moved up into the position of the supreme good. To promote the power of the Church and its control over all rival political forces was equivalent to promoting the supreme ends of Christianity. This increased the arrogance of Churchmen and took the moral check off their policies. . . .

5. The Kingdom ideal is the test and corrective of the influence of the Church. When the Kingdom ideal disappeared, the conscience of the Church was muffled. It became possible for the missionary expansion of Christianity to halt for centuries without creating any sense of shortcoming. It became possible for the most unjust social conditions to fasten themselves on Christian nations without awakening any consciousness that the purpose of Christ was being defied and beaten back. . . .

6. The Kingdom ideal contains the revolutionary force of Christianity. When this ideal faded out of the systematic thought of the Church, it became a conservative social influence and increased the weight of the other stationary forces in society. If the Kingdom of God had remained part of the theological and Christian consciousness, the Church could not, down to our times, have been salaried by autocratic class governments to keep the democratic and economic impulses of the people under check.

7. Reversely, the movements for democracy and social justice were left without a religious backing for lack of the Kingdom idea. The Kingdom of God as the fellowship of righteousness would be advanced by the abolition of industrial slavery and the disappearance of the slums of civilization; the Church would only indirectly gain through such social changes. Even today many Christians cannot see any religious importance in social justice and fraternity because it does not increase the number of conversions nor fill the Churches. Thus the practical conception of salvation, which is the effective theology of the common man and minister, has been cut back and crippled for lack of the Kingdom ideal.

8. Secular life is belittled as compared with Church life. Services rendered to the Church get a higher religious rating than services rendered to the community. . . .

9. When the doctrine of the Kingdom of God is lacking in theology, the salvation of the individual is seen in its relation to the Church and

to the future life, but not in its relation to the task of saving the social order. . . .

10. Finally, theology has been deprived of the inspiration of great ideas contained in the idea of the Kingdom and in labor for it. The Kingdom of God breeds prophets; the Church breeds priests and theologians. The Church runs to tradition and dogma: the Kingdom of God rejoices in forecasts and boundless horizons. . . . The Kingdom of God is to theology what outdoor color and light are to art. It is impossible to estimate what inspirational impulses have been lost to theology and to the Church, because it did not develop the doctrine of the Kingdom of God and see the world and its redemption from that point of view. . . .

In the following brief propositions I should like to offer a few suggestions, on behalf of the social gospel, for the theological formulation of the doctrine of the Kingdom. Something like this is needed to give us "a theology for the social gospel."

1. The Kingdom of God is divine in its origin, progress and consummation. It was initiated by Jesus Christ, in whom the prophetic spirit came to its consummation, it is sustained by the Holy Spirit, and it will be brought to its fulfillment by the power of God in his own time. The passive and active resistance of the Kingdom of evil at every stage of its advance is so great, and the human resources of the Kingdom of God so slender, that no explanation can satisfy a religious mind which does not see the power of God in its movements. The Kingdom of God, therefore, is miraculous all the way, and is the continuous revelation of the power, the righteousness, and the love of God. The establishment of a community of righteousness in mankind is just as much a saving act of God as the salvation of an individual from his natural selfishness and moral inability. The Kingdom of God, therefore, is not merely ethical, but has a rightful place in theology. This doctrine is absolutely necessary to establish that organic union between religion and morality, between theology and ethics, which is one of the characteristics of the Christian religion. When our moral actions are consciously related to the Kingdom of God they gain religious quality. Without this doctrine we shall have expositions of schemes of redemption and we shall have systems of ethics, but we shall not have a true exposition of Christianity. The first step to the reform of the Churches is the restoration of the doctrine of the Kingdom of God.

2. The Kingdom of God contains the teleology of the Christian religion. It translates theology from the static to the dynamic. It sees, not doctrines or rites to be conserved and perpetuated, but resistance to be

overcome and great ends to be achieved. Since the Kingdom of God is the supreme purpose of God, we shall understand the Kingdom so far as we understand God, and we shall understand God so far as we understand his Kingdom. . . .

3 Since God is in it, the Kingdom of God is always both present and future. Like God it is in all tenses, eternal in the midst of time, it is the energy of God realizing itself in human life. . . . No theories about the future of the Kingdom of God are likely to be valuable or true which paralyze or postpone redemptive action on our part. To those who postpone, it is a theory and not a reality. It is for us to see the Kingdom of God as always coming, always pressing in on the present, always big with possibility and always inviting immediate action. We walk by faith. Every human life is so placed that it can share with God in the creation of the Kingdom, or can resist and retard its progress. The Kingdom is for each of us the supreme task and the supreme gift of God. By accepting it as a task, we experience it as a gift. By laboring for it we enter into the joy and peace of the Kingdom as our divine fatherland and habitation.

4. Even before Christ, men of God saw the Kingdom of God as the great end to which all divine leadings were pointing. Every idealistic interpretation of the world, religious or philosophical, needs some such conception. Within the Christian religion the idea of the Kingdom gets its distinctive interpretation from Christ. (a) Jesus emancipated the idea of the Kingdom from previous nationalistic limitations and from the debasement of lower religious tendencies, and made it world-wide and spiritual. (b) He made the purpose of salvation essential in it. (c) He imposed his own mind, his personality, his love and holy will on the idea of the Kingdom. (d) He not only foretold it but initiated it by his life and work. . . .

5. The Kingdom of God is humanity organized according to the will of God. Interpreting it through the consciousness of Jesus we may affirm these convictions about the ethical relations within the Kingdom: (a) Since Christ revealed the divine worth of life and personality, and since his salvation seeks the restoration and fulfillment of even the least, it follows that the Kingdom of God, at every stage of human development, tends toward a social order which will best guarantee to all personalities their freest and highest development. This involves the redemption of social life from the cramping influence of religious bigotry, from the repression of self assertion in the relation of upper and lower classes, and from all forms of slavery in which human beings are treated as mere means to serve the ends of others. (b) Since love is the supreme law of

Christ, the Kingdom of God implies a progressive reign of love in human affairs. We can see its advance wherever the free will of love supersedes the use of force and legal coercion as a regulative of the social order. This involves the redemption of society from political autocracies and economic oligarchies; the substitution of redemptive for vindictive penology; the abolition of constraint through hunger as part of the industrial system; and the abolition of war as the supreme expression of hate and the completest cessation of freedom. (c) The highest expression of love is the free surrender of what is truly our own, life, property, and rights. A much lower but perhaps more decisive expression of love is the surrender of any opportunity to exploit men. No social group or organization can claim to be clearly within the Kingdom of God which drains others for its own ease, and resists the effort to abate this fundamental evil. This involves the redemption of society from private property in the natural resources of the earth, and from any condition in industry which makes monopoly profits possible. (d) The reign of love tends toward the progressive unity of mankind, but with the maintenance of individual liberty and the opportunity of nations to work out their own national peculiarities and ideals.

6. Since the Kingdom is the supreme end of God, it must be the purpose for which the Church exists. The measure in which it fulfills this purpose is also the measure of its spiritual authority and honor. The institutions of the Church, its activities, its worship, and its theology in the long run must be tested by its effectiveness in creating the Kingdom of God. For the Church to see itself apart from the Kingdom, and to find its aims in itself, is the same sin of selfish detachment as when an individual selfishly separates himself from the common good. The Church has the power to save in so far as the Kingdom of God is present in it. If the Church is not living for the Kingdom, its institutions are part of the "world." In that case it is not the power of redemption but its object. It may even become an anti-Christian power. If any form of Church organization which formerly aided the Kingdom now impedes it, the reason for its existence is gone.

7. Since the Kingdom is the supreme end, all problems of personal salvation must be reconsidered from the point of view of the Kingdom. It is not sufficient to set the two aims of Christianity side by side. There must be a synthesis, and theology must explain how the two react on each other. The entire redemptive work of Christ must also be reconsidered under this orientation. Early Greek theology saw salvation chiefly as the redemption from ignorance by the revelation of God and from earthli-

ness by the impartation of immortality. It interpreted the work of Christ accordingly, and laid stress on his incarnation and resurrection. Western theology saw salvation mainly as forgiveness of guilt and freedom from punishment. It interpreted the work of Christ accordingly, and laid stress on the death and atonement. If the Kingdom of God was the guiding idea and chief end of Jesus—as we now know it was—we may be sure that every step in his life, including his death, was related to that aim and its realization, and when the idea of the Kingdom of God takes its due place in theology, the work of Christ will have to be interpreted afresh.

8. The Kingdom of God is not confined within the limits of the Church amid its activities. It embraces the whole of human life. It is the Christian transfiguration of the social order. The Church is one social institution alongside of the family, the industrial organization of society and the State. The Kingdom of God is in all these, and realizes itself though them all. . . .

Source: Walter Rauschenbusch, *A Theology of This Social Gospel* (New York: Macmillan, 1917), 131–45.

30

Baptists and Religious Liberty, 1920

George Washington Truett

S OUTHERN BAPTISTS COUNT IT A high privilege to hold
their Annual Convention this year in the national capital, and they
count it one of life's highest privileges to be citizens of our one great,
united country. . . .

It behooves us often to look backward as well as forward. We should
be stronger and braver if we thought oftener of the epic days and deeds
of our beloved dead. The occasional backward look would give us poise
and patience and courage and fearlessness and faith. The ancient Hebrew
teachers and leaders had a genius for looking backward to the days and
deeds of their mighty dead. They never wearied of chanting the praises
of Abraham and Isaac and Jacob, of Moses of Joshua and Samuel; and
thus did they bring to bear upon the living the inspiring memories of the
noble actors and deeds of bygone days. Often such a cry as this rang in
their ears: "Look unto the rock whence ye were hewn, and the hole of the
pit whence ye were digged. Look unto Abraham, your father, and unto
Sarah that bare you; for when he was but one I called him, and I blessed
him, and made him many."

The Doctrine of Religious Liberty

We shall do well, both as citizens and as Christians, if we will hark
back to the chief actors and lessons in the early and epoch-making strug-
gles of this great Western democracy, for the full establishment of civil
and religious liberty—back to the days of Washington and Jefferson and
Madison, and back to the days of our Baptist fathers, who have paid such
a great price, through the long generations, that liberty, both religious
and civil, might have free course and be glorified everywhere.

Years ago, at a notable dinner in London, that world-famed statesman, John Bright, asked an American statesman, himself a Baptist, the

noble Dr. J. L. Curry, "What distinct contribution has your America made to the science of government?" To that question Dr. Curry replied: "The doctrine of religious liberty." After a moment's reflection, Mr. Bright made the worthy reply: "It was a tremendous contribution."

Supreme Contribution of the New World

Indeed, the supreme contribution of the new world to the old is the contribution of religious liberty. This is the chiefest contribution that America has thus far made to civilization. And historic justice compels me to say that it was pre-eminently a Baptist contribution. The impartial historian, Mr. Bancroft, when he says: "Freedom of conscience, unlimited freedom of mind, was from the first the trophy of the Baptists." And such historians will concur with the noble John Locke who said: "The Baptists were the first propounders of absolute liberty, just and true liberty, equal and impartial liberty." Ringing testimonies like these might be multiplied indefinitely.

Not Toleration, but Right

Baptists have one consistent record concerning liberty throughout their long and eventful history. They have never been a party to oppression of conscience. They have forever been the unwavering champions of liberty, both religious and civil. Their contention now is, and has been, and please God, must ever be, that it is the natural and fundamental and indefeasible right of every human being to worship God or not, according to the dictates of his conscience, and, as long as he does not infringe upon the rights of others, he is to be held accountable alone to God for all religious beliefs and practices. Our contention is not for mere toleration, but for absolute liberty. There is a wide difference between toleration and liberty. Toleration implies that somebody falsely claims the right to tolerate. Toleration is a matter of expediency, while liberty is a matter of principle. Toleration is a gift from man, while liberty is a gift from God. It is the consistent and insistent contention of Baptist people, always and everywhere, that religion must be forever voluntary and uncoerced, and that it is not the prerogative of any power, whether civil or ecclesiastical, to compel men to conform to any religious creed or form of worship, or to pay taxes for support of a religious organization to which they do not belong and in whose creed they do not believe. God wants free worshipers and no other kind.

A Fundamental Principle

. . . How is it, then, that Baptists, more than any other people in the world, have forever been the protagonists of religious liberty, and its compatriot, civil liberty? They did not stumble upon this principle. Their uniform, unyielding and sacrificial advocacy of such principle was not and is not an accident. It is, in a word, because of our essential and fundamental principles. Ideas rule the world. A denomination is molded by its ruling principles, just as a nation is thus molded and just as an individual life is thus molded. Our fundamental essential principles have made our Baptist people, of all ages and countries, to be the unyielded protagonist of religious liberty, not only for themselves, but as well for everybody else.

The Fundamental Baptist Principles

Such a fact provokes the inquiry: What are these fundamental Baptist principles which compel Baptists in Europe, in America, in some far-off seagirt island, to be forever contending for unrestricted religious liberty? First of all, and explaining all the rest, is the doctrine of the absolute Lordship of Jesus Christ. That doctrine is for Baptists the dominant fact in all their Christian experience, the nerve center of all their Christian life, the bedrock of all their church polity, the sheet anchor of all their hopes, the climax and crown of all their rejoicing. They say with Paul: "For to this end Christ both died and rose again, that he might be Lord both of the dead and the living."

The Absolute Lordship of Christ

From the germinal conception of the absolute Lordship of Christ, all our Baptist principles emerge. Just as yonder oak came from the acorn, so our many-branched Baptist life came from the cardinal principle of the absolute Lordship of Christ. The Christianity of our Baptist people, from Alpha to Omega, lives and moves and has its whole being in the realm of the doctrine of the Lordship of Christ. "One is your Master, even Christ, and all ye are brethren." Christ is the one head of the church. All authority has been committed unto Him, in heaven and on earth, and He must be given the absolute pre-eminence in all things. One clear note is ever to be sounded concerning Him, even this, "Whatsoever He saith unto you, do it."

147

The Bible Our Rule of Faith and Practice

How shall we find our Christ's will for us? He has revealed it in His Holy Word. The Bible and the Bible alone is the rule of faith and practice for Baptists. To them the one standard by which all creeds and conduct and character must be tried is the Word of God. They ask only one question concerning all religious faith and practice, and that question is, "What saith the Word of God?" Not traditions, nor customs, nor councils, nor confessions, nor ecclesiastical formularies, however venerable and pretentious, guide Baptists, but simply the will of Christ as they find it revealed in the New Testament. The immortal B. H. Carroll has thus stated it for us: "The New Testament is the law of Christianity. All the New Testament is the law of Christianity. The New Testament is all the law of Christianity. The New Testament always will be all the law of Christianity." . . .

Infant Baptism Unthinkable

It follows, inevitably, that Baptists are unalterably opposed to every form of sponsorial religion. If I have fellow Christians in this presence today who are protagonists of infant baptism, they will allow me frankly to say, and certainly I would say it in the most fraternal, Christian spirit, that to Baptists infant baptism is unthinkable from every viewpoint. First of all, Baptists do not find the slightest sanction for infant baptism in the Word of God. That fact, to Baptists, makes infant baptism a most serious question for the consideration for the whole Christian world. Nor is that all. As Baptists see it, infant baptism tends to ritualize Christianity and reduce it to lifeless forms. It tends also and inevitably, as Baptists see it, to the secularizing of the church and to the blurring and blotting out of the line of demarcation between the church and the unsaved world. . . .

The Ordinances Are Symbols

Again, to Baptists, the New Testament teaches that salvation through Christ must precede membership into His church, and must precede the observation of the two ordinances in His church, namely, baptism and the Lord's Supper. These ordinances are for the saved and only the saved. These two ordinances are not sacramental, but symbolic. They are teaching ordinances, portraying in symbolic truths an immeasurable and everlasting moment to humanity. To trifle with these symbols, to pervert their forms and at the same time to pervert the truths they are designed to symbolize, is indeed a most serious matter. Without ceasing and without wavering, Baptists are, in conscience, compelled to contend that these two teaching ordinances shall be maintained in the churches just as they were placed there in the wisdom and authority of Christ. . . .

The Church a Pure Democracy

To Baptists, the New Testament also clearly teaches that Christ's church is not only a spiritual body but it is also a pure democracy, all its members being equal, a local congregation, and cannot subject itself to any outside control. Such terms, therefore, as "The American Church," or "The bishop of this city or state," sound strangely incongruous to Baptist ears. In the very nature of this case, also, there must be no union between church and state, because their nature and functions are utterly different. Jesus stated the principle in two sayings, "My Kingdom is not of this world," and "Render unto Caesar the things that are Caesar's, and unto God the things that are God's." Never, anywhere, in any clime, has a true Baptist been willing, for one minute, been for the union of church and state, never for a moment. . . .

A Free Church in a Free State

That utterance of Jesus, "Render unto Caesar the things that are Caesar's, and unto God the things that are God's," is one of the most revolutionary and history-making utterances that ever fell from those lips divine. That utterance, once for all, marked the divorcement of church and state. It marked a new era for the creeds and deeds of men. It was the sunrise gun of a new day, the echoes of which are to go on and on and on until in every land, whether great or small, the doctrine shall have absolute supremacy everywhere of a free church in a free state.

In behalf of our Baptist people I am compelled to say that the forgetfulness of the principles that I have just enumerated, in our judgment, explains many of the religious ills that now afflict the world. All went well with the early churches in their earlier days. They were incomparably triumphant days for the Christian faith. Those early disciples of Jesus without prestige and worldly power, yet aflame with the love of God and the passion of Christ, went out and shook the pagan Roman Empire from the center to circumference, even in one brief generation. Christ's religion needs no prop of any kind from any worldly source, and to the degree that it is thus supported is a millstone hanged about its neck.

An Incomparable Apostasy

Presently there came an incomparable apostasy in the realm of religion, which shrouded the world in spiritual night through the long hundreds of years. Constantine, the Emperor, saw something in the religion of Christ's people which awakened his interest, and now we see him uniting religion to the state and marching up the marble steps of the Emperor's palace, with the church robed in purple. Thus and there was begun the most baneful misalliance that ever fettered and cursed a suffering world. For long centuries, even from Constantine to Pope Gregory VII, the conflict between church and state waxed stronger and stronger, and the encroachments and usurpations became more deadly and devastating. When Christianity first found its way into the city of the Caesars it lived at first in cellars and alleys, but when Constantine crowned the union of the church and state, the church was stamped with the impress of the Roman idea and fanned with the spirit of the Caesars. Soon we see a Pope emerging, who himself became a Caesar, and soon a group of councilors may be seen gathered around the Pope, and the supreme power of the church is assumed by the Pope and his councilors. . . .

The Reformation Incomplete

The coming of the sixteenth century was the dawning of a new hope for the world. With that century came the Protestant Reformation. Yonder goes Luther with his theses, which he nails over the church door in Wittenberg, and the echoes of the mighty deed shake the Papacy, shake Europe, shake the whole world. Luther was joined by Melanchthon and Calvin and Zwingli and other mighty leaders. Just at this point emerges one of the most outstanding anomalies of all history. Although Luther and his compeers protested vigorously against the errors of Rome, yet when these mighty men came out of Rome, and mighty men they were, they brought with them some of the grievous errors of Rome. The Protestant Reformation of the Sixteenth century was sadly incomplete—it was a case of arrested development. Although Luther and his compeers grandly sounded the battle cry of justification by faith alone, yet they retained the doctrine of infant baptism and a state church. They shrank from the logical conclusions of their own theses. . . .

. . . The early colonies of America were the forum of the working out of the most epochal battles that earth ever knew for the triumph of religious and civil liberty.

America and Religious and Civil Liberty

Just a brief glance at the struggle in those early colonies must now suffice us. Yonder in Massachusetts, Henry Dunster, the first president of Harvard, was removed from the presidency because he objected to infant baptism. Roger Williams was banished, John Clarke was put in prison, and they publicly whipped Obadiah Holmes on Boston Common. In Connecticut the lands of our Baptist fathers were confiscated and their goods sold to build a meeting house and support a preacher of another denomination. In old Virginia, "mother of states and statesmen," the battle for religious and civil liberty was waged all over her nobly historic territory, and the final triumph recorded there was such as to write imperishable glory upon the name of Virginia until the last syllable of recorded time. Fines and imprisonments and persecutions were everywhere in evidence in Virginia for conscience's sake. . . .

. . . They dared to be odd, to stand alone, to refuse to conform, though it cost them suffering and even life itself. They dared to defy traditions and customs, and deliberately chose the way of non-conformity, even though in many cases it meant a cross. They pleaded and suffered, they offered their protests and remonstrances and memorials, and thank God, mighty statesmen were won to their contention. Washington and Jefferson and Madison and Patrick Henry, and many others, until at last it was written into our country's Constitution that church and state must in this land be forever separate and free, that neither must ever trespass upon the distinctive functions of the other. It was preeminently a Baptist achievement. . . .

The Present Call

And now, my fellow Christians, and fellow citizens, what is the present call to us in connection with the priceless principle of religious liberty? That principle, with all the history and heritage accompanying it, imposes upon us obligations to the last degree meaningful and responsible. Let us today and forever be highly resolved that the principle of religious liberty shall, please God, be preserved inviolate through all our days and the days of those who come after us. . . .

The Price to Be Paid

Are we willing to pay the price that must be paid to secure for humanity the blessings they need to have? We say that we have seen God in the face of Jesus Christ, that we have been born again, that we are the true friends of Christ, and would make proof of our friendship for Him by doing His will. Well, then, what manner of people ought we to be in all holy living and godliness? Surely we should be a holy people, remembering the apostolic characterization, "Ye are a chosen generation, a royal priesthood, a holy nation, a peculiar people: That we should shew forth the praises of Him who hath called you out of darkness into His marvelous light, who in times past were not a people but are now the people of God."

Let us look again to the strange passion and power of the early Christians. They paid the price for spiritual power. Mark well this record: "And they overcame him by the blood of the Lamb, and by the word of their testimony; and they loved not their lives unto death." O my fellow Christians, if we are to be in the true succession of the mighty days and deeds of the early Christian era, or of those mighty days and deeds of our Baptist fathers in the later days, then selfish ease must be utterly renounced for Christ and His cause, and our every gift and grace and power utterly dominated by the dynamic of His cross. Standing here today in the shadow of our country's capital, compassed as we are with so great a cloud of witnesses, let us today renew our pledge to God, and to one another, that we will give our best to church and to state, to God and to humanity, by His grace and power, until we fall on the last sleep.

Source: George Washington Truett, *Baptists and Religious Liberty* (Nashville: Baptist Sunday School Board, 1920), 3–36.

31

THE IMPACT OF J. FRANK NORRIS ON BAPTIST LIFE

The Fruits of Norrisism, L. R. Scarbrough, ca. 1925

Foreword

THIS TRACT IS A DISCUSSION of some of the fruits of an old cult under a new name. The following are some of the characteristics of this cult—Norrisism:

1. It is toward true religion what socialism and bolshevism are to politics and industry; wholly destructive in spirit and methods.

2. It is anti-missionary and anti-institutional. It gives nothing to associational, state or home missions and only enough to foreign missions to get representation in the convention. It spends most of its money on itself—some times in court trials for perjury, arson and murder, and in sending out free literature seeking to destroy the causes other people try to build.

3. It thrives on sensationalism, misrepresentation and false accusations of good men and true causes. It masquerades under the cloak of anti-evolutionism, anti-modernism, anti-Catholicism in order to ride into public favor and cast poisonous suspicion on the leadership of the causes of constructive Christianity.

4. In its chief leadership it is the embodiment of autocratic ecclesiasticism. All the privileges and rights of the church heading up in the pastor.

5. It uses the pulpit, the press, and the radio to create suspicion, to foment class prejudices and to vent its hatred against innocent personalities and institutions.

6. It divides and splits families, churches, associations and strikes its poisonous fangs at the brotherhood of Christianity.

7. It lowers the standards of right conduct, individual righteous-ness, ministerial ethics, personal integrity, and gives to the world a false conception of the character, spirit and methods of Christianity.

8. The only people or causes it praises are those who bow down to its dictum or fail in any wise to cross its path.

9. The individual, the preacher or church who joins in sympathy with this cult will sooner or later cease to co-operate with the mission, educational or benevolent enterprises fostered by God's people.

10. It has some noble names upon the escutcheon of its false ac-cusations and public misrepresentations; [B. H.] Carroll, [J. B.] Gambrell, [G. W.] McDaniel, [F. M.] McConnell, [E. Y.] Mullins, C. V. Edwards, [Samuel Palmer] Brooks, [John R.] Sampey, [F. S.] Groner, [T. B.] Ray, [A. T.] Robertson, Forrest Smith, Cullen Thomas, [G. W.] Truett and others—multitudes of false accusa-tions, such as: infidelity, graft, heresy, theft and suchlike, and groundless insinuations have gone out against these good men for years. . . .

Source: L. R. Scarborough, *The Fruits of Norrisism* (Fort Worth, TX: Southwestern Baptist Theological Seminary, n.d.).

Formation of the Baptist Bible Fellowship, Noel Smith, 1950

Reasons for Baptist Bible Fellowship "That is Final"—It Was

The following statement is self-explanatory—Editor:

It is commonly known among us that there has been for many months a widespread and deep-rooted restlessness among our people, both the ministers and the laity, because of the manner in which the affairs of the World Fundamental Baptist Missionary Fellowship and the Bible Baptist Seminary have been handled.

We have felt that our voice in the conduct of these affairs has not been commensurate with the responsibilities which we have been asked to assume, and for the amount of which we have contributed to the work of these institutions. We have sensed, and deeply sensed, the absence of the constitutional principles and procedure which should be the basis of representative government, especially the government of Christian institutions into whose treasuries so many people, many of them poor, are constantly asked to put their money.

This accumulated restlessness came to a head at the annual meeting of the World Fundamental Baptist Missionary Fellowship, which was held in the First Baptist Church of Fort Worth the week of May 21.

Tuesday morning, May 23, was Seminary day. Dr. J. Frank Norris was in charge of the Seminary program. Dr. Norris spoke on the history of the Seminary.

In the meantime, as was generally known, Dr. Norris had made revolutionary changes in the management and personnel of the Seminary. Those changes were made without any general notice to the Fellowship, and we believe they were made in violation of every constitutional principle.

Dr. Norris' position was that he had made these changes—including the taking over of the Seminary finances—in accordance with the constitution and by-laws of the Seminary. There was considerable discussion regarding the legality of the by-laws.

Mr. G. Beauchamp Vick, president of the Seminary, pointed out that the changes made by Dr. Norris had stripped him (Vick) of all authority. Mr. Vick also reminded the Fellowship that the 'election' of the new Seminary "trustees," who in turn "elected" Rev. Jock Troup of Scotland as "president," had taken place early Monday morning before hardly any of the messengers to the Fellowship had reached Fort Worth.

Mr. Vick asked how many in the large audience had attended the Monday "session" where the new trustees were "elected." Fourteen hands were raised. Meantime Dr. Frank Godsoe had stated that it seemed to him that 150 had voted for the "election" of the new trustees.

During the discussion, Rev. Wendell Zimmerman, pastor of the Baptist Temple of Kansas City, called the Fellowship's attention to the fact that the by-laws which Dr. Norris claimed had authorized his acts (copies of them had been distributed among the audience) were an altogether different set of by-laws from those published in the Seminary's catalog for the year 1948–49.

Mr. Zimmerman raised the question as to which set of by-laws was the official document.

Mr. Zimmerman moved that a committee be appointed to make an investigation and report back to the Fellowship.

The presiding officer, Rev. W. E. Dowell of Springfield, Missouri, held that the motion was open for discussion.

There was little discussion, except by Dr. Norris. Dr. Norris' conduct and defiant language convinced us that he was opposed to an investigation by such a committee. Of course we do not remember his words verbatim, but substantially they were these:

"We are going to follow these by-laws regardless of any investigation. You can appoint all the committees you want to. We are going to follow these by-laws. These are the by-laws on which this Seminary has been recognized. They cannot be changed. They are on record in Austin. And that is final."

We consider the attitude of Dr. Norris and his defiant language on such a basic matter as this, a profound insult to every one of us, and to every man, woman and child whom God has given us the honor of representing. During the last two years our churches have, in addition to raising the $1300 a week for the current expenses of the Seminary, paid approximately $125,000 on the Seminary's indebtedness.

In view of this we believe that we and our people (and all Christian people, for that matter) have a moral (and legal) right to know whether the authority governing an institution involving such huge sums of money, is the authority of a constitution or the emotional whims of a single man. We believe that we have the moral (and legal) right to know whether the by-laws which Dr. Norris claims gave him the authority to make the revolutionary changes he made, are the official by-laws of the Bible Baptist Seminary, or whether they are not the official by-laws of the Bible Baptist Seminary.

Dr. Norris has spoken. "That is final."

For us it is final. We can not, and we will not, ask our hard-working, trusting and generous people to continue to pour their sacrificial gifts into an institution dominated by a man with an attitude like that of Dr. J. Frank Norris.

We and our people have worked for this Seminary. We have given our money into its treasury. We gave this money as an offering to our Lord. We gave it honestly, generously and gladly. We did the best we could. We leave the case with Him. . . .

Source: "Reasons for Baptist Bible Fellowship," *Baptist Bible Tribune*, 23 June 1950. Permission granted by the *Bible Baptist Tribune*.

Experiences with J. Frank Norris, J. M. Dawson, 1964

Popularity underwent a severe test when my former associate in the *Baptist Standard*, the Rev. J. Frank Norris, pastor of the influential First Baptist Church, Fort Worth, commenced criticism in the columns of his widely circulated *Fundamentalist*. Of course, at first I was only one of the Baylor University group assailed for alleged heresies charged against President S. P. Brooks and members of the faculty who worshipped at First Church. Perhaps Norris thought I was an easy mark, because I accented social obligations as well as sound Baptist doctrines. Or he could have imagined the sickly young pastor, who never boasted a weight beyond one hundred and twenty-nine pounds, almost a habitué of hospitals, would wilt quickly under the paper's "barrage." One brother pastor confirmed this when he remarked, "Dawson doesn't have a robust personality, looks sallow, and might soon throw in the sponge."

A brief summary of Norris' doings between the time of my former connection with him and his attack on Baylor may be inserted here. After my leaving the *Baptist Standard* he continued as editor, also pastored the McKinney Avenue Baptist Church, Dallas. His utterances and practices there incurred the distrust of several Dallas Baptist pastors. It leaked out that Norris desired some other church. Dr. B. H. Carroll, who had admired the abilities of the young man as a student, upon assuming the presidency of Southwestern Baptist Theological Seminary and joining Fort Worth's pastorless First Church, recommended the restless Dallas preacher. Soon after Norris took over the Fort Worth Church, Carroll withdrew his membership because of Norris' sensational sermons. This produced quite a flare-up, with predictions that Norris was through. Instead the resourceful pastor spread accusations that Brooks, Truett, and Dawson have pressured the great Dr. Carroll with threats of denominational disapproval of the Seminary. Norris changed the name of his new publication to the *Searchlight* and said he would expose secret cabals and dispel malicious suspicions.

While this publicity met resentment from many Baptists, it won large audiences and many accessions to his church. So quick was the growth, the demand for a new edifice rose to a clamor. One night the old church burned down. Norris was indicted for arson, but upon standing trial he was acquitted. The local Baptist Association expelled him, but the adverse action only caused him to intensify his efforts to complete vindication.

Norris felt immensely encouraged by evidences, both within Texas and beyond its borders, that his crusade against Baylor University was being hailed as courageous. Inside the state "folks from the forks of the creek," who he said had long been denied a hearing, were speaking up. Informed people noted with anxiety that radical reactionary Baptist newspapers, particularly those representing splinter groups, proudly wearing the name of Fundamentalists throughout the country, were sounding off in his favor.

Men of some importance in the nation applauded Norris' announcement that he intended to establish a new theological seminary in Fort Worth. With a powerful radio station supplementing his paper, he broadcast his Sunday sermons in which he set forth his charges against his alma mater, "for teaching evolution, salvation by education and other heresies." By his sustained drive he caused several of Baylor University's most highly rated teachers to resign, notably Professor Samuel Grove Dow, author of a textbook on sociology.

Since Baylor trustees, such as Truett and myself, who were under accusation, were appointed by the Baptist General Convention, that body deemed it wise to make a full investigation into its institution's teachings. The Convention named a large representative and responsible committee to undertake this. This committee of inquiry—not quite unanimously—at the next session of the Convention found "literalistic believers in the Bible, who refused to reckon with the results of science along with some inclined toward the materialistic, who relied entirely on scientific research—both positions repulsive to lovers of truth." The committee asserted that it endorsed neither position, though the Convention should say that it was "not committed to any theory of evolution, though opposed to Darwinian evolution." It advised that all complaints be communicated directly to the president and the trustees—not decided on the hustings or on the Convention floor. The Convention overwhelmingly adopted the report.

Appointment of the investigating committee at first had pleased the warring editor-pastor so much that he had apologized to the Convention and promised future cooperation. A peace party within the fold maneuvered a resolution of reconciliation into adoption at the Galveston Convention and everybody hoped for a new era. But Norris was outraged by the final report, castigated the reporting committee as being puppets in the hands of leaders who hated him, and conspired to silence him. He opened new war on the convention and all its works.

Something other than Baylor's alleged heresies contributed to Norris' fight on me. Next year Texas Baptists accepted a quota of $15,000,000 in the Southern Baptist $75,000,000 campaign. On the state's staff the Convention named me as publicity director. The organized movement vigorously promoted the very institutions and objects Norris opposed. He denounced me as an evolutionist, a Unitarian, a rationalist, the creator of "Dawsonism." When I spoke as a fraternal delegate to the Northern Baptists he advertised me as allied with "Fosdickism," and in the Convention city of Milwaukee, he hired a sound-truck, placarded with depicted evils of Fosdickism and Dawsonism, to traverse the streets. Perhaps my Dallas *News* column in the Sunday book review magazine had added fuel to Norris' fire, for he could easily extract from the reviewed quotes which he handled to suit his purposes, frequently without regard to accuracy. And undoubtedly I was a bit careless in some of my book reviews in not guarding against phraseology which he could twist in a manner to disturb good people.

One night over the radio his misinterpretations were so palpably false that his wife felt compelled to correct them. I smiled, because I knew Texas Baptists believed that Lillian Norris, Jim Gaddy's daughter, would tell the truth. She said Dr. Norris had taken another's words for mine.

The Southern Baptist 75 Million Campaign, superbly led by Dr. L. R. Scarborough of Fort Worth, succeeded. Texas Baptists subscribed their quota. Norris was exasperated. It could have been that his distemper to some degree accounted for his shooting to death an opponent who visited his study to protest the pastor's arraignment of Fort Worth's politics. The shocking tragedy puzzled the public, but fellow Baptists failed to express sympathy for the killer. A member of my church, former Governor Pat M. Neff, regarded as the state's ablest defense lawyer, declined to accept Norris' case. There was no sign of general rejoicing when on a change of venue to Austin, Norris was acquitted. But acquittal in the courts gained him more power.

With subsequent fortunes of Norris I shall not here deal, but with more personal features of the Norris unpleasantness I must press on a little further. Ignoring his flagellations did not stop him. In a fresh attack he picked at vulnerable articles of mine published in the international *Homiletic Review* of New York. My succeeding Professor Gaius Atkins of Auburn Theological Seminary as book editor of the magazine did not mitigate my errors in the view of Norris. My election to the presidency of the Texas Institute of Letters also magnified my guilt in his sight. When in the latter capacity I persuaded my friend Carr Collins of Dallas to offer a thousand dollars annually for the best book written by a Texan, Norris fumed that I was attempting to corrupt Southwestern culture!

In the city of his alma mater, with the joint action of the Rev. A. Reilly Copeland of the Tabernacle Baptist Church, he conducted mass meetings, gave out interviews to newspapers, and laid copies of his own explosive publication on every door step. On Sundays my church members went from the sanctuary to their cars to find the *Searchlight's* red-bannered front pages denouncing "Dawsonism Worse Than Fosdickism." Yet my deacons and members uniformly stood loyally by me.

In the eyes of the militant Fundamentalist (he spelled the word with a capital) my interfaith contacts increased my guilt. Thus when Rector Everett Jones of Waco's St. Paul's Episcopal Church, Methodist Edmond Heinsohn of Southwestern University's church and I formed an association for discussion of theological and sociological questions, in his view this made me a public enemy. When I preached in Waco's liberal synagogue, presided over by Rabbi Macht, I became "intolerable." Incidentally many Jewish friends there welcomed me—A. M. Goldstein, L. Fred, and the Misses Novich, who unfailingly sent us Christmas and Easter greetings! When Congressman W. H. Judd, a Congregationalist, spoke in First Church to the Waco Council of Women, it was too much—Norris heralded this hospitality as an overture to the "insufferable Federal Council of Churches."

His last serious attack came in November, 1943. I was to preach the annual sermon for the General Convention of Texas. In a special edition of the *Searchlight*, in handbills and by pickets at the entrances of First Baptist Church, Dallas, he challenged the messengers to allow the heretic to proceed. Never could I have asked for a more perfect setting. The vast sanctuary was filled to overflowing. Pastor Truett, though ill, appeared on the platform beside me to offer the prayer. My gifted soloist, Miss Mildred Cook, sang "O Divine Redeemer." Within a simple outline I presented "The Christian View of Man," as exhibited in the Scriptures: 1. What man is ideally. 2. What man is actually. 3. What man will be finally under grace. Instant, emphatic vocal approval and subsequent letters from every section of the state gave ample evidence that my message met with favor. Norris had little to say that day, nor did he assail the published copy, as carried in part by the Dallas newspapers, by the *Baptist Standard* in full, likewise by Baptist papers elsewhere in the nation. I regret to say Norris continued to arraign me. . . .

That he was a man of ability and could precipitate a really serious episode in Baptist history is attested by the fact that institutions and research agencies are currently rehearsing just how much of a stir he created in denominational affairs. . . .

Source: J. M. Dawson, *A Thousand Months to Remember* (Waco: Baylor University Press, 1964), 129–34. Permission granted by Baylor University Press.

32

THE COOPERATIVE PROGRAM, 1924

Southern Baptist Convention

Recommendations

FIRST. THAT A SIMULTANEOUS EVERY-MEMBER canvass of every Baptist church in the South be conducted from November 30th to December 7th, 1924, for subscriptions to cover denominational needs for the calendar year 1925, ever keeping before our people the ideal of an annual increase over each year's gifts.

Second. That in this, and future campaigns, their emphasis shall be placed upon the need for permanency in our financial plans through the Bible principles of Stewardship and Tithing.

Third. That we recognize the right of individuals and churches to designate their gifts, but it is earnestly hoped that contributions will be made to the whole program. It is urged that pastors, denominational representatives and all others of our workers shall present the whole program and press upon the people the importance of unity in its support. If, notwithstanding, there be individuals who of their own accord wish their gifts to go to special objects and who indicate the same when the gift is made, this gift shall not be charged against the sums allocated to the object to which it was given. Any solicitation of such gifts through this Every-Member Canvass will be regarded as a breach of comity and opposed to the spirit of the campaign. All designated gifts of individuals and churches made subsequent to and above the campaign pledge shall go to the causes for which they are designated without being charged against the percentage which those causes are due to receive from the general fund, but these designated gifts shall not be considered as counting on the amounts already pledged by churches or on the total amount of the pledges of the members of the church. Bequests shall be considered as "subsequent" gifts.

Fourth. Participating South-wide Causes shall, after the simultaneous campaign, have the right to approach individuals in soliciting large gifts provided such solicitation be approved by the state organizations of the states in which this is to be done.

An emergency now existing in the Building Program of the Southern Baptist Theological Seminary, we recommend that the Seminary be given the right of approach to individuals, after the simultaneous campaign, for large gifts to the Building Fund, payable within one year.

Fifth. We recommend that there be a General Committee, with headquarters in Nashville, for the promotion of this program, consisting of the General Secretaries, State Secretaries, Secretary of Laymen's Movement, President and Secretary of the W.M.U., Presidents of the three South wide Institutions and ten others, three of whom shall be women and the remainder Pastors and Laymen. The expenses of the meetings of the Committee to be borne by the several States, boards and Institutions represented, except for the ten members at large, whose expenses shall be charged to general expenses. We favor the election by the Committee of a competent General Director, who shall be under the direction of the Committee. The Committee to employ such other help as may seem advisable.

Sixth. We recommend that we undertake to raise for South-wide objects during 1925 the sum of $7,500,000.00, the same to be allocated as follows:

	Foreign Missions. 47%
Home Missions 20%	
	Christian Education 20%
Ministers' Relief and Annuities 10%	
	New Orleans Hospital. . . . 3%
Total 100%	

The percentages recommended for Home and Foreign Missions have been arranged for the purpose of restoring to those Boards the funds heretofore loaned to the two Seminaries and the Baptist Bible Institute.

The 20% allocated to Christian Education to be apportioned as follows:

Southern Baptist Seminary 10%
W.M.U. Training School 1%
Southwestern Baptist Seminary 4%
S. W. Training School 1/2%
Bible Institute 3%
Education Board 1%
Negro Seminary. 1/2%
Total 20%

Seventh. That hereafter the General Committee of the Convention shall ask from the various South-wide interests, prior to the meeting of the Southern Baptist Convention, a detailed written statement of their needs for the coming year and that, with these statements before them, the General Committee shall make a South-wide budget which shall be reported to the Convention at its annual session in a ratio of distribution based on this annual budget.

Eighth. That this Convention requests the states in the interest of exercising the spirit of co-operation, the interest of a unified program and in the interest of all our Convention causes, to leave the percentages of distribution of South-wide funds to this Convention or its General Committee. That the General Committee be instructed to confer with the several states for the adjustment of this matter.

Ninth. That monthly remittances shall be insisted upon from all Treasurers of all funds for South-wide objects on such percentage of total collections as shall be agreed upon at the outset of the campaign.

Tenth. That State Treasurers be asked to take out of the total receipts all expenses before they divide and remit to the various objects the amounts due them according to the percentages of collections.

Eleventh. That the Special Days in the Sunday Schools, as heretofore provided for by the Southern Baptist Convention and the several State Boards, shall continue to be a part of this Campaign.

In making these recommendations, your Committee is keenly sensible to the fact that all of this proposed machinery shall be but sounding brass and clanging cymbal unless it be infilled and vitalized by the Spirit of God. We, therefore, call all our people everywhere to constant and persistent intercession in behalf of all our great causes which Christ has committed to our trust.

We believe that Southern Baptists should go forward, and forward together, year by year, in high and holy endeavor until His Kingdom shall stretch from shore to shore and His name shall be known from the river to the ends of the earth.

Source: *Annual*, SBC, 1924, 68–69.

33

THE TRAIL OF BLOOD, 1931

J. M. Carroll

FOURTH LECTURE—17th, 18th, 19th Centuries

1. THIS LECTURE BEGINS WITH the beginning of the seventeenth century (A.D. 1601). We have passed very hurriedly over much important Christian history, but necessity has compelled this.

2. This three-century period begins with the rise of an entirely new denomination. It is right to state that some historians give the date of the beginning of the Congregational Church (at first called "Independents") as 1602. However, Schaf-Herzogg, in their Encyclopedia, place its beginning far back in the 16th century, making it coeval with the Lutheran and Presbyterian. In the great reformation wave many who went out of the Catholic Church were not satisfied with the extent of the reformation led by Luther and Calvin. They decided to repudiate also the preacher rule and government idea of the churches and return to the New Testament democratic idea as had been held through the fifteen preceding centuries by those who had refused to enter Constantine's hierarchy.

3. The determined contention of this new organization for this particular reform brought down upon its head bitter persecution from Catholic, Lutheran, Presbyterian and Church of England adherents—all the established churches. However, it retained many other of the Catholic made errors, such for instance as infant baptism, pouring or sprinkling for baptism, and later adopted and practiced to an extreme degree the church and state idea. And, after refugeeing to America, themselves, became very bitter persecutors.

4. The name "Independents" or as now called "Congregationalists," is derived from their mode of church government. Some of the distinguishing principals of the English Congregationalists as given in the Schaff- Herzogg Encyclopedia are as follows:

(1) That Jesus Christ is the only head of the church and that the Word of God is its only statute book.

(2) That visible churches are distinct assemblies of Godly men gathered out of the world for purely religious purposes, and not to be confounded with the world.

(3) That these separate churches have full power to choose their own officers and to maintain discipline.

(4) That in respect to their internal management they are each independent of all other churches and equally independent of state control.

5. How markedly different these principals are from Catholicism, or even Lutheranism, or Presbyterianism or the Episcopacy of the Church of England. How markedly similar to the Baptists of today, and of all past ages, and to the original teachings of Christ and His apostles.

6. In 1611, the King James English Version of the Bible appeared. Never was the Bible extensively given to the people before. From the beginning of the general dissemination of the Word of God began the rapid decline of the Papal power, and the first beginnings for at least many centuries, of the idea of "religious liberty. . . ." . . .

8. During all the seventeenth century, persecutions of Waldenses, Ana-Baptists and Baptists (in some places the "Ana" was now being left off) continued to be desperately severe; in England by the Church of England, as John Bunyan and many others could testify; in Germany by the Lutherans; in Scotland by the Church of Scotland (Presbyterian); in Italy, in France and in every other place where the papacy was in power, by the Catholics. There is now no peace anywhere for those who are not in agreement with the state churches, or some one of them.

9. It is a significant fact well established in credible history that even as far back as the fourth century those refusing to go into the Hierarchy, and refusing to accept the baptism of those baptized in infancy, and refusing to accept the doctrine of "Baptismal Regeneration" and demanding rebaptism for all those who came to them from the Hierarchy, were called "Ana-Baptists." No matter what other names they then bore, they were always referred to as "Ana-Baptists." Near the beginning of the sixteenth century, the "Ana" was dropped, and the name shortened to

simply "Baptist," and gradually all other names were dropped. Evidently, if Bunyan had lived in an earlier period his followers would have been called "Bunyanites" or "Ana-Baptists." Probably they would have been called by both names as were others preceeding him.

10. The name "Baptist" is a "nickname," and was given to them by their enemies (unless the name can be rightfully attributed to them as having been given to them by the Savior Himself, when He referred to John as "The Baptist"). To this day, the name has never been officially adopted by any group of Baptists. The name, however, has become fixed and is willingly accepted and proudly borne. It snugly fits. It was the distinguishing name of the forerunner of Christ, the first to teach the doctrine to which the Baptists now hold.

Where did these Baptists come from? They did not come out of the Catholics during the Reformation. They had large churches prior to the Reformation.

Source: J. M. Carroll, *The Trail of Blood* (Lexington, KY: Ashland Avenue Baptist Church, 1931).

34

THE BAPTIST WAY, 1945

Ben M. Bogard

PART I
The Scriptural Way

T HE BIBLE IS THE ALL-SUFFICIENT rule of faith and practice and it is as much a rule of practice as it is of faith.

The commission given by our Master in Matt. 28:19, 20, commands the church to "teach all things whatsoever I have commanded you." The specification of one thing in law is the prohibition of everything else. Since what the church is to teach is specified, viz., "all things whatsoever I have commanded," it follows that all things not commanded are forbidden. It follows that the church is shut up to the things commanded. There is therefore no place for the exercise of private opinion except it be in our effort to understand the things commanded. Any doctrine or institution that is outside of the purview of the Scriptures is wrong. . . .

By the Scriptures, the all-sufficient rule of faith and practice, must every doctrine and every truth be tried. If it be allowed that reason or sanctified common sense shall determine in matters of faith and practice, it shall still be an open question as to whose reason and whose sanctified common sense shall make the decision. If reason or common sense shall be the rule of any part of faith and practice then it is certain that we shall see division, contention, strife. Let the Bible be the rule of faith and practice and our only difficulty shall be understanding our rule. . . .

If Baptists forsake this cardinal and fundamental principle, it shall not be long until they shall cease to be Baptists. They shall be at sea without chart or compass.

In the following chapters we shall examine what the Scriptures teach concerning the Way of Salvation, Baptism, the Lord's Supper, Church Policy, Missions, and Providence. While we hear the Word of God on these subjects, let us remember that this Word is the only and all-sufficient rule of faith and practice.

CHAPTER II
The Way of Baptism

The church only having authority to baptize, it follows that all baptisms administered without church authority are null and void. For this reason Baptists have in all ages refused to recognize the baptisms of those who were not baptized by the authority of a Scriptural church. It was to the church the commission was given and the church institution to which the commission was given is in the world today, and if the Lord meant what He said, He is with that church today. The baptisms of that institution are valid and no other is.

Scriptural baptism is the immersion of a saved person by authority of a Scriptural church.

Since God called the forerunner, John the Baptist—the baptizer—called him "Baptist" because he did the baptizing, it follows that, if God made no mistake, that a CHURCH THAT BAPTIZES should be called a Baptist Church; a baptizing church. Since the baptizing church is a missionary church it is perfectly right to call it a Missionary Baptist Church.

CHAPTER III
The Way of the Lord's Supper

The Lord's Supper is a commemorative ordinance to be observed by the church in memory of the broken body and shed blood of the Savior. 1 Cor. 11:24: "This do in remembrance of me."

Only baptized believers have a right to partake of the Supper. The commission given by our Master commands that the newly made disciples be baptized and then "teach them to observe all things whatsoever I have commanded you," Matt. 28:19, 20. One of the things the Lord had commanded was the partaking of the Memorial Supper. The new disciples were first to be baptized then taught to observe the other things which had been commanded. To partake of the Supper before baptism is to violate this law, and if we encourage any to thus violate the law of the Lord on this subject we shall be partakers of their sin. To invite unbaptized people to partake of the Lord's Supper is a sin. Open Communion is therefore a sin—a transgression of the Master's law concerning the Supper. . . .

Note the order here indicated:

1. "Gladly received his word"—disciples.

2. "Were baptized"—baptized disciples.

3. "The same day were added"—church members.

4. "Continued in apostolic doctrine"—sound in faith.

5. "And in fellowship"—united in faith and love.

6. Lastly, "breaking of bread"—partaking of the Lord's Supper.

This is the Divine order, and no man has a right to change it. If we observe this order we have Close Communion, the doctrine for which Baptists have always contended.

CHAPTER IV
The Way of Church Polity

There are three forms of church government or polity: the Episcopalian, the Presbyterian, and the Congregational. Episcopacy is government by bishops; Presbyterianism is government by presbyters or preachers; Congregationalism is government by the people—a pure democracy.

Baptists are Congregationalists. They do not claim the right to make or repeal laws, but recognize and obey the unchanging law of their King Jesus Christ. But in the execution of these laws of the Lord there is a pure democracy. . . .

In the New Testament we learn the following facts:

1. The congregation received members. . . .

2. The congregations excluded members from their fellowship. . . .

3. The congregations elected their own officers. . . .

4. The congregations elected their own missionaries. . . .

The conclusion is clear. It was to "the church" that the Commission was given. It is therefore the duty of the congregation to do all that the Commission enjoins. The congregation is the unit in all the work contemplated in the Commission. There is not the slightest hint in the New Testament of their being authority on earth above a congregation of baptized disciples. Where we read of "elders that rule well," the literal rendering is the elders that "lead well." The "elder" or bishop, which are the Scriptural terms for pastor, is a leader of his flock over which the Holy Ghost has made him overseer. But he leads by teaching, by example, and not by authority. To exercise authority is expressly forbidden by our Master. Matt. 20:25, 26: "Ye know that the princes of the Gentiles exercise dominion over them, and they that are great exercise authority upon them. But it shall not be so among you." In 1 Peter 5:3: "Neither as being lords (masters) over God's heritage, but being examples to the flock."

The Episcopal and Presbyterian bodies have men of authority—men in control. The Master said: "It shall not be so among you." The superintendent of missions, so common among Baptists, has authority to superintend the work of missionaries. The Master said: "It shall not be so among you." Baptists should recognize only one Master, even Jesus Christ and only one Superintendent of Missions, even the Holy Spirit.

A gospel church may exist with or without officers. The churches (Acts 14:23) in which elders were elected existed as gospel churches before they had elders, and if they could exist as gospel churches before they had elders, it follows that if the elders should die or move away, the churches could exist again as gospel churches without them. Elders or pastors are not necessary to the existence of a church. A church is a gospel church with them or without them. So with the deacons. The church at Jerusalem was a gospel church (Acts 6) before the deacons were elected. If all the deacons should die or move away, it would continue to be a gospel church. As Pendleton put it in his Church Manual: "Officers are not necessary to 'the being of a church, but they are necessary to its well being.' . . ."

Evils of Conventionism

1. Conventionism ignores the law of Christ and sets up rules of its own.
2. Conventionism gives one man authority over another, and the Master said, "It shall not be so among you." (Matt. 20:25, 26).
3. Conventionism tends toward centralization and destroys congregationalism.
4. Conventions are unknown to the Scriptures.
5. Conventionism fosters liberalism and decries orthodoxy.
6. Conventionism is an invention of man and not a revelation of God.
7. Conventionism is a breeder of strife and confusion among the churches.
8. Conventionism is a departure from the faith and practice of the fathers.
9. Conventionism incurs needless expenses, and unjustly calls upon the churches to pay the debts they had no part in making.
10. Conventionism has a bad spirit. Those it can't control it seeks to ruin.
11. Conventionism is responsible in a large measure for Hardshellism, since the extremes of Conventionism drove many into repudiating all mission work.

12. Conventionism is fast becoming a schism, and unless reform or revolution comes speedily it must be treated as such.

13. Conventionism and Hardshellism are both departures from the historic faith and practice of the ancient Baptists. . . .

What is called the association is not an organization in the common acceptance of the term at all. It is only an intelligent working together of independent organizations. It is only the associated work—working at the same thing at the same time and the same way, but working as individual churches, independent and free. Beyond this they cannot go without violating the law of the Master, who told the individual church, as such, to "go teach all nations, baptizing them," etc. (Matt. 28:19, 20).

Source: Ben Bogard, *The Baptist Way Book* (Texarkana, TX: Bogard Press, 1945), 1, 2, 14–20, 47, 48, 72. Permission granted by the Baptist Sunday School Committee and Bogard Press.

35

RUSSIAN BAPTIST HISTORY FROM 1929 TO 1963, 1967

I N 1929, IN THE PRESENCE of the law on freedom of religion, there was published the Resolution of the Central Executive
Committee and the Sovnarkom, "Concerning Religious Associations,"
which reduced religious freedom to nil. Already by the summer of this
year the publication of the journals, "*Khristianin*" and "*Baptist*," was
forbidden, which have heretofore not been revived. At the same time
congregations were closed. Atheists sought the possibility of deposing
the church through their actions on the leadership of the fraternal unions.
Many brethren workers of the union applied all their energies to preserve
the brotherhood's faithfulness to the Lord and to all suggestions of co-
operation with the authorities and curtailment of preaching the Gospel
they answered: "We submit unconditionally to all governmental laws,
if they do not violate our convictions. If you promulgate laws that we,
believers, must not preach the Gospel to anyone, then such a law for us
is not binding, since the law of God is above the laws of the state. If you
publish a law that people will not believe in God, then also that law is
not binding for us."

For such faithfulness to the Lord they all, with few exceptions, accepted imprisonment and several, such as Odintsov, Bukreev, Kostiukov,
Vins, and many others, gave their lives. . . .

In 1935 the Union of Baptists was closed and the Union of Evangelical
Christians also curtailed its spiritual activity. Societies of Evangelical
Christians and Baptists everywhere were closed and prayer houses were
confiscated.

But the year 1937 was especially hard for our brotherhood. It is difficult to determine the number of believers who were imprisoned in those
years and who died through torture in the severe conditions of Siberia,

the Far East, and on Solovki Island. The terms of imprisonment were so long that for many they seemed to be for life. Thrown in to the wild taiga forests, deprived of the right of correspondence, tormented by hunger and weakened by labor, the true children of God died by the thousands. Only a few of those condemned returned home as invalid, old men, after the nightmares they experienced. . . .

The Church of Christ in those years went through a long, deathly darkness. In 1940, in all the country, there remained only a few open congregations. To enemies of the work of God it seemed that religion had already ceased. In reality, the Church continued to live even in these improbable conditions. In the congregations where sin did not rule, the following picture was observed: the presbyter was arrested; the church elected another for leading meetings; he was taken; a third was elected. And so on until all were awarded bonds. The modest, wretched apartments of believers, the forests and ravines were the places of worship services. Many expected deliverance from the Lord, which they saw in the imminent advent of Christ for the church.

Thus passed the mournful path of the Church of Christ in our country. This was a period of cruel persecutions in the life of our brotherhood in all of its hundred years' existence. From these tears the Lord also delivered His elect.

The same ruler under whom believers were suppressed so unimaginably, according to the will of God, at the end of the last war permitted the opening of prayer houses.

The ensuing period of the life of our brotherhood was a period of new revival. . . . In October, 1944, the All-Union Council of Evangelical Christians and Baptists [AUCECB] was formed. Into its founding entered the workers of the former unions who had been freed from the places of confinement, after they had given consent to form the Union on specified conditions.

For the supervision of the life of the churches the AUCECB named its commissioners, the so-called senior presbyters. In 1947, the work of registration of the congregations was begun, after which few churches received official permission for conducting services. Societies and groups of believers who did not manage to organize themselves in this short period began to be refused registration by local organs of the state for various pretenses. After 1948 registration of congregations was completely ceased, as a result of which a significant part of the congregations suffered persecution. . . .

The church languished under such violence from the secular authorities, and workers of the AUCECB and the senior presbyters everywhere taught that such obedience was pleasing to God, seducing the weak and unstable souls who accepted the interference of outsiders in the inner life of the church as the will of the Lord. The vigilant children of God saw that the actions of the authorities and of the workers of the AUCECB coincided. It became clear to them that the persecutors who had become convinced of the futility of persecutions and repression had decided to suppress the Church using for this purpose its own ministers.

But the life of Christ found a place in the midst of the sorrowing people of God. "Philips" were found who baptized new converts, despite bans. There were found good pastors, who in secrecy from the leadership of the congregation visited believers in their homes and established them in the faith, encouraged and exhorted them to renewed prayer for the work of God. There were also benefactors who found the means for support of the needy. Meetings for young people and for exhortation were held without the knowledge of the presbyter. The children of God did all of this, subjecting themselves to danger, and many of them had to accept bonds for their zeal. There were also separate groups and whole congregations who did not want to be reconciled with apostasy and began independent services, protecting themselves from every kind of influence from the AUCECB. It was this way in Baku, Tashkent, Khar'kov, Kiev, Voronezh, Simferopol, Ordzhonikidze, and elsewhere.

In 1960, the AUCECB, to please the authorities, worked out the infamous "Situation of the Union of ECB" and the Letter of Instruction to the senior presbyters which strengthened the spiritual restrictions which existed earlier in the life of the church. On the strength of these documents our brotherhood was artificially divided into registered and unregistered societies, since the AUCECB turned from the latter and they were doomed to suffering under the intensified repressions. The ministers of these societies were falsely accused of parasitism and exiled. . . .

In August 1961, [several ministers] formed the Initiating Group for the Calling of an All-Union Congress of ECB [Evangelical Christian Baptists] Churches and accused the ministers of the AUCECB of conscious apostasy from the evangelical truth and, having given the initiative for a congress, called the people of God to intensified prayers and fasts on Fridays for the sake of revival in the country. Their call was accepted by numerous groups of believers and separate congregations. In support of the initiative for a congress thousands of petitions were sent to the government. . . .

From 1961 to 1963 was a difficult period for our brotherhood. In meetings there was little room for preaching the pure gospel. Preachers of the registered congregations, distorting the Word of God, represented the revival that was beginning as displeasing to God. . . .

The awakened churches suffered intensified persecution. Their meetings were broken up, believers were summoned to organs of authority with the demands that they renounce petitions concerning the congress, searches were conducted in their apartments, and children were taken away from their parents for religious education. At this time, on false charges, around 200 brothers and sisters were convicted, and in the courts senior presbyters and ministers of registered congregations frequently represented the adherents of the movement for the congress as enemies of the state. . . .

Source: *Vestnik Spaseniia*, No. 3 (1967), 24–29, translated by PDS. Cited in Paul D. Steeves, *Church and State in the U.S.S.R.: A Sourcebook* (Deland, FL: Stetson University Press, 1973, 1976), 136–38. Permission granted by Paul D. Steeves.

36

ORIGINS OF THE CONSERVATIVE RESURGENCE

Death in the Pot, K. Owen White, 1961

"SINCE THE PARABLE INCLUDES THE historical and the non-historical, one can say with Richardson: 'We must learn to think of the stories of Genesis—the creation, the fall, Noah's ark, the tower of Babel—in the same way as we think of the parables of Jesus; **they are profoundly symbolical** (though not allegorical) **stories, which aren't to be taken as literally true** (like the words of the textbooks of geology), but which yet bear a meaning that cannot be paraphrased or stated in any other way without losing something of their quality of existential truth.'"

"Adam originally must have meant 'mankind,' not just one person." "The particular problem of Chapter 5 is the longevity of the antediluvians. **It is difficult to believe that they actually lived as long as stated.** In all probability, the Priestly writer simply exaggerated the ages in order to show the glory of an ancient civilization.". . .

"There developed **the tradition** that this was what happened to Lot's wife—**perhaps not exactly historical** . . ."

"Suddenly, what had been a thought of meditation gripped the inner being of Abraham until **he thought he heard it as a clear call from God**, 'Go sacrifice Isaac.'"

Does this sound like [J. P.] Boyce, [J. A.] Broadus, [E. Y.] Mullins, [A. T.] Robertson, [J. R.] Sampey, [J. B.] Gambrell, [B. H.] Carroll, [L. R.] Scarborough, and other great Southern Baptist leaders? The quotations listed above are from *The Message of Genesis*, written by Dr. Ralph Elliott, now teaching at Midwestern Seminary, Kansas City, Mo.

Being a graduate of Southern Seminary and having served as pastor of Southern Baptist churches for more than 30 years, I love and believe in my denomination and have a burning passion for it to remain true to the Bible as the Word of God. I have a deep concern that our seminaries shall sound a clear, ringing note in their interpretation of the Scriptures and that young preachers shall come from their halls with not an "uncertain sound."

The book from which I have quoted is liberalism, pure and simple! It stems from the rationalistic theology of Wellhausen and his school which led Germany to become a materialistic godless nation. This is "the wisdom of the world" which seeks to find a "reasonable, acceptable" solution to every problem which involves the supernatural.

Several great denominations in the last generation have drifted from the faith of our fathers, have lost their conviction that the Bible is authoritative and dependable, and now have little evangelistic witness. The drift came from liberalism in their seminaries and their literature.

If the appeal is made for "academic freedom," let it be said that we gladly grant any man the right to believe what he wants to—but, we do not grant him the right to believe and express views in conflict with our historic position concerning the Bible as the Word of God **while he is teaching in one of our schools, built and supported by Baptist funds**.

The book in question is "poison." This sort of rationalistic criticism can lead only to further confusion, unbelief, deterioration, and ultimate disintegration as a great New Testament denomination. It has happened to other denominations; it can happen to us! Modernism is insidious, dangerous, and destructive.

What can be done?

- Invite men with such views to find a place of service with groups or denominations of like theological inclinations.
- Ask the trustees of our institutions to consider seriously the dangers involved in such theological views and to exercise caution in their approval of faculty members.
- Urge our Sunday School Board to be alert to any trend in the direction of liberalism in our publications.

This is not an incidental matter. It involves the total responsibility of every one of us individually, of our churches and our denomination, in declaring plainly, positively, and unequivocally "the whole counsel of God."

In this brief statement I have made no attempt to review the book. The quotations speak for themselves. I have merely emphasized certain words and phrases in these quotations to shed light upon the particular doctrinal or historical truth in question. The influence of this sort of teaching would substitute intuition for inspiration, reason for revelation, and futility for faith. It is quite true of course that in our study and interpretation of God's Word we are not to forsake common sense, but we also need to remember the words of Isaiah 55:8, 9. "For my thoughts are not your thoughts, neither are your ways my ways, saith the Lord. For as the heavens are higher than the earth, so are my ways higher than your ways, and my thoughts than your thoughts."

"There is death in the pot!"

Source: *Baptist Standard*, 10 January 1962, 7. Permission granted by the *Baptist Standard*.

Why I Preach That the Bible Is Literally True, W. A. Criswell, 1969

The Most Important Question in the World Today

The most important question for the religious world today is this: "Is the Bible the Word of God?" If the Bible is the Word of God we have an absolutely trustworthy guide for all the answers our souls desire to know. We have a starting point from whence we can proceed to the conquest of the whole realm of religious truth. We have an assurance of our salvation and of the glories of the world to come. But if the Bible is not the Word of God, if it is the mere product of man's speculation, if it is not altogether trustworthy in regard to religious and eternal truth, then we are all in a trackless wilderness not knowing where to go or where to turn.

Truly, there is no sadder or more tragic sight than to look upon a minister or a professor of divinity attacking and ridiculing the Word of God, the anchor of the human soul. There is a depth of hypocrisy about ministers attacking the Bible that is unusually heinous. We have public halls, houses of assembly, scholastic academics, and civic auditoriums where the Bible and Christianity may be assaulted without interruption. But to see a minister of the gospel mount the pulpit to find fault with the Word of God and to decry it as a revelation of the truth of heaven is of all things most sad. In our day the Bible is assailed by infidel pseudoscientists, by rash materialists, by cheap secularists, by blaspheming communists, and by all the vice of earth and all the venom of perdition. For the minister to link hands with these enemies with the kingdom of God is unbelievable. If there ever was a time when our wobbling world needed to hear a clamant voice calling it back to the changeless verities of the Word of God, that time is now.

Modern, liberal critics leave behind them a world of jumbled confusion. They tell us that God has revealed Himself but refuse to pin themselves down as to exactly what the revelation is. In fact, upon occasion, we find them glorifying in the uncertainty of their preaching because this offers them an opportunity for the exercise of "the leap of faith." The basic thesis of their dialectical theology is that the acts of God in history cannot be detected apart from "a leap of faith" and the revealed Words of God can never be identified with any words. They avow that divine acts are beyond history and divine words are beyond language. There is a segment of neoorthodoxy that distinguishes between God's Word and the human expression of the word. The so-called word of God can be recognized only in the area of experience. This would mean that not even the words of Jesus are a valid external authority. Only those words of Jesus are valid which one feels to be appropriate to Jesus according to the judgment of one's own mind, which seems to mean that one's own mind becomes one's own Jesus.

They would have us believe that a miracle is not a marvelous or wondrous event that happened in history but that it is merely an interpretation which believing people gave to an event which moved them to such an expression and such an interpretation. For example, the miraculous deliverance of Israel through the waters of the sea was not a thing that actually happened. Rather, what we read in the Bible is just the empty interpretation of people who thought that it happened. It was a miracle only in their minds. The resurrection of Christ is likewise categorized as a human, fallible interpretation. Christ did not rise from the dead. The real truth is that his disciples thought that he rose from the dead, and what we have in the Bible is just the record of their cogitations. The Bible, to these men, does not contain timeless, divine truths, but it is only a purely human testimony to the response evoked by an event in their lives. Scripture, therefore, is true only to the degree in which it evokes an experience in us. What Jesus did on the cross has no meaning, according to these theologians, except what the interpreter would like to make it mean, and the interpreter, of course, could make it mean anything.

Thus, the entire Bible becomes a Book from which one may pick and choose what appeals to one's mind. Experience becomes the supreme authority. Bible teaching becomes secondary. In this way all of religion is reduced to a speculative, human experience, and there is no ultimate standard nor is there any ultimate truth. Religious experience thus becomes an object of one's own interpretation of truth and as such it can prove anything. Truly, falling back upon experience alone leaves the church and human soul in a limbo of doubt and agonizing uncertainty. Cutting theology off from the control of the biblical text cannot do aught but lead to its death. The theology which delights in the absence of final truth and revelation is absolutely nonsense. It cannot escape the just charge of pure meaninglessness. It cannot finally escape from the ultimate despair of materialistic, subjective existentialism.

The destructive results of the critics' work can be seen on every hand as they busy themselves seeking errors, contradictions, and historical inaccuracies in the Bible. They have torn apart God's beautiful flower. They cannot see it any more. As vivisectionists they have cut up the living body until for them and for those who believe them it is has died. Though they cannot destroy the Word of God, they have destroyed for themselves and for those who listen to them its vital life. It has become a dismembered cadaver. The critical spirit not only kills the will to worship and destroys confidence in the God Who revealed himself in the Bible but it also throws the whole life into unending doubt. It loosens the foundation stones of truth; it casts a shadow upon faith; it weakens the hold upon spiritual reality. The soul of man cannot feed upon negations. It cannot eat a stone when it demands and cries for bread.

The results of all of this doubt can be seen throughout the length and breadth of the Christian church. For many today, the question of what Jesus thought about Scripture cannot be seriously faced because the evidence against biblical infallibility is so overwhelming that it is hardly relevant. Negative biblical criticism has conducted a wide campaign of brainwashing to this effect. The results of modern critical teaching in the last century have rendered untenable to those who are influenced by it the whole conception of the Bible as a verbally inspired Book. No longer can we appeal to the Book with absolute certainty for infallible guidance in all matters of faith and conduct. Therefore, without an infallible guide and without an inerrant Bible, the church is lost in this modern sea of conflicting storms and currents. The fruits of modern critical theology leave the minister without any sure word to say. We have no revelation of God to help us in our hour of greatest extremity and need.

Modern criticism does nothing but destroy the church and plow up our hope in Christ. It has no other result than to leave us desolate in heart, chaotic in mind, and utterly lost in soul. It offers us nothing but it takes away from us everything. If we do not have a sure revelation of God in the Bible, we are of all men most miserable.

A Closer Look at Modern, Liberal Theologians

For a moment let us look further at these modern liberals. An intelligent gentleman who sat for a time under the ministry of a liberal preacher made the following observations: "I find that so called liberals can be the most illiberal of men. They often degenerate into religious critics and sensors. They indulge in flings at the orthodox and have little to say that is positive and constructive." This is so true. I have, myself, felt the bitter sting of these unchristian castigations. Instead of winning people to Christ and sending out missionaries and building up the household of faith, they indulge in nothing but seeking to destroy the faith of those who believe in God's word and who love God's Son. It is safe to challenge the whole Christian world for the name of a man who stands out as a winner of souls who also does not believe in the inspiration of the Bible as it has been loved through the generations.

What they preach is sometimes an amazing thing to behold. When I was in the seminary, some of us went to hear a liberal preacher in the City. To our amazement he was preaching from Shakespeare. At the conclusion of the service we went up to him and said: "We thought that a Christian minister ought to preach the Bible, but you are preaching Shakespeare." "Why?" He replied, "I preached the Bible last year and finished it. Now I am preaching Shakespeare!" The Bible was no more to him than any other book from which he might gain a starting point to lecture on the drivel that might come into his mind.

As we examine these liberals, we find that they are consumed with presuppositions and have closed minds to any other truth. They presuppose that there is nothing miraculous and nothing supernatural in the world and they assail the Bible with those definite a priori conclusions. Therefore, they are not able to judge the Bible objectively, and what they write as "assured results of critical analysis" is nothing other than an empty accounting of what they have previously concluded.

As we look more closely at these critics, do we find agreement among them? Do these liberals agree in what they say? No, they do not. They may unanimously deny the inspiration of the Bible, the divinity of Christ, the personality of the Holy Spirit, the fall of man, and the atonement of Christ for our sins; they may deny prophecies, miracles, the resurrection of the dead, and the final judgments, yet when it comes to the pretendedly assured results of their studies, not any two of them affirm the same thing, and their numerous publications create a flood of disputable, self-contradictory, and naturally destructive hypothesis.

When we take our stand apart from the Bible, we fall into a fool's paradise of rationalism. We have lost all sense of spiritual direction and grope in an inky, murky blackness as in a fog and in a mist. When reason substitutes for the supernatural, invisible, eternal things of God, it talks as a blind man does about colors and discourses about things of which it knows nothing about.

When the modern liberal theologians attempt to palm off their denials of the Holy Scriptures by labeling them "the findings of science" or "the consensus of scholarship," there are some people who take them seriously and are ready to throw away their Bibles. But one man, however, was not in that class. This man was Premier Winston Churchill. Let us read again what he said:

> We regret, with scorn, all those learned and labored myths that Moses was but a legendary figure upon whom the priesthood and the people hung their essential social, moral and religious ordinances.

> We believe the most scientific view, the most up-to-date and rationalistic conception will find its fullest satisfaction in taking the Bible story *literally*, and in identifying one of the greatest human beings with the most decisive leap forward ever discernable in the human story.[1]

Amen and Amen! . . .

An Appeal to Our Ministers to Be True to the Book

Let me speak to Southern Baptists. If our preachers, evangelists, pastors, churches, and institutions are true to that expression of faith, we shall live. If we repudiate it, we shall die. God will remove our lampstand out of its place, and we shall no longer continue to be a lighthouse in a stormy sea. As theological liberalism that denies the Word of God has destroyed other churches, the same theological liberalism will destroy us. There is no exception to this judgment whether in individual congregations or in denominational associations. Like many others we can continue to exist, having a form of godliness and denying the power thereof, but we shall be dead, spiritually dead, evangelistically dead. Our witness in power and saving grace shall have ceased.

Which way shall we go? There is no common ground between infidelity and Christianity. God himself says so and God himself calls us to be an obedient separation. "Be ye not unequally yoked together with unbelievers: for what fellowship hath righteousness with unrighteousness? and what communion hath light with darkness? And what concord hath Christ with Belial? or what part hath he that believeth with an infidel? And what agreement hath the temple of God with idols? for ye are the temple of the living God; as God hath said, I will dwell in them, and walk in them; and I will be their God, and they shall be my people. Wherefore come out from among them, and be ye separate, saith the Lord, and touch not the unclean thing; and I will receive you, and will be a Father unto you, and ye shall be my sons and daughters, saith the Lord Almighty" (2 Cor. 6:14–18).

Even our Lord asked us to be on one side or the other. "I know thy works, that thou art neither cold nor hot: I would thou wert cold or hot. So then because thou art lukewarm, and neither cold nor hot, I will spue thee out of my mouth" (Rev. 3:15–16). And again Jesus said, "He that is not with me is against me; and he that gathereth not with me scattereth abroad" (Matt. 12:30).

In the spirit of the captain of the conquering armies of Israel, Joshua of old, I am prepared to say that *as for me and my people we shall serve the Lord, stand by the Book, preach its treasures, love its words, serve its Savior, and humbly seek to obey his mandates.*

Will you?

Source: W. A. Criswell, *Why I Preach That the Bible Is Literally True* (Nashville: Broadman Press, 1969), 150–54, 159.
1. Winston S. Churchill, *Amid These Storms: Thoughts and Adventures* (New York: Charles Scribner's Sons, 1932), 293.

A Hill on Which to Die,
Paul Pressler, 1999

Marching to Zion

The issue over which the conservatives and liberals have parted ways in the SBC is, and always has been, the nature of Scripture—not an interpretation of Scripture, but what Scripture *is*. We were concerned about the fact that some professors in our institutions ridiculed and mocked students who held to the inerrancy of Scripture. We were concerned because conservative, traditional Baptist beliefs were not adequately presented in some of our institutions. If the individuals in authority had been willing to listen to our legitimate and genuine concerns, we never would have worked to change the direction of the convention.

Year after year, our efforts failed as we attempted to reason with the group in charge. Therefore, we saw that no other way existed to effect change except to get the establishment's attention by electing a conservative SBC president and setting the wheels of change in motion. Thus, we began to prepare for the watershed 1979 Southern Baptist Convention meeting in Houston. . . .

It also became necessary to travel to communicate the message. The message was simple and a homiletically correct three-pointer: first, we have a problem. That could be illustrated in the writings of seminary and college professors in our Baptist institutions. Demonstrating that a problem existed was easy. Many graduates of Southern Baptist schools were now pastors of churches and knew the problems very well, since they recently had been students in those institutions. The second point was to show that a methodology existed to correct the problem. Few Southern Baptists knew how the system worked and how trustees were elected. They were ready to be educated. Thirdly, we needed to motivate people to attend the annual meeting of the SBC.

At no time was I more impressed with how much we needed to communicate the means of correcting the problem than when I met with Dr. W.A. Criswell, the respected, longtime pastor of First Baptist Church of Dallas, Texas. Dr. Criswell was attending a meeting of the International Conference on Biblical Inerrancy in Chicago October 26 to 28, 1978, when he learned firsthand about plans to start the conservative movement.

Paige and I were among the forty to fifty Southern Baptists attending that conference. Paige called a meeting to discuss the problems in the SBC. Among those present was Maxey Jarman of Nashville, a great Baptist lay leader who expressed approval of our desire to correct the direction of the convention. Dr. Criswell got up after Paige and I made a presentation and said this movement was definitely something that needed to be done, and affirmed his support. He further encouraged the group by saying that Paige and I were "fine young men" who could lead.

Later Jerry Vines spoke in Dallas at Criswell College, and I went to the meetings. One night about 11 o'clock, Jerry, Paige, and I went to Dr. Criswell's home, where we talked for a long time about the problems and the methodology to correct them. We explained very carefully how the SBC president appoints the Committee on committees, which nominates all the trustees of the SBC-boards, agencies, and commissions. We talked about how a real impact could be made on our institutions through a continuation of conservative appointments.

After discussing this thoroughly, Dr. Criswell put his hands on the desk, pushed back, and looked at the three of us. His exact words still ring in my ears: "If I had only known what you have explained to me tonight when I was president of the convention, things could have been different."

He continued by illustrating: "Do you know what happened? How I made the appointments to the Committee on Committees? I received a call from Portor Routh (who was then executive secretary of the convention), and he said to me that I had to make the appointments in the near future. I said 'Porter, I don't know who to appoint. How about your drawing up the list for me and letting me sign it?' And that's exactly what happened. Porter Runch drew up the list, and I signed what he gave me. I didn't know most of the men whom I appointed."

Then Dr. Criswell advised: "If you want to be successful, you must do two things. You must have presidents elected who not only are theologically conservative, but who will use their power as president to appoint other like-minded persons who desire to see changes made. Secondly, you must get to know people throughout the United States so that a president will have a reservoir of people from whom to make appointments in each state." These were wise words from Dr. Criswell, and his counsel proved a very valuable stimulus to Jerry, Paige, and me. The practical steps for proceeding were falling into place.

I needed to start visiting people, primarily pastors, and explain to them what could be done. When we had a week off in court or when I did not have oral arguments, I traveled. I would go from town to town for prearranged meetings with one to ten people in a community and explain to them what we were doing. I would illustrate the problem and then explain the methodology of dealing with it. Then I sought to motivate people to attend the SBC annual meeting and to be a voice there. Many people with whom I met had been looking for ways to express their concerns and to accomplish the needed changes.

When a reporter once asked me the greatest number of talks I made in a week regarding the convention situation, I told him that one week I made about forty or fifty. As that was reported, that figure immediately became inflated, and I was accused of making forty to fifty talks *every* week and neglecting my court duties. Such was not the case. Although

I had numerous meetings, I had worked them carefully around the court schedule so that I neglected nothing.

About March or April of 1979, I called to make an appointment with Dr. W. M. Shamburger, pastor of First Baptist Church of Tyler, Texas. I briefly explained the purpose of my visit, but he said he was too busy to meet. Shortly after that an unwarranted attack against us appeared in the *Texas Baptist Standard* and then in other media. I have always wondered who gave them their information.

Although I am not a person who remembers dreams, I did have one which recurred during a three- to four-month period in the winter of 1978 and spring of 1979. Each time I dreamed it, I related it to Nancy. In the dream I saw a long line of people marching down Main Street in Houston and headed to the Summit, where the Southern Baptist Convention annual meeting would be held in June 1979. I remembered seeing two bright lines in the middle of the street (as if it were a no-passing zone) and no cars, only people. We were marching in a long line which was strung out, and as we marched, we sang a hymn, "We're Marching to Zion." I had no idea what the dream meant, nor did I try to understand it. To me at that time, it was just a strange experience and showed my preoccupation with convention events. But before long, I would understand clearly why the dream would be critical to what occurred in the days ahead.

Source: Paul Pressler, *A Hill on Which to Die: One Southern Baptist's Journey* (Nashville: Broadman & Holman, 1999), 93–96.

37

The Resurgence of Calvinism

By His Grace and for His Glory,
Thomas Nettles, 1986 (2001)

S INCE IT FIRST APPEARED IN 1986, *By His Grace and For His Glory* went through three printings with Baker Book House. I thank them for their willingness to undertake the project and keep it before the public for several years. It has now been out of print for over three years. Requests for copies come to me regularly. Others in the business of locating, buying, and selling books tell me that they periodically receive requests for it. Others tell me that the used book market seldom has it available. In light of these realities, I am pleased that Founders Press sought my consent for a republication of *By His Grace and For His Glory*. Thanks also to Mr. Josh Priola for commandeering the initial stages of this process.

Since 1986, the issues this book treats have become more visible, more widely embraced by church members, pastors, denominational servants, more controversial and ardently opposed by some, and the frequent subject of discussion groups in churches and a variety of denominational gatherings. The attention focused on the Doctrines of Grace is good; it is healthy to give intense thought to issues of God's holiness, His sovereignty, and His efficacious and infinitely wise design in the justification of sinners under the curse of His law. Though I think I understand a small portion of the dynamic involved, it is still mysterious to me how one related set of truths has the power to engender such a frame of love, humility, joy, gratitude, and transformation in one group and at the same time, among people professing faith in the same gospel, such a fervent opposition, resentment, fear, and strategic attempts to exclude, or at least know how to deal with, those who cordially confess these doctrines. It is sad as well as mysterious, but perhaps normal. The most deeply persevering advocates of the Doctrines of Grace once stood strongly in opposition to them.

The last fifteen years of the twentieth century produced a healthy phenomenon of Southern Baptists expanding their discussion beyond inerrancy into the whole corpus of theology. These ongoing theological discussions culminated in the adoption of a modestly but strategically revised *The Baptist Faith and Message* in 2000. So sensitive had some people become to Calvinism that even the statement, "God is all powerful and all knowing; and His perfect knowledge extends to all things, past, present, and future, including the future decisions of His free creatures," underwent scrutiny as a thinly veiled attempt to impose Calvinism on the confession. Two observations may be made. One, the articles on election and regeneration, which remained unchanged, and the article on God the Son, which had slight but clarifying verbal changes, already contained the lion's share of historic Baptist Calvinism. The confessional mother of the BF&M, the New Hampshire Confession of Faith (1833), was an intentionally Calvinistic document aimed at disarming a Free Will Baptist assault on the Baptist churches of New England. Absence of Calvinism in the 1925 BF&M would have presented an odd historical anomaly. Two, the fear of imposing Calvinism in the article on omniscience demonstrates that the heresy of open theism has always loomed as the Achilles heel of Arminianized theologies, and the only doctrinally and biblically consistent guard against it is the historic Calvinism discussed by the subjects of this book. The same case could be made for other defining doctrines such as inerrancy, original sin, substitutionary propitiatory atonement, the deity of Christ, and regenerate church membership.

The number of publications devoted to historic Baptist doctrine has been very encouraging during the last fifteen years. Broadman/Holman has published the large *Baptist Theologians* volume edited by Timothy George and David Dockery as well as a second smaller and amended edition entitled *Theologians of the Baptist Tradition*. Other books dealing with Baptist theology and identity come regularly from BH. A new press, Particular Baptist Press, has published several meaty and finely-bound volumes on Baptist history and theology as has Joshua Press located in Canada. The Center for Church Reform, operating from Washington, DC, has published helpful volumes on Baptist theology and polity. Smyth & Helwys has sought to engage the issue also from the easily recognizable perspective of the Cooperative Baptist Fellowship. In spite of many shortcomings, they have managed to provoke study and discussion of several important issues of Baptist theological identity.

. . . Even in light of any nuancing of judgment such interaction and examination might entail, I am more convinced of the fundamental thesis of the book than I was fifteen years ago. I would like to spend time on John Spilsbery, William Kiffin, and Hanserd Knollys and their heroic stance for Baptist ecclesiology and clear presentation of the Doctrines of Grace. I would expand treatment of Richard Furman and Basil Manly, Sr. I would discuss the Separate Baptists and their Whitefieldian Calvinism, the Philadelphia Association and the pastors in that association such as P. P. VanHorn, Thomas Ustick, John Gano, William Staughton, and Oliver Hart. These Baptist witnesses were faithful unto death and found their greatest consolation and confidence in the Lord Jesus Christ as the Bible presents him to us through the blood of the eternal covenant. The leaders saw the pastoral wisdom and church as a purifying dynamic of these truths. They put no confidence in the flesh for they understood that they had no goodness nor moral aptitude to commend themselves or turn themselves to God; they knew that nothing could separate them from the love of God for God placed it upon them unconditionally before the foundation of the world; they worshipped by the Spirit of God for they knew that He had opened their hearts to believe; they feared no condemnation because they trusted to the efficacy of Christ's sacrificial death; they struggled valiantly against the formidable foes of the world, the flesh and the devil because they were strengthened with all might according to His glorious power in whose hands they were secure. "Now to Him who is able to keep you from stumbling, and to make you stand in the presence of His glory blameless with great joy, to the only God our Savior, through Jesus Christ our Lord, be glory, majesty, dominion and authority, before all time and now and forever. Amen." (Jude 24, 25 NASB). . . .

In the course of this book we have sought to answer this question: What place does Calvinism have in Baptist life? Historical, dogmatic, and practical areas have received the energies of our investigation. Before these answers are summarized, perhaps we should explore why the question has even been asked.

No doubt some will feel peeved at not only my answers but my question and methods. They may believe the entire enterprise is irrelevant. They may argue, "Certainly no benefit comes from resurrecting antiquated ideological systems when the complexities of the present have far outstripped the usefulness of those systems. It is far better to adopt contemporary modes and categories of thought in which to perpetuate whatever is experientially beneficial from the past. In that way, the faith is not embarrassed by its being identified with what finally proves untenable." The lack of systematic coherence and doctrinal absolutes provides a handy way out of any conflict with modern thought. The absolutizing of human experience, of which there is always plenty, offers a supposed nonfalsifiable explanation of meta-physical reality. See how easy it is to rescue the faith from any attack upon it!

In the form of Process Theology, modern theological thinking has finally reached its logical antithesis to the God of Calvinism and the Bible. The god of Process Theology is hardly identifiable as a person, has no power to control history, has only a relative understanding of justice, and knows little more than man does about what is right and wrong in the terribly complex problems that confront us today. Process Theology views history as moving and fluctuating and undulating with no ultimate goal or purpose and, in the process, "god" is being formed. It is, therefore, essentially atheistic.

That is the only resting place for theology, once the sovereign God of the Bible has been compromised in any way. The Christian faith is devastated beyond recognition in this system, and any hope of justice and purpose in human affairs is crushed sadistically. The biblical hope of the beatific vision becomes completely excluded from consideration, for nothing beatific can be seen in such a god. Again, once the God of the Bible, as clearly set forth in the Reformed faith, is sidestepped, there remains only nihilistic despair.

It is for that reason the question has been asked—What place *does* Calvinism have in Baptist life? It is the belief of the author and the demonstration of history that true theism must present a God of absolute sovereignty. Only within this sphere can any human responsibility and justice be maintained. Once God's sovereignty is diminished for the supposed sake of human freedom, we take a path that will ultimately shatter all meaning and justice and leave us not only with no god but with no humanity. When this happens, there is also no gospel, no true Christian mission, no holiness to pursue, no standard to which we are to be conformed.

Now back to the answer—which has three parts: historical, theological, and practical. First, I have affirmed historically, and I hope demonstrated, that Calvinism was the dominant theology in the most enduring areas of Baptist life for the first 275 years of modern Baptist history. Its energy generated the establishment of churches, the missionary enterprise, and the agencies and institutions of Baptist life. This fact raises several interesting possibilities. First, we could decide that our forefathers were right. Therefore, their answer to the question, "How is a man made right with God?" is right, and their contemporary heirs must do everything within the realm of godliness to continue on that foundation. Or, second, if we decide that our forefathers were wrong, we must repent of our past, expose their errors, overtly reject on an institutional as well as individual basis the theological moorings established at first, and re-constitute on some other basis. (It might be noted that the current scene of theological anarchy would severely test any effort of that nature.) Or, third, we could conclude that no such thing as truth and error exists in theological categories.

The third option cannot be right, for then all further discussion, writ-ing, and investigation would be useless. On its own foundations, it be-comes impossible to affirm that even the statement itself is true. It can only be affirmed as "true" on the basis of the first option; but the first option categorically rejects the viability of the third. So the third option is self-defeating.

Option two must be rejected as well, for it leads inexorably, histori-cally, and logically to option three.

Option one must be right. The lesson of history then is the one that screams to us, "REPENT!" We must turn from our wicked ways and recapture our vision of the glory of God before the cherubim whisk it off to another place.

The second part of our answer has been theological and expositional. These doctrines are the soteriological portion of a system that in its whole and in its parts is comprehensive, coherent, cogent, and clear. Their scope is comprehensive since these doctrines give credible answers about God, man, sin, righteousness, heaven, hell, time, eternity, the natural, the su-pernatural, good, evil, justice, and mercy. These doctrines are coherent in that they stick together; they do not alienate themselves from one an-other, but rather mutually serve to explain and clarify each other. They are also cogent in that their harmony with other data is observable and remarkable. The most important aspect of this observation is that these doctrines harmonize with Scripture because they arise from Scripture. No other reason exists for the construction of such a view of the world than that the Bible itself clearly displays it. It may be called Calvinism for convenience, Augustinianism for patristic pedigree, or Jansenism to highlight its persistence in appearing under the most unlikely circum-stances, but at bottom it is pure dominical and apostolic teaching.

Finally, this system of theology has such clarity that it has univer-sal appeal. The basic premises of the Doctrines of Grace are so simple, strong, and clear that many unschooled saints who have embraced the reality of which they speak have become undeniably effective exponents of the doctrines. But they are also a sun without a sphere and an ocean without a shore. He who gazes into these doctrines can gaze for eternity and never reach the end of their grandeur and brightness; and he who plunges in can swim forever and never exhaust the routes and currents that might be taken.

Because of these theological and expositional qualities, Calvinism has been unparalleled in producing hope, character, and self-sacrifice at every level of society. The theological answer, therefore, should be: Calvinism should still occupy the place of universal adherence in Baptist life. To reject it is not theological progress, but decline; not theological wisdom, but folly; not theological erudition, but fragmentation.

We have sought the third part of the answer from three practical categories. How do these doctrines affect one's understanding of God's intentions toward the individual? How do they affect the coexistence of the body of the regenerate with the body of the unregenerate? How do they affect the activity of the regenerate toward the unregenerate? Thus, chapters on assurance of salvation, liberty of conscience, and evangelism close the discussion. The answer that is given affirms that the Doctrines of Grace produce a more defensible, coherent, and biblical construction of each of these practical areas. Therefore, if we are to maintain a proper foundation for personal counseling in spiritual matters, the Doctrines of Grace must inform all of our dealings. If we are to maintain a pure church in a free society, we must understand and propagate the nature of God's purposes with his fallen race. And if our evangelism is to be uncompromising in its adherence to the gospel, we cannot forfeit that view of salvation as presented to us in those doctrines fondly embraced by the Baptist forefathers.

> To him who is able to keep you from falling and to present you before his glorious presence without fault and with great joy—to the only God our Savior be glory, majesty, power and authority, through Jesus Christ our Lord, before all ages, now and forevermore! Amen [Jude 24–25, NIV].

Source: Thomas Nettles, *By His Grace and For His Glory: A Historical, Theological, and Practical Study of the Doctrines of Grace in Baptist Life* (repr., Cape Coral, FL: Founders Press, 2001), 11, 12, 425–28. Permission granted by the Founder's Press.

Founder's Ministries—An Attempt at Self-Identification, Tom Ascol, 1992

"WHO ARE THEY?" THIS QUESTION, or a variation of it, is often asked when interested parties are first introduced to the Southern Baptist Founders Conference or *Founders Journal*. It is a question which, on one level, defies a quick and simple answer—largely because of the difficulty of identifying the "they" being asked about. Since there is no official Southern Baptist Founders organization which can be joined, there is no membership roll to determine who "they" are.

Are "they" the people who attend or have attended the annual conference? If so, then the answer would need to be broad enough to include the peculiarities (and idiosyncrasies) of several hundred men (mostly pastors) and women. Most share a deep interest in doctrinal and devotional Christianity. Within this number, however, would be found a variety of theological convictions and church affiliations. One need not pass a confessional litmus test in order to attend.

Any attempt, therefore, to draw a profile of the typical attendee (a sort of "Founder Fred") would inevitably tend toward caricature.

Moreover, there are those who appreciate the ministry of the Founders conference and journal who would object to being closely identified with either. This must be understood when trying to ascertain exactly who it is that has become involved with or supportive of the conference and/or journal.

On another level, however, the question, "Who are they?" suggests a desire to understand the rationale and purpose behind the efforts of those who plan the conference and publish the journal. This concern can be decisively, though not simplistically, addressed by considering the beginnings and abiding concerns of both efforts.

Historical Background

The conference, which this year celebrates its 10th anniversary, was born in a prayer meeting on November 13, 1982. On that day seven men gathered in a motel room in Euless, Texas, to consider the feasibility of planning a conference which would be based upon the doctrines of grace as historically articulated by our Southern Baptist forebears.

After spending half of the day in prayer, it was agreed to attempt such an effort. A Statement of Principles was drafted, assignments were made, and the result was the first Founders Conference.

That original statement still obtains. It describes the "Motive" of the conference as follows:

> To glorify God, honor His gospel, and strengthen His churches by providing encouragement to Southern Baptists in historical, biblical, theological, practical, and ecumenical studies.

The conference's "Purpose" is also clearly stated:

> To be a balanced conference in respect to doctrine and devotion expressed in the Doctrines of Grace and their experimental application to the local church, particularly in the areas of worship and witness. This is to be accomplished through engaging a variety of speakers to present formal papers, sermons, expositions, and devotions, and through the recommendation and distribution of literature consistent with the nature of the conference.

In keeping with this stated purpose the decision was made in 1990 to begin publishing a quarterly journal. The *Founders Journal* is currently being mailed to 36 states and 8 foreign countries.

Abiding Concerns

This historical background gives some information about how we began, but it does not adequately address who and what we are. The following attempt at self-identification is perhaps better understood as a set of goals toward which we continually strive rather than ones which we have attained with finality.

We desire to be orthodox without being obnoxious. Surely such is possible. We believe that truth matters. There is such a thing as objective, absolute, unchanging, and unchangeable truth. God has revealed it. Through his Word and his Spirit, men can come to know it. Such knowledge is both desirable and necessary for genuine, vibrant Christianity. Therefore the Bible should be studied, proclaimed, and applied with a deep sense of submission to its authority.

This does not mean that we believe that wisdom ends with us. Neither do we make any claim to have a corner on the truth. Therefore we renounce theological pride and spiritual haughtiness. We are willing to learn from those with whom we disagree. Our goal is to contend for the truth of the gospel in that spirit of the gospel which recognizes that if one understands all mysteries and possesses all knowledge yet has not love, he is nothing (1 Cor. 13:2).

Secondly, we want to be confessional, yet contemporary. Our faith is unashamedly consistent with the great, time-honored confessions of our forefathers. It consciously arises from the historic stream of that "exalted system of Pauline truth which is technically called Calvinism" (to borrow John Broadus's description).

Our identification with historic Calvinism does not mean that we use the designation pridefully or require it as a test of fellowship. It is a mere tag; a nickname which says nothing other than "God is sovereign in creation, providence, and salvation." C. H. Spurgeon's sentiments are our own:

> We only use the term "Calvinism" for shortness. That doctrine which is called "Calvinism" did not spring from Calvin; we believe that it sprang from the great founder of all truth. Perhaps Calvin himself derived it mainly from the writings of Augustine. Augustine obtained his views, without doubt, through the Holy Spirit of God, from diligent study of the writings of Paul, and Paul received them from the Holy Ghost and from Jesus Christ, the great founder of the Christian Church. We use the term then, not because we impute an extraordinary importance to Calvin's having taught these doctrines. We should be just as willing to call them by any other name, if we could find one which would be better understood, and which on the whole would be as consistent with fact.

Neither does our identification with historic, orthodox, evangelical Calvinism mean that we embrace the caricatures and misrepresentations that have often been associated with the designation. Specifically, John Calvin is not our final authority. We affirm the supreme and final authority of the Bible.

We do not deny or de-emphasize human responsibility in salvation. We affirm the absolute responsibility of man and insist that it be held as fervently as the absolute sovereignty of God. We do not deny or de-emphasize evangelism. Though we do challenge the legitimacy of much that parades under the banner of evangelism today, we strongly affirm the necessity to be zealous, bold, and compassionate in evangelistic efforts. Let it be clearly said that we are not Hyper-Calvinists. We strongly believe in the duty of all men to repent and believe the gospel, and we renounce Hyper-Calvinism as deadly, pernicious error.

If we must be labelled, call us evangelical Calvinists. Personally, I prefer the moniker, "Historic Southern Baptists." It is an appropriate designation because the truths that we hold dear were held historically not only by Augustine, Luther, Calvin, the Puritans, Edwards, and Whitefield, as well as by the English Baptists Fuller, Pearce, Ryland, Carey, and Spurgeon, but also (and, for the purpose of denominational identity, more importantly) by great early Southern Baptist statesmen such as R. B. C. Howell, R. Fuller, W. B. Johnson, B. Manly (Sr. & Jr.), J. A. Broadus, J. P. Boyce, J. L. Dagg, P. H. Mell, B. H. Carroll, M. McGregor, J. B. Gambrell, and J. M. Frost—to name but a few! Hence the names "Southern Baptist **Founders** Conference" and "*Founders Journal.*"

These names do not suggest that we are trying to live in the past or that we have been overtaken with wistful nostalgia. Rather, they demonstrate that, in our belief and practice, we are standing in the historic stream of orthodox Christianity. What we are trying to do is proclaim and apply the old gospel in a new day. After all, if what our forefathers believed was true in their day, it is still true today.

We are Southern Baptist, though not sectarian. Much that is of spiritual value is being done in and through the Southern Baptist Convention. We want to affirm and encourage such efforts. We are consciously Southern Baptist and recognize the propriety of serving within the SBC borders. At the same time, we adhere firmly to the autonomy of each local church. Therefore, we have no political agenda which we are seeking to have implemented in the convention.

As Southern Baptists, we have great appreciation of and fellowship with those of other churches and denominations with whom we share fundamental, biblical convictions. We desire to maintain a genuine catholic spirit toward all who believe the gospel.

Finally, *our goal is to be doctrinally and devotionally balanced.* The doctrines of grace are intellectually satisfying. Spurgeon noted that one evidence of Calvinism's being truth from God is the fact that even simple believers without formal theological training can grasp its teachings.

With this advantage, however, comes an ever present danger. There is a temptation to embrace the doctrines of grace intellectually without being embraced by the grace of the doctrines experientially. May the Lord deliver us from "intellectual Calvinism" and grant us in its place what older writers have called, "experimental Calvinism."

God's truth was never intended to illuminate the understanding while leaving the affections and the will untouched. To be properly received it must reach all three. Doctrinal precision and devotional warmth are equally important for balanced, vibrant Christian living.

This sheds some light on who we are, where we have been, and where we hope to go. We long to see a widespread recovery of the old gospel which was known and loved by our convention's founders. We long to see a real revival of true religion which that gospel is calculated to promote. We long to see churches strengthened, members and pastors encouraged, and men, women and children soundly converted to Christ. To this end we work and pray.

Source: *Founder's Journal* (Spring 1992). Permission granted by the *Founders' Journal.*

38

PEACE COMMITTEE REPORT, 1987

Southern Baptist Convention

Introduction

D URING THE 1985 ANNUAL MEETING of the Southern Baptist Convention in Dallas, June 11–13, 1985, a special committee was created to attempt to determine the sources of the current controversy in the Southern Baptist Convention and to make findings and recommendations to resolve it. The motion, overwhelmingly adopted, says:

"With gratitude for God's bountiful blessings on us as Southern Baptists and with recognition of our unparalleled opportunity to confront every person on earth with the gospel of Christ by the year 2000 and with acknowledgment of divisions among us, which, if allowed to continue, inevitably will impede our progress, impair our fellowship, and imperil our future; and after much prayer, we offer the following motion:

That a special committee be authorized by this Convention, in session in Dallas, June, 1985; and

That this committee seek to determine the sources of the controversies in our Convention, and make findings and recommendations regarding these controversies, so that Southern Baptists might effect reconciliation and effectively discharge their responsibilities to God by cooperating together to accomplish evangelism, missions, Christian education, and other causes authorized by our Constitution, all to the glory of God. "By this shall all men know that ye are my disciples, if ye have love one to another" (John 13:35) (John 17:21); and

That this committee follow the 1963 Baptist Faith and Message Statement in regard to theological issues, and operate within the Constitution and Bylaws of the Southern Baptist Convention; and . . . .

That all Southern Baptists be urged to exercise restraint, to refrain from divisive action and comments, and to reflect Christian love, while this committee is doing its work; and

That the following persons be designated to serve on the special committee: Charles G. Fuller, Chairman; Harmon M. Born, Doyle E. Carlton, Jr., Mrs. Morris H. Chapman, *William O. Crews, Robert E. Cuttino, Mrs. A. Harrison Gregory, Jim Henry, William E. Hull, Herschel H. Hobbs, Albert McClellan, Charles W. Pickering, William E. Poe, Ray E. Roberts, Adrian P. Rogers, *Cecil E. Sherman, John Sullivan, Daniel G. Vestal, Jerry Vines, Edwin H. Young, *Charles F. Stanley, *W. Winfred Moore,

> *NOTE: William O. Crews was elected president of Golden Gate Baptist Theological Seminary October 13, 1986, but was asked to remain as a member; Cecil E. Sherman resigned from the special committee October 22, 1986, and was replaced by Peter James Flamming; Charles F. Stanley and W. Winfred Moore served by virtue of office as president and first vice-president of the Convention, and were asked to remain after their terms of office expired.

Since its creation, the Peace Committee has met 14 times. Following each meeting, a report was given to Southern Baptists by Chairman Charles G. Fuller through the denominational news service, Baptist Press.

In keeping with its assignment, the Peace Committee has determined what it believes to be the primary sources of the controversy, has made findings in reference to those sources and, in this report, is making recommendations as to possible ways to effect reconciliation.

I. Sources of the Controversy

During its first meeting, the Peace Committee determined the primary source of the controversy is theological differences, but found there are political causes as well.

> **Theological Sources**: In meeting after meeting of the Peace Committee, talk turned to the nature of inspiration of the Scriptures, often to the point of preempting the committee's established agenda. Gradually, it became clear that while there might be other theological differences, the authority of the Word of God is the focus of differences. The primary source of the controversy in the Southern Baptist Convention is the Bible, more specifically, the ways in which the Bible is viewed.

All Baptists see the Bible as authoritative; the question is the extent and nature of its authority. The differences in recent years have developed around the phrase in Article I of the Baptist Faith and Message Statement of 1963, that the Bible "has . . . truth without any mixture of error, for its matter. . . ."

The action which created the Peace Committee instructed it to follow the Baptist Faith and Message Statement of 1963 in regard to theological issues. Although the statement includes a Preamble and seventeen articles, the committee has focused primarily on Article One, "The Scriptures."

> "The Holy Bible was written by men divinely inspired and is the record of God's revelation of Himself to man. It is a perfect treasure of divine instruction. It has God for its author, salvation for its end, and truth, without any mixture of error, for its matter. It reveals the principles by which God judges us; and therefore is, and will remain to the end of the world, the true center of Christian union, and the supreme standard by which all human conduct, creeds, and religious opinions should be tried. The criterion by which the Bible is to be interpreted is Jesus Christ."

Herschel H. Hobbs, a member of the Peace Committee and chairman of the committee which wrote the 1963 Baptist Faith and Message Statement, explained the phrase "truth without any mixture of error for its matters. . . ." by reference to II Timothy 3:16 which says, "all Scripture is given by inspiration of God." He explained: "The Greek New Testament reads 'all'—without the definite article—and that means every single part of the whole is God-breathed. And a God of truth does not breathe error." Dr. Hobbs made the comments during the 1981 annual meeting of the Southern Baptist Convention in Los Angeles, California.

Using Article I of the Baptist Faith and Message Statement of 1963 as a yardstick, Committee subcommittees visited each of the Southern Baptist seminaries and five other agencies, the Foreign Mission Board, the Home Mission Board, Baptist Sunday School Board, Historical Commission, and Christian Life Commission. Following those visits, the committee adopted a "Statement on Theological Diversity."

> "The Peace Committee has completed a preliminary investigation of the theological situation in our SBC seminaries. We have found significant theological diversity within our seminaries, reflective of the diversity within our wider constituency. These divergences are found among those

who claim to hold a high view of Scripture and to teach in accordance with, and not contrary to, the Baptist Faith and Message Statement of 1963.

Examples of this diversity include the following, which are intended to be illustrative but not exhaustive.

(1) Some accept and affirm the direct creation and historicity of Adam and Eve while others view them instead as representative of the human race in its creation and fall.

(2) Some understand the historicity of every event in Scripture as reported by the original source while others hold that the historicity can be clarified and revised by the findings of modern historical scholarship.

(3) Some hold to the stated authorship of every book in the Bible while others hold that in some cases such attribution may not refer to the final author or may be pseudonymous.

(4) Some hold that every miracle in the Bible is intended to be taken as an historical event while others hold that some miracles are intended to be taken as parabolic.

"The Peace Committee is working earnestly to find ways to build bridges between those holding divergent views so that we may all legitimately coexist and work together in harmony to accomplish our common mission. Please pray that we may find ways to use our diversity to win the greatest number to faith in Christ as Savior and Lord."

Early in its second year, the Peace Committee continued to discuss theological concerns, including the fact that there are at least two separate and distinct interpretations of Article I of the Baptist Faith and Message Statement of 1963, reflective of the diversity present in the Convention.

One view holds that when the article says the Bible has truth without any mixture of error for its matter it means all areas—historical, scientific, theological and philosophical. The other holds the "truth" relates only to matters of faith and practice.

The Committee discussed whether the faculties of the SBC seminaries adequately reflect the views of many Southern Baptists who believe in the first interpretation. A Peace Committee subcommittee met with the six seminary presidents to communicate the need for the faculties to reflect the beliefs of these Southern Baptists.

In October 1986, the Peace Committee held a prayer retreat at Glorieta Baptist Conference Center near Santa Fe, New Mexico, attended by the Peace Committee and leaders of all national agencies. During that meeting, the seminary presidents presented a statement of their intentions which has become known as the "Glorieta Statement:"

> We, the presidents of the six SBC seminaries, through prayerful and careful reflection and dialogue, have unanimously agreed to declare these commitments regarding our lives and our work with Southern Baptists.

> We believe that Christianity is supernatural in its origin and history. We repudiate every theory of religion which denies the supernatural elements in our faith. The miracles of the Old and New Testaments are historical evidences of God's judgment, love, and redemption.

> We believe that the Bible is fully inspired; it is "God-breathed" (II Tim. 3:16), utterly unique. No other book or collections of books can justify that claim. The sixty-six books of the Bible are not errant in any area of reality. We hold to their infallible power and binding authority.

> We believe that our six seminaries are fulfilling the purposes assigned to them by the Southern Baptist Convention. Nevertheless, we acknowledge that they are not perfect institutions. We recognize that there are legitimate concerns regarding them which we are addressing.

We commit ourselves therefore to the resolution of the problems which beset our beloved denomination. We are ready and eager to be partners in the peace process.

Specifically:

(1) We reaffirm our seminary confessional statements, and we will enforce compliance by the persons signing them.

(2) We will foster in our classrooms a balanced, scholarly frame of reference for presenting fairly the entire spectrum of scriptural interpretations represented by our constituencies. We perceive this to be both good education and good cooperation.

(3) We respect the convictions of all Southern Baptists and we repudiate the caricature and intimidation of persons for their theological beliefs.

(4) We commit ourselves to fairness in selecting faculty, lecturers, and chapel speakers across the theological spectrum of our Baptist constituency.

(5) We will lead our seminary communities in spiritual revival, personal discipleship, Christian lifestyle, and active churchmanship.

(6) We will deepen and strengthen the spirit of evangelism and missions on our campuses while emphasizing afresh the distinctive doctrines of our Baptist heritage.

(7) We have scheduled for Southern Baptists three national conferences.

A Conference on Biblical Inerrancy—*1987

A Conference on Biblical Interpretation—1988

A Conference on Biblical Imperatives—1989

*Note: The first conference, focusing on biblical inerrancy, was held at Ridgecrest Baptist Conference Center May 4–7, 1987, with more than 1,000 in attendance.

We share these commitments with the hope that all Southern Baptists will join us in seeking "the wisdom from above" in our efforts toward reconciliation:

"The wisdom from above is first pure, then peaceable, gentle, open to reason, full of mercy and good fruits, without uncertainty or insincerity" (James 3:17).

The Peace Committee affirmed the Glorieta Statement and ceased its official inquiry, referring unanswered questions and unresolved issues back to the administrators and the trustees of Southern Baptist Theological Seminary, Southeastern Baptist Theological Seminary, and

Midwestern Baptist Theological Seminary, hoping the results of their actions would be satisfactory to the Convention-at-large.

During the committee's December 1986 meeting, additional questions arose as to the meaning and the implementation of the Glorieta Statement.

The seminary presidents report that their efforts to implement the Statement have included an effort to recruit conservative scholars to fill faculty vacancies, expansion of reading lists, invitations to conservative scholars to address chapel and other events, a commitment to treat all persons fairly, and expanded evangelistic and missions activities on campus.

The question for the majority of the Peace Committee, however, remains not whether there is diversity in the Southern Baptist Convention, but how broad that diversity can be while still continuing to cooperate.

> **Political Sources**: In the opinion of the Peace Committee, the controversy of the last decade began as a theological concern. When people of good intention became frustrated because they felt their convictions on Scripture were not seriously dealt with, they organized politically to make themselves heard. Soon, another group formed to counter the first and the political process intensified.

The Peace Committee, primarily through its Political Activities Subcommittee, has studied charges and counter charges regarding political activity. It has looked at many issues, including:

Restructuring the Constitution and Bylaws of the Southern Baptist Convention to limit the appointive powers of the president; restructuring the way in which the annual meeting is held, specifically shifting the pre-Convention meetings to post-Convention meetings; cooperation between the Pastors' Conference and the SBC Forum; discussing the coverage of personalities and issues in the controversy by the official and unofficial news media outlets; the use of descriptive terms and labels for the various groups; "depoliticizing" the Convention by asking the various groups to "stand down" from political activities; instituting stricter means of messenger registration and voting to prevent misuse of the registration and voting processes at annual meetings.

A primary area of discussion was changing the Constitution and Bylaws of the Convention to restrict the appointive powers of the president. However, the majority of the committee's members feel the basic Convention structure has served Southern Baptists well and should not now be changed.

The Committee investigated numerous charges of political malfeasance and voter irregularity. It heard a detailed report, complete with statistical analysis, on messenger participation at annual meetings, presented by the SBC registration secretary and Convention manager, as well as the chairman of a special study committee appointed by the SBC Executive Committee. Although the reports included isolated instances of registration and ballot abuse, there was no evidence of widespread or organized misuse of the ballot by any political group and no evidence of massive voter irregularities related to annual meetings.

The Political Activities Subcommittee, as well as a special ad-hoc committee, dealt with the question of a parliamentarian for the annual meeting. The matter was deferred in 1986, because then SBC president Charles F. Stanley appointed a certified parliamentarian to assist him at the Atlanta annual meeting. The Committee is recommending a new by-law be prepared concerning the appointment of a certified parliamentarian and two assistant parliamentarians for the annual meeting.

A special subcommittee also looked into the possibility of "negative designation" or "selective support" of agencies through the Cooperative Program, but concluded that a change in the basic structure of the unified giving plan would not provide significant help in resolving the crisis.

Some of the issues have been brought forward as recommendations from the Peace Committee. Others were not deemed sufficiently significant to warrant recommendations at this time.

II. Findings

The Peace Committee has made findings on Scripture and on politics.

> **On Theology**: The Committee found there is significant diversity in the understanding of Article I "On Scripture" of the Baptist Faith and Message Statement of 1963. The Committee found there are at least two separate and distinct interpretations of the article. One holding "truth without any mixture of error for its matter," means all areas—historical, scientific, theological, and philosophical. The other holds "truth" relates only to matters of faith and practice.

The Committee, discussing whether the faculties of the SBC seminaries adequately reflect the views of many Southern Baptists who believe in the first interpretation, found there was not a theological balance represented in the faculties at Southern Baptist Theological Seminary or Southeastern Baptist Theological Seminary.

The committee adopted two statements concerning its findings on theology, one a "foundational" statement, and the other a more elaborate statement.

1. The *"Foundational Statement on Theology"*:—The Committee agreed the following Scripture references should be read as an introduction to the "Foundational Statement on Theology": Deuteronomy 4:2; Joshua 1:7; Psalm 119:160; Matthew 5:18; II Timothy 3:16; Revelation 22:10.

It is the conclusion of the majority of the Peace Committee that the cause of peace within the Southern Baptist Convention will be greatly enhanced by the affirmation of the whole Bible as being "not errant in any area of reality."

Therefore, we exhort the trustees and administrators of our seminaries and other agencies affiliated with or supported by the Southern Baptist Convention to faithfully discharge their responsibility to carefully preserve the doctrinal integrity of our institutions receiving our support, and only employ professional staff who believe in the divine inspiration of the whole Bible and that the Bible is "truth without any mixture of error."

The Committee also adopted the more elaborate statement on Scripture.

2. The *"Statement on Scripture"*: We, as a Peace Committee, affirm biblical authority for all of life and for all fields of knowledge. The Bible is a book of redemption, not a book of science, psychology, sociology, or economics. But, where the Bible speaks, the Bible speaks truth in all realms of reality and to all fields of knowledge. The Bible, when properly interpreted, is authoritative to all of life.

We, as a Peace Committee, reaffirm the Baptist commitment to the absolute authority of Scripture and to the historic Baptist position that the Bible has "truth without any mixture of error for its matter." We affirm that the narratives of Scripture are historically and factually accurate. We affirm that the historic accounts of the miraculous and the supernatural are truthful as given by God and recorded by the biblical writers.

We, as a Peace Committee, have found that most Southern Baptists see "truth without any mixture of error for its matter," as meaning, for example, that

(1) They believe in direct creation of mankind and therefore they believe Adam and Eve were real persons.

(2) They believe the named authors did indeed write the biblical books attributed to them by those books.

(3) They believe the miracles described in Scripture did indeed occur as supernatural events in history.

(4) They believe that the historical narratives given by biblical authors are indeed accurate and reliable as given by those authors.

We call upon Southern Baptist institutions to recognize the great number of Southern Baptists who believe this interpretation of our confessional statement and, in the future, to build their professional staffs and faculties from those who clearly reflect such dominant convictions and beliefs held by Southern Baptists at large.

However, some members of the Peace Committee differ from this viewpoint. They would hold that "truth without any mixture of error" relates only to faith and practice. They would also prefer a broader theological perspective. Yet, we have learned to live together on the Peace Committee in mutual charity and commitment to each other. We pledge our mutual efforts to fulfill the Great Commission, and we call on others within our Convention to make the same pledge.

> **On Politics**: The committee has found that the sources of the political aspect of the controversy are long standing. Historically, informal political groups or coalitions have emerged in Southern Baptist life. Prior to the last decade, most of these groups operated informally by word-of-mouth among mutual acquaintances interested in selecting the leadership of the Southern Baptist Convention. More recently, these groups have developed organized coalitions centered around theological perceptions and committed to electing leadership committed to a particular viewpoint. The effort has been largely successful, but led to the formation of a counter-effort which has increased hostility and turned up the heat on the controversy.

After its investigation, the Peace Committee found "that the extent of political activity . . . at the present time creates distrust, diminishes our ability to do missions and evangelism, is detrimental to our influence, and impedes our ability to serve our Lord."

The committee adopted two statements, one a "foundational" statement and the other a more elaborate statement.

1. The "Foundational Statement On Politics."—It is the unanimous conclusion of the Peace Committee that fairness in the appointive process will contribute to peace.

Therefore, we exhort the present and future presidents of the Southern Baptist Convention, the Committee on Committees, and the Committee on Boards to select nominees who endorse the Baptist Faith and Message Statement and are drawn in balanced fashion from the broad spectrum of loyal, cooperative Southern Baptists, representative of the diversity of our denomination.

The more elaborate statement on politics also was adopted.

2. The "Statement on Politics":—Politics are intrinsically a part of congregational polity, i.e., voting, public and private discussions, influencing others to share one's view.

Historically, informal political groups or coalitions have emerged in Southern Baptist life. Prior to the last decade, most of these groups operated informally by word-of-mouth among mutual acquaintances interested in selecting the leadership of the Southern Baptist Convention. More recently, these groups have developed organized coalitions centered on theological perceptions and individual leaders committed to a defined viewpoint. These coalitions have adopted political strategies for electing officers of the Convention, appointing committees, and changing or preserving the character of accepted institutions. These strategies have included extensive travel, numerous informational and ideological meetings, mailouts, a network of representatives who share in this common strategy, and sustained efforts to recruit messengers to attend the Convention.

We as a Peace Committee recognize that these political coalitions and strategies were born in part, at least, out of deep conviction and concern for theological issues.

But, we believe that the time has come for the Convention to move beyond this kind of politics. We find that the extent of political activity within the Southern Baptist Convention at the present time promotes a party spirit; creates discord, division, and distrust; diminishes our ability to do missions and evangelism; is detrimental to our influence; and impedes our ability to serve our Lord.

If allowed to continue unchecked, such political activity in the Convention can have disastrous consequences affecting our ability to serve our Lord and do His work.

Steps have been taken and additional steps are recommended in this report to resolve the theological issues involved in our present controversy. Because of our fear of the consequences of continued organized political activity within our Convention, and since steps have been and will continue to be taken to resolve theological issues, we feel that continued organized political activity within the Southern Baptist Convention is no longer necessary, desirable, or appropriate. We think the continuation of such political activity in the future would be unacceptable and could be disastrous.

We recommend that the Southern Baptist Convention request all organized political factions to discontinue the organized political activity in which they are now engaged. We think the following specific activities are out of place and request all groups to discontinue these specific political activities:

(1) Organized political activity;

(2) Political strategies developed by a group with central control;

(3) Holding information-ideological meetings;

(4) Extensive travel on behalf of political objectives within the Convention; and

(5) Extensive mail-outs to promote political objectives in the Convention.

In 1986, the Southern Baptist Convention adopted the report of the Peace Committee which found:

(1) Some spokesmen on both sides of the political spectrum have used intemperate, inflammatory, and unguarded language, i.e., "going for the jugular," "Holy War," "independent fundamentalists," "flaming liberal," and other pejorative terms.

(2) Some spokesmen on both sides of the political spectrum and the autonomous independent journals on both sides of the issue have labeled and attributed improper motives to people with whom they disagree.

(3) Distribution of news is necessary in a democratic society. There have been instances when news releases have been altered, distorting the intent of the article and oftentimes creating confusion. In some denominational papers and in some autonomous independent journals, there has been prejudice against the conservative political activists and in some autonomous independent journals there has been prejudice against the moderate side.

The Convention in Atlanta adopted the recommendation of the Peace Committee as follows:

—That the Convention deplore the use of the type of intemperate, inflammatory, and unguarded language used by some spokesmen on both sides of the political spectrum.

—That the Convention urge Baptist Press, the state Baptist papers, and the autonomous independent journals to be especially careful to be fair and accurate in reporting events in the Convention and refrain from labeling and attributing improper motives.

Despite these recommendations approved by the Southern Baptist Convention, the Peace Committee finds that some of the state Baptist papers and the autonomous journals—The Southern Baptist Advocate, SBC Today, Baptists United News, and The Baptist Laity Journal—have continued to use intemperate, inflammatory language and have labeled individuals and impugned motives.

We renew again our request to these papers and journals to contribute to the process of reconciliation and the promotion of our cooperative work together as we seek to do the work of Christ. We again call upon all state Baptist papers and the independent autonomous journals to comply with the action taken at the Atlanta Convention and outlined above. We call upon individual Southern Baptists to use their influence to help stop these divisive actions.

We, the Peace Committee, ask Baptist Press, all Baptist state papers, Baptist publications, and independent autonomous journals to refrain from using terms and labels, specifically terms such as fundamentalist, liberal, fundamental-conservative, and moderate-conservative.

III. Conclusions

The enabling resolution of the Southern Baptist Convention at the 1985 Dallas Convention commissioned this special committee to determine the sources of the controversies within the Convention and to make findings and recommendations that would make it possible for Southern Baptists to effect reconciliation and to continue to cooperate in carrying out evangelism, missions, Christian education, and other causes.

Making peace among all Southern Baptists was not to be the work of the committee. Reconciliation was, and still is, the key word. Surely, there must be peace; that is, there must be an end to hostility among us, which is peace. Committed Christians must live in peace. No recommendation of the committee is needed to effect peace—it is found in the heart of the believer.

Reconciliation may be a first cousin to peace, but it rests on a different foundation. To reconcile is to harmonize, to cause to be friendly again, to reunite, to accept our differences and to cooperate in all undertakings which enhance our mutual interests and goals. It was only through a subtle process of reconciliation, taking place over 142 years of history, that Southern Baptists have with God's blessing and His help, achieved a preeminent position in missions, education, and evangelism. We have kept our differences from creating hostility, until recently, and not only have we lived in peace, but with remarkable harmony and cooperation.

We must never try to impose upon individual Southern Baptists nor local congregations a specific view of how Scripture must be interpreted. If such an attempt is made, then reconciliation is not the goal nor is it possible to achieve.

There is but one way for us to survive *intact* as a denomination. It involves the recognition of some basic facts, among which are these:

(1) Changes are now taking place in the leadership of many Southern Baptist Convention boards.

(2) These changes will impact these boards and agencies for years to come.

(3) The role of many who have exercised leadership in the past will change as colleagues of different persuasions will fill leadership roles.

(4) This change will mean that some who have been in general agreement with Convention programs in the past will have less involvement, while those who previously have had difficulty in agreement with certain Convention programs will have more involvement.

(5) We have seen changes in Southern Baptist life in the past and we will see changes in the future. The important issue is that we must continue to be faithful stewards of the opportunities God has given Southern Baptists.

How then can we survive intact or substantially that way?

First, the hostility must cease within the heart of each of us. That brings peace.

Second, our leaders must have and must demonstrate a view of Baptist life that reaches beyond the limits of their own personal theology. No effort should be made or should be permitted to be made which would seek to eliminate from Baptist life theological beliefs or practices which are consistent with the Baptist Faith and Message Statement and which have found traditional acceptance by substantial numbers of our people. Proponents of extreme positions at each end of the current Baptist theological spectrum should be encouraged to major on those things which lead to cooperative efforts and to minimize divisive issues and controversies.

Third, and most important, nothing must be allowed to stand in the way of genuine cooperation in missions, Christian education, evangelism, and our other traditional causes. While different leaders may arise, the nature and work of our Christian cooperative enterprise must continue unabated.

Finally, we should recognize and freely admit that the greatest source of our strength as a denomination lies in the thousands of local church congregations that support our cooperative undertakings. Through long years of experience, they have learned to trust our leaders, our agencies and institutions and, because of that trust, they have provided magnificent support and responded to that leadership.

We have proclaimed this to be God's way of doing His work. Through continued cooperation in His enterprises, we can continue this mighty work. If we insist on having our way, drawing lines which exclude from places of leadership and responsibility those who do not hold our specific viewpoint, we can destroy what God has created in the Southern Baptist Convention. If, however, we can maintain a cooperative spirit and let our sense of Christian love bridge the gap of the diversity among us, we can continue to bear effective witness to His kingdom enterprise throughout all the world. . . .

Source: *Annual*, SBC, 1987, 232–42.

39

DOCTRINAL STATEMENT OF THE BAPTIST MISSIONARY ASSOCIATION OF AMERICA, 1989

I. GOD

There is one living and true God, the creator of the universe (Exod. 15:11; Isa. 45:11; Jer. 27:5). He is revealed in the unity of the Godhead as God the Father, God the Son, and God the Holy Spirit, who are equal in every divine perfection (Exod. 15:11; Matt. 28:19; II Cor. 13:14).

A. God the Father is the supreme ruler of the universe. He providentially directs the affairs of history according to the purposes of His grace (Gen. 1; Ps. 19:1; Ps. 104; Heb. 1:1–3).

B. God the Son is the Savior of the world. Born of the virgin Mary (Matt. 1:18; Luke 1:26–35), He declared His deity among men (John 1:14, 18; Matt. 9:6), died on the cross as the only sacrifice for sin (Phil. 2:6–11), arose bodily from the grave (Luke 24:6, 7, 24–26; I Cor. 15:3–6), and ascended back to the Father (Acts 1:9–11; Mark 16:19). He is at the right hand of the Father, interceding for believers (Rom. 8:34; Heb. 7:25) until He returns to rapture them from the world (Acts 1:11; I Thess. 4:16–18).

C. God the Holy Spirit is the manifest presence of deity. He convicts of sin (John 16:8–11), teaches spiritual truths according to the written Word (John 16:12–15), permanently indwells believers (Acts 5:32; John 14:16, 17, 20, 23), and confers on every believer at conversion the ability to render effective spiritual service (I Peter 4:10, 11).

II. THE SCRIPTURES

A. The Scriptures are God's inerrant revelation, complete in the Old and New Testaments, written by divinely inspired men as they were moved by the Holy Spirit (II Tim. 3:16; II Peter 1:21). Those men wrote not in words of human wisdom but in words taught by the Holy Spirit (I Cor. 2:13).

B. The Scriptures provide the standard for the believer's faith and practice (II Tim. 3:16, 17), reveal the principles by which God will judge all (Heb. 4:12; John 12:48), and express the true basis of Christian fellowship (Gal. 1:8, 9; II John 9–11).

III. CREATION

A. The World—God created all things for His own pleasure and glory, as revealed in the biblical account of creation (Gen. 1; Rev. 4:11; John 1:2, 3; Col. 1:16).

B. The Angels—God created an innumerable host of spirit beings called angels. Holy angels worship God and execute His will; while fallen angels serve Satan, seeking to hinder God's purposes (Col. 1:16; Luke 20:35, 36; Matt. 22:29, 30; Ps. 103:20; Jude 6).

C. Man—God created man in His own image. As the crowning work of creation, every person is of dignity and worth and merits the respect of all other persons (Ps. 8; Gen. 1:27; 2:7; Matt. 10:28–31).

IV. SATAN

Satan is a person rather than a personification of evil (John 8:44), and he with his demons opposes all that is true and godly by blinding the world to the gospel (II Cor. 4:3, 4), tempting saints to do evil (Eph. 6:11; I Peter 5:8), and warring against the Son of God (Gen. 3:15; Rev. 20:1–10).

V. DEPRAVITY

Although man was created in the image of God (Gen. 1:26; 2:17), he fell through sin and that image was marred (Rom. 5:12; James 3:9). In his unregenerate state, he is void of spiritual life, is under the influence of the devil, and lacks any power to save himself (Eph. 2:1–3; John 1:13). The sin nature has been transmitted to every member of the human race, the man Jesus Christ alone being excepted (Rom. 3:23; I Peter 2:22). Because of the sin nature, man possesses no divine life and is essentially and unchangeably depraved apart from divine grace (Rom. 3:10–19; Jer. 17:9).

VI. SALVATION

A. The Meaning of Salvation—Salvation is the gracious work of God whereby He delivers undeserving sinners from sin and its results (Matt. 1:21; Eph. 2:8, 9). In justification He declares righteous all who put faith in Christ as Savior (Rom. 3:20–22), giving them freedom from condemnation, peace with God, and full assurance of future glorification (Rom. 3:24–26).

B. The Way of Salvation—Salvation is based wholly on the grace of God apart from works (Titus 3:5; Eph. 2:9). Anyone who will exercise repentance toward God and faith in the Lord Jesus Christ will be saved (Acts 16:30–32; Luke 24:47; Rom. 10:17).

C. The Provision of Salvation—Christ died for the sins of the whole world (John 1:29; 3:16; I John 2:1, 2). Through His blood, atonement is made without respect of persons (I Tim. 2:4–6). All sinners can be saved by this gracious provision (Heb. 2:9; John 3:18).

VII. DIVINE SOVEREIGNTY AND HUMAN FREEDOM

God's sovereignty and man's freedom are two inseparable factors in the salvation experience (Eph. 2:4–6). The two Bible truths are in no way contradictory, but they are amazingly complementary in the great salvation so freely provided by God, in His sovereignty purposed, planned and executed salvation in eternity while man's freedom enables him to make a personal choice in time, either to receive this salvation and be saved, or to reject it and be damned (Eph. 1:9–12; 1:13, 14; John 1:12, 13).

VIII. SANCTIFICATION

All believers are set apart unto God (Heb. 10:12–14) at the time of their regeneration (I Cor. 6:11). They should grow in grace (II Peter 1:5–8) by allowing the Holy Spirit to apply God's Word to their lives (I Peter 2:2), conforming them to the principles of divine righteousness (Rom. 12:1, 2; I Thess. 4:3–7) and making them partakers of the holiness of God (II Cor. 7:1; I Peter 1:15, 16).

IX. SECURITY

All believers are eternally secure in Jesus Christ (John 10:24–30; Rom. 8:35–39). They are born again (John 3:3–5; I John 5:1; I Peter 1:23), made new creatures in Christ (II Cor. 5:17; II Peter 1:4), and indwelt by the Holy Spirit (Rom. 8:9; I John 4:4), enabling their perseverance in good works (Eph. 2:10). A special providence watches over them (Rom. 8:28; I Cor. 10:13), and they are kept by the power of God (Phil. 1:6; 2:12, 13; I Peter 1:3–5; Heb. 13:5).

X. CHURCH

A. The Nature of the Church—A New Testament church is a local congregation (Acts 16:5; I Cor. 4:17) of baptized believers in Jesus Christ (Acts 2:41) who are united by covenant in belief of what God has revealed and in obedience to what He has commanded (Acts 2:41, 42).

B. The Autonomy of the Church—She acknowledges Jesus as her only Head (Eph. 5:23; Col. 1:18) and the Holy Bible as her only rule of faith and practice (Isa. 8:20; II Tim. 3:16, 17), governing herself by democratic principles (Acts 6:1–6; I Cor. 5:1–5) under the oversight of her pastors (Acts 20:28; Heb. 13:7,17,24).

C. The Perpetuity of the Church—Instituted by Jesus during His personal ministry on earth (Matt. 16:18; Mark 3:13–19; John 1:35–51), true churches have continued to the present and will continue until Jesus returns (Matt. 16:18; 28:20).

D. The Ordinances of the Church—Her two ordinances are baptism and the Lord's Supper. Baptism is the immersion in water of a believer as a confession of his faith in Jesus Christ (Matt. 28:19; Rom. 6:4) and is prerequisite to church membership and participation in the Lord's Supper (Acts 2:41, 42). The Lord's Supper is the sacred sharing of the bread of communion and the cup of blessing by the assembled church (Acts 20:7) as a memorial to the crucified body and shed blood of Jesus Christ (Luke 22:19, 20; I Cor. 11:23–26). Both ordinances must be administered by the authority of a New Testament church (Matt. 28:18–20; I Cor. 11:23–26).

E. The Officers of the Church—Pastors and deacons are the permanent officers divinely ordained in a New Testament church (Phil. 1:1). Each church may select men of her choice to fill those offices under the leading of the Holy Spirit (Acts 6:1–6; 20:17, 18) according to the divinely given qualifications (I Tim. 3:1–13).

Pastors (elders, bishops) are authorized to oversee and teach the churches under the Lordship of Jesus Christ (Acts 20:28; Heb 13:7, 17, 24; I Peter 5:1–4). Each church is responsible to follow them as they follow Christ (I Cor. 11:1; I Thess. 1:6; Heb. 13:17) and to provide a livelihood for them that they might fulfill their ministries (I Tim 5:17, 18; Phil. 4:15–18). Pastors are equal in the service of God (Matt. 23:8–12).

Deacons (ministers, servants) are servants of the churches and assistants to the pastors, particularly in benevolent ministries. Each church may select her own deacons according to her needs, and no church is bound by the act of another church in that selection (Acts 6:1–6).

F. The Ministry of the Church—Her mission is evangelizing sinners by preaching the gospel (Matt. 28:19; Luke 24:45–47), baptizing those who believe (Acts 2:41; 8:12, 35–38), and maturing them by instruction (Matt. 28:20; Acts 2:42) and discipline (Matt. 18:17, 18; I Cor. 5:1–5).

G. The Fellowship of the Church—She is free to associate with true churches in furthering the faith (II Cor. 11:8; Phil 4:10, 15, 16) but is responsible to keep herself from those who hold doctrines or practices contrary to Holy Scripture (Gal. 1:8, 9; I John 2:19). In association with other churches, each church is equal and is the sole judge of the measure and method of her cooperation (Matt. 20:25–28). In all matters of polity and practice, the will of each church is final (Matt. 18:18).

XI. CIVIL AUTHORITY

Human government was instituted by God to protect the innocent and punish the guilty. It is separate from the church, though both church and state exercise complementary ministries for the benefit of society (Matt. 22:21).

Christians should submit to the authority of the government under which they live, obeying all laws which do not contradict the laws of God, respecting officers of government, paying taxes, rendering military service, and praying for the welfare of the nation and its leaders (Rom. 13:1–7; I Peter 2:13, 17; I Tim. 2:1, 2). They should vote, hold office, and exercise influence to direct the nation after the principles of Holy Scripture.

Civil authority is not to interfere in matters of conscience or disturb the institutions of religion (Acts 4:18–20), but it should preserve for every citizen the free exercise of his religious convictions.

Churches should receive no subsidy from the government, but they should be exempt from taxation on property and money used for the common good through worship, education, or benevolence.

XII. LAST THINGS

A. Return—Our risen Lord will return personally in bodily form to receive His redeemed unto Himself. His return is imminent (I Thess. 4:13–17; Rev. 22:20).

B. Resurrections—After Jesus returns, all of the dead will be raised bodily, each in his own order: the righteous dead in "the resurrection of life" and the wicked dead in "the resurrection of damnation" (John 5:24–29; I Cor. 15:20–28).

C. Judgments—Prior to the eternal state, God will judge everyone to confer rewards or to consign to punishment (Matt. 25:31–46; II Cor. 5:10; Rev. 20:11–15).

D. Eternal States—Heaven is the eternal home of the redeemed (John 14:1–3) who, in their glorified bodies (I Cor. 15:51–58), will live in the presence of God forever (I Thess. 4:17) in ultimate blessing (Rev. 21, 22).

Hell is the place of eternal punishment and suffering (Luke 16:19–31) for the devil, his angels (Matt. 25:41), and the unredeemed (Rev. 20:10–15).

ADDENDUM

NOTE: The following statements are not to be binding upon the churches already affiliated with this association, or to require adoption by churches petitioning this body for privilege of cooperation, or to be a test of fellowship between brethren or churches. However, they do express the preponderance of opinion among the churches of the Baptist Missionary Association of America.

1. We believe in the premillennial return of Christ to earth, after which He shall reign in peace upon the earth for a thousand years (Rev. 20:4–6).
2. We believe the Scriptures to teach two resurrections: the first of the righteous at Christ's coming; the second of the wicked at the close of the thousand-year reign (I Thess. 4:13–17; Rev. 20:6,12–15).
We endorse the New Hampshire Confession of Faith as a representative compendium of what Baptists have historically believed through the centuries. This confession was consulted and provided a pattern and guide for the formulation of these doctrinal statements. As there are several versions and editions, we refer particularly to the edition in J. E. Cobb's Church Manual third edition, published by the Baptist Publications Committee of Texarkana, TX.

Source: Permission granted by the BMAA Web site http://www.baptist-newsservice.org/doctrinal.php.

40

THE COOPERATIVE BAPTIST FELLOWSHIP

Address to the Public: The Founding Document of the Cooperative Baptist Fellowship, ca. 1990

THE COOPERATIVE BAPTIST FELLOWSHIP IS *a group of moderate Southern Baptists and ex-Southern Baptists. Born in August 1990, as a result of the fundamentalist-moderate controversy within the Southern Baptist Convention (1979–1990), it did not adopt the name "Cooperative Baptist Fellowship" until May 10, 1991, and after the adoption of the following document. Because the name of the organization originally proposed was the "United Baptist Fellowship," that was the term used in this document when presented to the Assembly. It has been replaced here by "Cooperative Baptist Fellowship," the name ultimately adopted for the organization.*

Presented to the General Assembly as "information" on behalf of the "Interim Steering Committee," the document is the result of two people, Cecil E. Sherman and Walter B. Shurden. Sherman's is the primary hand. A brief history of the document is found in the archives of the Cooperative Baptist Fellowship at Mercer University in Macon, Georgia.

Designed primarily to distinguish moderate Southern Baptists from fundamentalist Southern Baptists "An Address to the Public" gives insight into what moderate Southern Baptists believe to be consistent with the Baptist tradition of freedom and responsibility. After providing a cursory background to the fundamentalist-moderate controversy, the document lists some of the major issues in the conflict. It then commits mod-

erates to the building of a new organization that will embody Baptists principles and extend the missionary work of their people.[1]

"An Address to the Public" from the Interim Steering Committee of the Cooperative Baptist Fellowship, Adopted May 9, 1991

Introduction

Forming something as fragile as the Cooperative Baptist Fellowship is not a move we make lightly. We are obligated to give some explanation for why we are doing what we are doing. Our children will know what we have done; they may not know why we have done what we have done. We have reasons for our actions, they are:

I. Our Reasons Are Larger Than Losing.

For twelve years the Southern Baptist Convention in annual session has voted to sustain the people who lead the fundamentalist wing of the SBC. For twelve years the SBC in annual session has endorsed the arguments and the rationale of the fundamentalists. What has happened is not a quirk or a flash or an accident. It has been done again and again.

If inclined, one could conclude that the losers have tired of losing. But the formation of Cooperative Baptist Fellowship does not spring from petty rivalry. If the old moderate wing of the SBC were represented in making policy and were treated as welcomed representatives of competing ideas in the Baptist mission task, then we would co-exist, as we did for years, along side fundamentalism and continue to argue our ideas before Southern Baptists.

But this is not the way things are. When fundamentalists won in 1979, they immediately began a policy of exclusion. Non-fundamentalists are not appointed to any denominational positions. Rarely are gentle fundamentalists appointed. Usually only the doctrinaire fundamentalists, hostile to the purposes of the very institutions they control, are rewarded for service by appointment. Thus, the boards of SBC agencies are filled by only one kind of Baptists. And this is true whether the vote to elect was 60–40 or 52–48. It has been since 1979 a "winner take all." We have no voice.

In another day Pilgrims and Quakers and Baptists came to America for the same reason. As a minority, they had no way to get a hearing. They found a place where they would not be second-class citizens. All who attended the annual meeting of the SBC in New Orleans in June

---

1 Walter B. Shurden, *The Struggle for the Soul of the SBC* (Macon, GA: Mercer University Press, 1993), 309.

of 1990 will have an enlarged understanding of why our ancestors left their homes and dear ones and all that was familiar. So forming the Cooperative Baptist Fellowship is not something we do lightly. Being Baptist should ensure that no one is ever excluded who confesses, "Jesus is Lord (Philippians 2:11)."

II. Our Understandings Are Different

Occasionally, someone accuses Baptists of being merely a contentious, controversial people. That may be. But the ideas that divide Baptists in the present "controversy" are the same ideas that have divided Presbyterians, Lutherans, and Episcopalians. These ideas are strong and central; these ideas will not be papered over. Here are some of these basic ideas:

1. Bible

Many of our differences come from a different understanding and interpretation of Holy Scripture. But the difference is not at the point of the inspiration or authority of the Bible. We interpret the Bible differently, as will be seen below in our treatment of the biblical understanding of women and pastors. We also, however, have a different understanding of the nature of the Bible. We want to be biblical—especially in our view of the Bible. That means that we dare not claim less for the Bible than the Bible claims for itself. The Bible neither claims nor reveals inerrancy as a Christian teaching. Bible claims must be based on the Bible, not on human interpretations of the Bible.

2. Education

What should happen in colleges and seminaries is a major bone of contention between fundamentalists and moderates. Fundamentalists educate by indoctrination. They have the truth and all the truth. As they see it, their job is to pass along the truth they have. They must not change it. They are certain that their understandings of the truth are correct, complete and to be adopted by others.

Moderates, too, are concerned with the truth, but we do not claim a monopoly. We seek to enlarge and build upon such truth as we have. The task of education is to take the past and review it, even criticize it. We work to give our children a larger understanding of spiritual and physical reality. We know we will always live in faith; our understandings will not be complete until we get to heaven and are loosed from the limitations of our mortality and sin.

3. *Mission*

What ought to be the task of the missionary is another difference between us. We think the mission task is to reach people for faith in Jesus Christ by preaching, teaching, healing and other ministries of mercy and justice. We believe this to be the model of Jesus in Galilee. That is what he went about in his mission task. Fundamentalists make the mission assignment narrower than Jesus did. They allow their emphasis on direct evangelism to undercut other biblical ministries of mercy and justice. This narrowed definition of what a missionary ought to be and do is a contention between us.

4. *Pastor*

What is the task of the pastor? They argue the pastor should be the ruler of the congregation. This smacks of the bishops' task in the Middle Ages. It also sounds much like the kind of church leadership Baptists revolted against in the seventeenth century.

Our understanding of the role of the pastor is to be a servant/shepherd. Respecting lay leadership is our assignment. Allowing the congregation to make real decisions is of the very nature of Baptist congregationalism. And using corporate business models to "get results" is building the Church by the rules of a secular world rather than witnessing to the secular world by way of a servant church.

5. *Women*

The New Testament gives two signals about the role of women. A literal interpretation of Paul can build a case for making women submissive to men in the Church. But another body of scripture points toward another place for women. In Gal. 3:27–28, Paul wrote, "As many of you as are baptized into Christ have clothed yourselves with Christ. There is no longer Jew or Greek, there is no longer slave or free, there is no longer male and female; for all of you are one in Christ Jesus (NRSV)."

We take Galatians as a clue to the way the church should be ordered. We interpret the reference to women the same way we interpret the reference to slaves. If we have submissive roles for women, we must also have a place for the slaves in the Church.

In Galatians Paul follows the spirit of Jesus who courageously challenged the conventional wisdom of his day. It was a wisdom with rigid boundaries between men and women in religion and in public life. Jesus deliberately broke those barriers. He called women to follow him; he treated women as equally capable of dealing with sacred issues. Our model for the role of women in matters of faith is the Lord Jesus.

6. *Church*

An ecumenical and inclusive attitude is basic to our fellowship. The great ideas of theology are the common property of all the church. Baptists are only a part of that great and inclusive Church. So, we are eager to have fellowship with our brothers and sisters in the faith and to recognize their work for our Savior. We do not try to make them conform to us; we try to include them in our design for mission. Mending the torn fabric of both Baptist and Christian fellowship is important to us. God willing, we will bind together the broken parts into a new company in preview of the great fellowship we shall have with each other in heaven.

It should be apparent that the points of difference are critical. They are the stuff which a fellowship such as the Southern Baptist Convention is made of. We are different. It is regrettable, but we are different. And perhaps we are most different at the point of spirit. At no place have we been able to negotiate about these differences. Were our fundamentalist brethren to negotiate, they would compromise. And that would be sin by their understanding. So, we can either come to their position, or we can form a new fellowship.

III. *We Are Called to Do More Than Politic*

Some people would have us continue as we have over the last twelve years, and continue to work with the SBC with a point of view to change the SBC. On the face of it this argument sounds reasonable. Acting it out is more difficult.

To change the SBC requires a majority vote. To effect a majority in annual session requires massive, expensive, contentious activity. We have done this, and we have done it repeatedly.

But we have never enjoyed doing it. Something is wrong with a religious body that spends such energy in overt political activity. Our time is unwisely invested in beating people or trying to beat people. We have to define the other side as bad and we are good. There is division. The existence of the Cooperative Baptist Fellowship is a simple confession of that division; it is not the cause of that division.

We can no longer devote our major energies to SBC politics. We would rejoice, however, to see the SBC return to its historic Baptist convictions. Our primary call is to be true to our understanding of the gospel. We are to advance the gospel in our time. When we get to heaven, God is not going to ask us, "Did you win in Atlanta in June of 1991?" If we understand the orders we are under, we will be asked larger questions. And to spend our time trying to reclaim a human institution (people made the SBC; it is not a scriptural entity) is to make more of that institution than we ought to make. A denomination is a missions delivery system; it is not meant to be an idol. When we make more of the SBC than we ought, we risk falling into idolatry. Twelve years is too long to engage in political activity. We are called to higher purposes.

Conclusion

- That we may have a voice in our Baptist mission . . . for that is our Baptist birthright . . .
- That we may work by ideas consistent with our understanding of the gospel rather than fund ideas that are not our gospel . . .
- That we may give our energies to the advancement of the Kingdom of God rather than in diverse, destructive politics . . . .

For these reasons we form the Cooperative Baptist Fellowship. This does not require that we sever ties with the old Southern Baptist Convention. It does give us another mission delivery system, one more like our understanding of what it means to be a Baptist and what it means to do the gospel. Therefore, we create a new instrument to further the Kingdom and enlarge the Body of Christ.

Source: *Address to the Public: The Founding Document of the Cooperative Baptist Fellowship* (Atlanta, GA: Cooperative Baptist Fellowship, n.d.). Permission granted by the Cooperative Baptist Fellowship.

Who We Are:
Identity, Vision, Mission, Core Values, Initiatives;
What Fellowship People Do, Cooperative Baptist Fellowship, ca. 1990

We are a Fellowship of Baptist Christians and Churches who share a passion for the Great Commission of Jesus Christ and a commitment to Baptist principles of faith and practice. More than 1,850 churches contributed to the Fellowship in fiscal year 2004–05.

Founded in 1991, CBF provides resources to churches and is engaged in a global missions enterprise with 163 field personnel and affiliates working among the most neglected people groups in the world.

The Fellowship partners with American Baptist Churches, U.S.A. to provide health insurance and retirement benefits through the Church Benefits Board to CBF-related churches and organizations. Thirteen theology schools and seminaries with a combined enrollment of more than 2,000 students are supported by the Fellowship through scholarships for about 80 students and operational funds for some schools. The Fellowship maintains a Council on Endorsement and has endorsed more than 520 chaplains and pastoral counselors.

The Fellowship is governed by a national Coordinating Council whose members serve three-year terms. The Fellowship's General Assembly elects one-third of the council each year to replace those council members who rotate off. The Fellowship has a paid staff of 55 fulltime and 7 part-time employees in addition to 163 Global Missions field personnel. The Fellowship's home office is the Atlanta Resource Center, and it also operates a Global Missions office in Dallas, Texas. CBF partners with 18 state and regional CBF organizations.

The Fellowship has an annual budget of $17 million, and the CBF Foundation has more than $33 million under management.

Our Identity

We are a fellowship of Baptist Christians and churches who share a passion for the Great Commission of Jesus Christ and a commitment to Baptist principles of faith and practice

Our Vision

Being the presence of Christ in the world

Our Mission

Serving Christians and churches as they discover and fulfill their God-given mission

Our Core Values

Baptist Principles:

Soul Freedom—We believe in the priesthood of all believers. We affirm the freedom and responsibility of every person to relate directly to

God without the imposition of creed or the control of clergy or government.

Bible Freedom—We believe in the authority of Scripture. We believe the Bible, under the Lordship of Christ, is central to the life of the individual and the church. We affirm the freedom and right of every Christian to interpret and apply Scripture under the leadership of the Holy Spirit.

Church Freedom—We believe in the autonomy of every local church. We believe Baptist churches are free, under the Lordship of Christ, to determine their membership and leadership, to order their worship and work, to ordain whomever they perceive as gifted for ministry, and to participate as they deem appropriate in the larger Body of Christ.

Religious Freedom—We believe in freedom of religion, freedom for religion, and freedom from religion. We support the separation of church and state.

Biblically Based Global Missions

All of us are called to be co-laborers in the task of fulfilling our Lord's Great Commission. We believe the Bible teaches that . . .

- God is the one triune God, Creator of all people in God's own image.
- All people are separated from God by sin.
- Christ is the Savior and Redeemer for all peoples.
- The Holy Spirit convicts and converts all who believe in Christ, teaches the church in the voice of the Living Christ, and empowers the church and all believers for the mission of Christ in the world.
- Christ calls us to minister redemptively to the spiritual, physical, and social needs of individuals and communities.

Every believer and every church is responsible for sharing the Gospel with all people.

We want to enable believers and churches to work cooperatively with other Great Commission Christians to activate this global missions calling in their communities and throughout the world.

Resource Model

We are committed to discovering and providing resources that will empower churches to fulfill their mission in their particular contexts and will equip individuals to fulfill their calling under the Lordship of Christ. We prefer to cooperate in mutually beneficial ways with other organizations rather than to establish, own, and control our own institutions.

Justice and Reconciliation

We are committed to a biblical vision of justice and mercy. We believe the call of Christ extends to every area and relationship of life.

Lifelong Learning and Ministry

We believe in lifelong learning for laity and clergy for the ministry of the church. We are committed to Baptist theological education that affords intellectual and spiritual freedom to both students and professors in an atmosphere of reverence for biblical authority and respect for open inquiry and responsible scholarship.

Trustworthiness

We will organize, make decisions and carry our mission in ways that earn trust. United in our mission and our shared commitments, we will celebrate God's gift of diversity among *individuals* and churches of the Fellowship.

Effectiveness

We will organize in ways that encourage flexibility, responsiveness, and accountability. We will monitor our processes and organizational structures in light of our stated mission.

Our Strategic Initiatives

Faith Formation

Encouraging all persons in their journeys toward Christ-likeness by identifying and responding to the critical needs of congregations in the following areas:
- *Evangelism and outreach*—Biblically wholesome and effective evangelism and outreach.
- *Spiritual growth*—In areas such as corporate worship, spiritual disciplines, Bible study, Christian ethics and discipleship.

Building Community

Nurturing authentic community within and beyond congregations by identifying and responding to the critical needs in the following areas:
- *Congregational health*—Developing and sustaining healthy congregations.

- *Baptist identity and relationships*—Understanding and embracing the Baptist values that have shaped our identity and to engage in meaningful Baptist partnerships and dialogue.
- *Reconciliation and justice*—Bringing wholeness to relationships within and beyond congregations through acts of reconciliation and justice.
- *Marriage and family ministries*—Developing healthy individuals, marriages, and families.
- *Ecumenical and interfaith dialogue*—Meaningful ecumenical partnerships and interfaith dialogue.
- *Chaplains and pastoral counselors*—Ministry in specialized settings and endorsement of chaplains and pastoral counselors.

Leadership Development

Developing effective Christian leaders by identifying and responding to the critical needs of congregations in the following areas:

- *Congregational leadership development*—Developing effective leaders among both laity and clergy.
- *Theological education*—Building a strong foundation of theological education for church leaders.
- *Collegiate ministry*—Effective collegiate student ministry, including the nurture and development of future leaders for churches and the larger CBF community.

Global Missions and Ministries

Engaging in holistic missions and ministries in a world without borders by identifying and responding to the critical needs of congregations in the following areas:

- *Partnership missions with local churches*—Engaging in effective missions and ministries in their communities and around the world.
- *Most neglected peoples*—Establishing an effective Christian witness among the world's unevangelized and marginalized peoples.
- *Church planting*—Assisting at the start of churches via research, recruitment, fundraising, training, and counsel.

Source: *Who We Are* (Atlanta, GA: Cooperative Baptist Fellowship, n.d.).

41

THE BAPTIST FAITH AND MESSAGE, 1925, 1963, 2000

Southern Baptist Convention

A Comparison of the 1925, 1963, and 2000 Baptist Faith and Message

Preamble to the 1925 Baptist Faith and Message

The report of the Committee on State-ment of Baptist Faith and Message was presented as follows by E. Y. Mullins, Kentucky:

REPORT OF THE COMMITTEE ON BAPTIST FAITH AND MESSAGE

Your committee beg leave to report as follows:

Your committee rec-ognize that they were appointed "to con-sider the advisability of issuing another statement of the Bap-

Preamble to the 1963 Baptist Faith and Message

Committee on Baptist Faith and Message

The 1962 session of the Southern Baptist Convention, meet-ing in San Francisco, California, adopted the following motion:

"Since the report of the Committee on Statement of Baptist Faith and Message was adopted in 1925, there have been vari-ous statements from time to time which have been made, but no over-all statement which might be help-ful at this time as suggested in Section 2 of that report, or

Preamble to the 2000 Baptist Faith and Message

The 1999 session of the Southern Baptist Convention, meeting in Atlanta, Georgia, adopted the following motion addressed to the President of the Convention:

"I move that in your capacity as Southern Baptist Conven-tion chairman, you appoint a blue ribbon committee to review the *Baptist Faith and Message* statement with the responsibil-ity to report and bring any recommendations to this meeting next June in Orlando."

tist Faith and Message, and report at the next Convention."

In pursuance of the instructions of the Convention, and in consideration of the general denominational situation, your committee have decided to recommend the New Hampshire Confession of Faith, revised at certain points, and with some additional articles growing out of present needs, for approval by the Convention, in the event a statement of the Baptist faith and message is deemed necessary at this time.

The present occasion for a reaffirmation of Christian fundamentals is the prevalence of naturalism in the modern teaching and preaching of religion. Christianity is supernatural in its origin and history. We repudiate every theory of religion which denies the supernatural elements in our faith.

As introductory to the doctrinal articles, we recommend the adoption by the Convention of the following introductory statement which might be used as an interpretation of the 1925 Statement."

"We recommend, therefore, that the president of this Convention be requested to call a meeting of the men now serving as presidents of the various state conventions that would qualify as a member of the Southern Baptist Convention committee under Bylaw 18 to present to the Convention in Kansas City some similar statement which shall serve as information to the churches, and which may serve as guidelines to the various agencies of the Southern Baptist Convention. It is understood that any group or individuals may approach this committee to be of service. The expenses of this committee shall be borne by the Convention Operating Budget."

Your committee thus constituted begs leave to present its report as follows:

President Paige Patterson appointed the committee as follows: Max Barnett (OK), Steve Gaines (AL), Susie Hawkins (TX), Rudy A. Hernandez (TX), Charles S. Kelley, Jr. (LA), Heather King (IN), Richard D. Land (TN), Fred Luter (LA), R. Albert Mohler, Jr. (KY), T. C. Pinckney (VA), Nelson Price (GA), Adrian Rogers (TN), Roger Spradlin (CA), Simon Tsoi (AZ), Jerry Vines (FL). Adrian Rogers (TN) was appointed chairman.

Your committee thus constituted begs leave to present its report as follows:

Baptists are a people of deep beliefs and cherished doctrines. Throughout our history we have been a confessional people, adopting statements of faith as a witness to our beliefs and a pledge of our faithfulness to the doctrines revealed in Holy Scripture.

Our confessions of faith are rooted in historical precedent, as the church in every

statement of the historic Baptist conception of the nature and function of confessions of faith in our religious and denominational life, believing that some such statement will clarify the atmosphere and remove some causes of misunderstanding, friction, and apprehension. Baptists approve and circulate confessions of faith with the following understanding, namely:

1. That they constitute a consensus of opinion of some Baptist body, large or small, for the general instruction and guidance of our own people and others concerning those articles of the Christian faith which are most surely conditions of salvation revealed in the New Testament, viz., repentance towards God and faith in Jesus Christ as Saviour and Lord.

2. That we do not regard them as complete statements of our faith, having any quality of finality or infallibility. As in the

Throughout its work your committee has been conscious of the contribution made by the statement of "The Southern Baptist Faith and Message" adopted by the Southern Baptist Convention in 1925. It quotes with approval its affirmation that "Christianity is supernatural in its origin and history. We repudiate every theory of religion which denies the supernatural elements in our faith."

Furthermore, it concurs in the introductory "statement of the historic Baptist conception of the nature and function of confessions of faith in our religious and denominational life. . . ." It is, therefore, quoted in full as a part of this report to the Convention:

"(1) That they constitute a consensus of opinion of some Baptist body, large or small, for the general instruction and guidance of our own people and others concerning those articles of the Christian

age has been called upon to define and defend its beliefs. Each generation of Christians bears the responsibility of guarding the treasury of truth that has been entrusted to us [2 Timothy 1:14]. Facing a new century, Southern Baptists must meet the demands and duties of the present hour.

New challenges to faith appear in every age. A pervasive anti-supernaturalism in the culture was answered by Southern Baptists in 1925, when the *Baptist Faith and Message* was first adopted by this Convention. In 1963, Southern Baptists responded to assaults upon the authority and truthfulness of the Bible by adopting revisions to the *Baptist Faith and Message*. The Convention added an article on "The Family" in 1998, thus answering cultural confusion with the clear teachings of Scripture. Now, faced with a culture hostile to the very notion of truth, this

past so in the future Baptist should hold themselves free to revise their statements of faith as may seem to them wise and expedient at any time.

3. That any group of Baptists, large or small, have the inherent right to draw up for themselves and publish to the world a confession of their faith whenever they may think it advisable to do so.

4. That the sole authority for faith and practice among Baptists is the Scriptures of the Old and New Testaments. Confessions are only guides in interpretation, having no authority over the conscience.

5. That they are statements of religious convictions, drawn from the Scriptures, and are not to be used to hamper freedom of thought or investigation in other realms of life.

faith which are most surely held among us. They are not intended to add anything to the simple conditions of salvation revealed in the New Testament, viz., repentance towards God and faith in Jesus Christ as Savior and Lord.

"(2) That we do not regard them as complete statements of our faith, having any quality of finality or infallibility. As in the past so in the future, Baptists should hold themselves free to revise their statements of faith as may seem to them wise and expedient at any time.

"(3) That any group of Baptists, large or small, have the inherent right to draw up for themselves and publish to the world a confession of their faith whenever they may think it advisable to do so.

"(4) That the sole authority for faith and practice among Baptists is the Scriptures of the Old and New Testaments. Confessions are only guides in interpretation, hav-

generation of Baptists must claim anew the eternal truths of the Christian faith.

Your committee respects and celebrates the heritage of the *Baptist Faith and Message*, and affirms the decision of the Convention in 1925 to adopt the *New Hampshire Confession of Faith*, "revised at certain points and with some additional articles growing out of certain needs. . . ." We also respect the important contributions of the 1925 and 1963 editions of the *Baptist Faith and Message*.

With the 1963 committee, we have been guided in our work by the 1925 "statement of the historic Baptist conception of the nature and function of confessions of faith in our religious and denominational life. . . ." It is, therefore, quoted in full as a part of this report to the Convention:

(1) That they constitute a consensus of opinion of some Baptist body, large

ing no authority over the conscience.

"(5) That they are statements of religious convictions, drawn from the Scriptures, and are not to be used to hamper freedom of thought or investigation in other realms of life."

The 1925 Statement recommended "the New Hampshire Confession of Faith, revised at certain points, and with some additional articles growing out of certain needs. . . ." Your present committee has adopted the same pattern. It has sought to build upon the structure of the 1925 Statement, keeping in mind the "certain needs" of our generation. At times it has reproduced sections of that Statement without change. In other instances it has substituted words for clarity or added sentences for emphasis. At certain points it has combined articles, with minor changes in wording, to endeavor to relate certain doctrines to

or small, for the general instruction and guidance of our own people and others concerning those articles of the Christian faith which are most surely held among us. They are not intended to add anything to the simple conditions of salvation revealed in the New Testament, viz., repentance toward God and faith in Jesus Christ as Saviour and Lord.

(2) That we do not regard them as complete statements of our faith, having any quality of finality or infallibility. As in the past so in the future, Baptists should hold themselves free to revise their statements of faith as may seem to them wise and expedient at any time.

(3) That any group of Baptists, large or small, have the inherent right to draw up for themselves and publish to the world a confession of their faith whenever they may think it advisable to do so.

(4) That the sole authority for faith and

each other. In still others—e.g., "God" and "Salvation"—it has sought to bring together certain truths contained throughout the 1925 Statement in order to relate them more clearly and concisely. In no case has it sought to delete from or to add to the basic contents of the 1925 Statement.

Baptists are a people who profess a living faith. This faith is rooted and grounded in Jesus Christ who is "the same yesterday, and today, and forever." Therefore, the sole authority for faith and practice among Baptists is Jesus Christ whose will is revealed in the Holy Scriptures.

A living faith must experience a growing understanding of truth and must be continually interpreted and related to the needs of each new generation. Throughout their history Baptist bodies, both large and small, have issued statements of faith which comprise a consensus of their beliefs. Such

practice among Baptists is the Scriptures of the Old and New Testaments. Confessions are only guides in interpretation, having no authority over the conscience.

(5) That they are statements of religious convictions, drawn from the Scriptures, and are not to be used to hamper freedom of thought or investigation in other realms of life.

Baptists cherish and defend religious liberty, and deny the right of any secular or religious authority to impose a confession of faith upon a church or body of churches. We honor the principles of soul competency and the priesthood of believers, affirming together both our liberty in Christ and our accountability to each other under the Word of God.

Baptist churches, associations, and general bodies have adopted confessions of faith as a witness to the world, and as instruments of doc-

statements have never been regarded as complete, infallible statements of faith, nor as official creeds carrying mandatory authority. Thus this generation of Southern Baptists is in historic succession of intent and purpose as it endeavors to state for its time and theological climate those articles of the Christian faith which are most surely held among us.

Baptists emphasize the soul's competency before God, freedom in religion, and the priesthood of the believer. However, this emphasis should not be interpreted to mean that there is an absence of certain definite doctrines that Baptists believe, cherish, and with which they have been and are now closely identified.

It is the purpose of this statement of faith and message to set forth certain teachings which we believe.

trinal accountability. We are not embarrassed to state before the world that these are doctrines we hold precious and as essential to the Baptist tradition of faith and practice.

As a committee, we have been charged to address the "certain needs" of our own generation. In an age increasingly hostile to Christian truth, our challenge is to express the truth as revealed in Scripture, and to bear witness to Jesus Christ, who is *"the Way, the Truth, and the Life."*

The 1963 committee rightly sought to identify and affirm "certain definite doctrines that Baptists believe, cherish, and with which they have been and are now closely identified." Our living faith is established upon eternal truths. "Thus this generation of Southern Baptists is in historic succession of intent and purpose as it endeavors to state for its time and theological climate those articles of the

Christian faith which are most surely held among us."

It is the purpose of this statement of faith and message to set forth certain teachings which we believe.

Respectfully Submitted,

The Baptist Faith and Message Study Committee

Adrian Rogers, Chairman

1925 Baptist Faith and Message Statement	1963 Baptist Faith and Message Statement with 1998 Amendment	2000 Baptist Faith and Message Statement
I. The Scriptures	**I. The Scriptures**	**I. The Scriptures**
We believe that the Holy Bible was written by men divinely inspired, and is a perfect treasure of heavenly instruction; that it has God for its author, salvation for its end, and truth, without any mixture of error, for its matter; that it reveals the principles by which God will judge us; and therefore is, and will remain to the end of the world, the true center of Chris-	The Holy Bible was written by men divinely inspired and is the record of God's revelation of Himself to man. It is a perfect treasure of divine instruction. It has God for its author, salvation for its end, and truth, without any mixture of error, for its matter. It reveals the principles by which God judges us; and therefore is, and will remain to the end of the world, the	The Holy Bible was written by men divinely inspired and is God's revelation of Himself to man. It is a perfect treasure of divine instruction. It has God for its author, salvation for its end, and truth, without any mixture of error, for its matter. Therefore, all Scripture is totally true and trustworthy. It reveals the principles by which God judges us, and

tian union, and the supreme standard by which all human conduct, creeds and religious opinions should be tried.

Luke 16:29–31; 2 Tim. 3:15–17; Eph. 2:20; Heb. 1:1; 2 Peter 1:19–21; John 16:13–15; Matt. 22:29–31; Psalm 19:7–10; Psalm 119:1–8.

true center of Christian union, and the supreme standard by which all human conduct, creeds, and religious opinions should be tried. The criterion by which the Bible is to be interpreted is Jesus Christ.

Ex. 24:4; Deut. 4:1–2; 17:19; Josh. 8:34; Psalms 19:7–10; 119:11,89,105,140; Isa. 34:16; 40:8; Jer. 15:16; 36; Matt. 5:17–18; 22:29; Luke 21:33; 24:44–46; John 5:39; 16:13–15; 17:17; Acts 2:16ff.; 17:11; Rom. 15:4; 16:25–26; 2 Tim. 3:15–17; Heb. 1:1–2; 4:12; 1 Peter 1:25; 2 Peter 1:19–21.

therefore is, and will remain to the end of the world, the true center of Christian union, and the supreme standard by which all human conduct, creeds, and religious opinions should be tried. All Scripture is a testimony to Christ, who is Himself the focus of divine revelation.

Exodus 24:4; Deuteronomy 4:1–2; 17:19; Joshua 8:34; Psalms 19:7–10; 119:11,89,105,140; Isaiah 34:16; 40:8; Jeremiah 15:16; 36:1–32; Matthew 5:17–18; 22:29; Luke 21:33; 24:44–46; John 5:39; 16:13–15; 17:17; Acts 2:16ff.; 17:11; Romans 15:4; 16:25–26; 2 Timothy 3:15–17; Hebrews 1:1–2; 4:12; 1 Peter 1:25; 2 Peter 1:19–21.

II. God

There is one and only one living and true God, an intelligent, spiritual, and personal Being, the Creator, Preserver, and Ruler of the universe, infinite in holiness and all other perfections, to whom we

II. God

There is one and only one living and true God. He is an intelligent, spiritual, and personal Being, the Creator, Redeemer, Preserver, and Ruler of the universe. God is infinite in holiness and all other perfec-

II. God

There is one and only one living and true God. He is an intelligent, spiritual, and personal Being, the Creator, Redeemer, Preserver, and Ruler of the universe. God is infinite in holiness and all other perfec-

owe the highest love, reverence, and obedience. He is revealed to us as Father, Son, and Holy Spirit, each with distinct personal attributes, but without division of nature, essence, or being.

Gen. 1:1; 1 Cor. 8:4–6; Deut. 6:4; Jer. 10:10; Isa. 48:12; Deut. 5:7; Ex. 3:14; Heb. 11:6; John 5:26; 1 Tim. 1:17; John 1:14–18; John 15:26; Gal. 4:6; Matt. 28:19.

tions. To him we owe the highest love, reverence, and obedience. The eternal God reveals Himself to us as Father, Son, and Holy Spirit, with distinct personal attributes, but without division of nature, essence, or being.

1. God the Father

God as Father reigns with providential care over His universe, His creatures, and the flow of the stream of human history according to the purposes of His grace. He is all powerful, all loving, and all wise. God is Father in truth to those who become children of God through faith in Jesus Christ. He is fatherly in his attitude toward all men.

Gen. 1:1; 2:7; Ex. 3:14; 6:2–3; 15:11ff.; 20:1ff.; Levit. 22:2; Deut. 6:4; 32:6; 1 Chron. 29:10; Psalm 19:1–3; Isa. 43:3,15; 64:8; Jer. 10:10; 17:13; Matt. 6:9ff.; 7:11; 23:9; 28:19; Mark 1:9–11; John 4:24; 5:26; 14:6–13; 17:1–8; Acts 1:7; Rom. 8:14–

tions. God is all powerful and all knowing; and His perfect knowledge extends to all things, past, present, and future, including the future decisions of His free creatures. To Him we owe the highest love, reverence, and obedience. The eternal triune God reveals Himself to us as Father, Son, and Holy Spirit, with distinct personal attributes, but without division of nature, essence, or being.

A. God the Father

God as Father reigns with providential care over His universe, His creatures, and the flow of the stream of human history according to the purposes of His grace. He is all powerful, all knowing, all loving, and all wise. God is Father in truth to those who become children of God through faith in Jesus Christ. He is fatherly in His attitude toward all men.

Genesis 1:1; 2:7; Exodus 3:14; 6:2–3; 15:11ff.; 20:1ff.;

15; 1 Cor. 8:6; Gal.
4:6; Ephes. 4:6; Col.
1:15; 1 Tim. 1:17;
Heb. 11:6; 12:9;
1 Peter 1:17; 1 John
5:7.

2. God the Son

Christ is the eternal
Son of God. In His
incarnation as Jesus
Christ He was con-
ceived of the Holy
Spirit and born of the
virgin Mary. Jesus
perfectly revealed
and did the will of
God, taking upon
Himself the demands
and necessities of
human nature and
identifying Himself
completely with
mankind yet with-
out sin. He honored
the divine law by
His personal obedi-
ence, and in His
death on the cross
He made provision
for the redemption
of men from sin. He
was raised from the
dead with a glorified
body and appeared
to His disciples as
the person who was
with them before
His crucifixion. He
ascended into heaven
and is now exalted at
the right hand of God
where He is the One

*Leviticus 22:2; Deu-
teronomy 6:4; 32:6;
1 Chronicles 29:10;
Psalm 19:1–3; Isaiah
43:3,15; 64:8; Jere-
miah 10:10; 17:13;
Matthew 6:9ff.;
7:11; 23:9; 28:19;
Mark 1:9–11; John
4:24; 5:26; 14:6–13;
17:1–8; Acts 1:7;
Romans 8:14–15;
1 Corinthians 8:6;
Galatians 4:6; Ephe-
sians 4:6; Colossians
1:15; 1 Timothy 1:17;
Hebrews 11:6; 12:9;
1 Peter 1:17; 1 John
5:7.*

B. God the Son

Christ is the eternal
Son of God. In His
incarnation as Jesus
Christ He was con-
ceived of the Holy
Spirit and born of the
virgin Mary. Jesus
perfectly revealed and
did the will of God,
taking upon Himself
human nature with its
demands and neces-
sities and identifying
Himself completely
with mankind yet
without sin. He
honored the divine
law by His personal
obedience, and in
His substitutionary
death on the cross
He made provision

239

Mediator, partaking of the nature of God and of man, and in whose Person is effected the reconciliation between God and man. He will return in power and glory to judge the world and to consummate His redemptive mission. He now dwells in all believers as the living and ever present Lord.

Gen. 18:1ff.; Psalms 2:7ff.; 110:1ff.; Isa. 7:14; 53; Matt. 1:18–23; 3:17; 8:29; 11:27; 14:33; 16:16,27; 17:5; 27; 28:1–6,19; Mark 1:1; 3:11; Luke 1:35; 4:41; 22:70; 24:46; John 1:1–18,29; 10:30,38; 11:25–27; 12:44–50; 14:7–11; 16:15–16,28; 17:1–5, 21–22; 20:1–20,28; Acts 1:9; 2:22–24; 7:55–56; 9:4–5,20; Rom. 1:3–4; 3:23–26; 5:6–21; 8:1–3,34; 10:4; 1 Cor. 1:30; 2:2; 8:6; 15:1–8,24–28; 2 Cor. 5:19–21; 8:9; Gal. 4:4–5; Ephes. 1:20; 3:11; 4:7–10; Phil. 2:5–11; Col. 1:13–22; 2:9; 1 Thess. 4:14–18; 1 Tim. 2:5–6; 3:16; Titus 2:13–14; Heb. 1:1–3;

for the redemption of men from sin. He was raised from the dead with a glorified body and appeared to His disciples as the person who was with them before His crucifixion. He ascended into heaven and is now exalted at the right hand of God where He is the One Mediator, fully God, fully man, in whose Person is effected the reconciliation between God and man. He will return in power and glory to judge the world and to consummate His redemptive mission. He now dwells in all believers as the living and ever present Lord.

Genesis 18:1ff.; Psalms 2:7ff.; 110:1ff.; Isaiah 7:14; 53; Matthew 1:18–23; 3:17; 8:29; 11:27; 14:33; 16:16,27; 17:5; 27; 28:1–6,19; Mark 1:1; 3:11; Luke 1:35; 4:41; 22:70; 24:46; John 1:1–18,29; 10:30,38; 11:25–27; 12:44–50; 14:7–11; 16:15–16,28; 17:1–5, 21–22; 20:1–20,28; Acts 1:9; 2:22–24; 7:55–56; 9:4–5,20;

4:14–15; 7:14–28; 9:12–15,24–28; 12:2; 13:8; 1 Peter 2:21–25; 3:22; 1 John 1:7–9; 3:2; 4:14–15; 5:9; 2 John 7–9; Rev. 1:13–16; 5:9–14; 12:10–11; 13:8; 19:16.

3. God the Holy Spirit

The Holy Spirit is the Spirit of God. He inspired holy men of old to write the Scriptures. Through illumination He enables men to understand truth. He exalts Christ. He convicts of sin, of righteousness and of judgment. He calls men to the Saviour, and effects regeneration. He cultivates Christian character, comforts believers, and bestows the spiritual gifts by which they serve God through His church. He seals the believer unto the day of final redemption. His presence in the Christian is the assurance of God to bring the believer into the fulness of the stature of Christ. He enlightens and empowers

Romans 1:3–4; 3:23–26; 5:6–21; 8:1–3,34; 10:4; 1 Corinthians 1:30; 2:2; 8:6; 15:1–8,24–28; 2 Corinthians 5:19–21; 8:9; Galatians 4:4–5; Ephesians 1:20; 3:11; 4:7–10; Philippians 2:5–11; Colossians 1:13–22; 2:9; 1 Thessalonians 4:14–18; 1 Timothy 2:5–6; 3:16; Titus 2:13–14; Hebrews 1:1–3; 4:14–15; 7:14–28; 9:12–15,24–28; 12:2; 13:8; 1 Peter 2:21–25; 3:22; 1 John 1:7–9; 3:2; 4:14–15; 5:9; 2 John 7–9; Revelation 1:13–16; 5:9–14; 12:10–11; 13:8; 19:16.

C. God the Holy Spirit

The Holy Spirit is the Spirit of God, fully divine. He inspired holy men of old to write the Scriptures. Through illumination He enables men to understand truth. He exalts Christ. He convicts men of sin, of righteousness, and of judgment. He calls men to the Saviour, and effects regeneration. At the

241

the believer and the church in worship, evangelism, and service.

Gen. 1:2; Judg. 14:6; Job 26:13; Psalms 51:11; 139:7ff.; Isa. 61:1–3; Joel 2:28–32; Matt. 1:18; 3:16; 4:1; 12:28–32; 28:19; Mark 1:10,12; Luke 1:35; 4:1,18–19; 11:13; 12:12; 24:49; John 4:24; 14:16–17,26; 15:26; 16:7–14; Acts 1:8; 2:1–4,38; 4:31; 5:3; 6:3; 7:55; 8:17,39; 10:44; 13:2; 15:28; 16:6; 19:1–6; Rom. 8:9–11,14–16,26–27; 1 Cor. 2:10–14; 3:16; 12:3–11; Gal. 4:6; Ephes. 1:13–14; 4:30; 5:18; 1 Thess. 5:19; 1 Tim. 3:16; 4:1; 2 Tim. 1:14; 3:16; Heb. 9:8,14; 2 Peter 1:21; 1 John 4:13; 5:6–7; Rev. 1:10; 22:17.

moment of regeneration He baptizes every believer into the Body of Christ. He cultivates Christian character, comforts believers, and bestows the spiritual gifts by which they serve God through His church. He seals the believer unto the day of final redemption. His presence in the Christian is the guarantee that God will bring the believer into the fullness of the stature of Christ. He enlightens and empowers the believer and the church in worship, evangelism, and service.

Genesis 1:2; Judges 14:6; Job 26:13; Psalms 51:11; 139:7ff.; Isaiah 61:1–3; Joel 2:28–32; Matthew 1:18; 3:16; 4:1; 12:28–32; 28:19; Mark 1:10,12; Luke 1:35; 4:1,18–19; 11:13; 12:12; 24:49; John 4:24; 14:16–17,26; 15:26; 16:7–14; Acts 1:8; 2:1–4,38; 4:31; 5:3; 6:3; 7:55; 8:17,39; 10:44; 13:2; 15:28; 16:6; 19:1–6; Romans 8:9–11,14–16,26–27;

1 Corinthians 2:10–14; 3:16; 12:3–11,13; Galatians 4:6; Ephesians 1:13–14; 4:30; 5:18; 1 Thessalonians 5:19; 1 Timothy 3:16; 4:1; 2 Timothy 1:14; 3:16; Hebrews 9:8,14; 2 Peter 1:21; 1 John 4:13; 5:6–7; Revelation 1:10; 22:17.

III. The Fall of Man

Man was created by the special act of God, as recorded in Genesis. "So God created man in his own image, in the image of God created he him; male and female created he them" (Gen. 1:27). "And the Lord God formed man of the dust of the ground, and breathed into his nostrils the breath of life; and man became a living soul" (Gen. 2:7).

He was created in a state of holiness under the law of his Maker, but, through the temptation of Satan, he transgressed the command of God and fell from his original holiness and righteousness; whereby his posterity inherit a nature

III. Man

Man was created by the special act of God, in His own image, and is the crowning work of His creation. In the beginning man was innocent of sin and was endowed by his Creator with freedom of choice. By his free choice man sinned against God and brought sin into the human race. Through the temptation of Satan man transgressed the command of God, and fell from his original innocence; whereby his posterity inherit a nature and an environment inclined toward sin, and as soon as they are capable of moral action become transgressors and are under condemnation.

III. Man

Man is the special creation of God, made in His own image. He created them male and female as the crowning work of His creation. The gift of gender is thus part of the goodness of God's creation. In the beginning man was innocent of sin and was endowed by his Creator with freedom of choice. By his free choice man sinned against God and brought sin into the human race. Through the temptation of Satan man transgressed the command of God, and fell from his original innocence whereby his posterity inherit a nature and an environment inclined toward sin. There-

corrupt and in bondage to sin, are under condemnation, and as soon as they are capable of moral action, become actual transgressors.

Gen. 1:27; Gen. 2:7; John 1:23; Gen. 3:4–7; Gen. 3:22–24; Rom. 5:12,14,19,21; Rom. 7:23–25; Rom. 11:18,22,32–33; Col. 1:21.

Only the grace of God can bring man into His holy fellowship and enable man to fulfill the creative purpose of God. The sacredness of human personality is evident in that God created man in His own image, and in that Christ died for man; therefore every man possesses dignity and is worthy of respect and Christian love.

Gen. 1:26–30; 2:5,7,18–22; 3; 9:6; Psalms 1; 8:3–6; 32:1–5; 51:5; Isa. 6:5; Jer. 17:5; Matt. 16:26; Acts 17:26–31; Rom. 1:19–32; 3:10–18,23; 5:6,12,19; 6:6; 7:14–25; 8:14–18,29; 1 Cor. 1:21–31; 15:19,21–22; Eph. 2:1–22; Col. 1:21–22; 3:9–11.

fore, as soon as they are capable of moral action, they become transgressors and are under condemnation. Only the grace of God can bring man into His holy fellowship and enable man to fulfill the creative purpose of God. The sacredness of human personality is evident in that God created man in His own image, and in that Christ died for man; therefore, every person of every race possesses full dignity and is worthy of respect and Christian love.

Genesis 1:26–30; 2:5,7,18–22; 3; 9:6; Psalms 1; 8:3–6; 32:1–5; 51:5; Isaiah 6:5; Jeremiah 17:5; Matthew 16:26; Acts 17:26–31; Romans 1:19–32; 3:10–18,23; 5:6,12,19; 6:6; 7:14–25; 8:14–18,29; 1 Corinthians 1:21–31; 15:19,21–22; Ephesians 2:1–22; Colossians 1:21–22; 3:9–11.

IV. The Way of Salvation

The salvation of sinners is wholly of grace, through the

IV. Salvation

Salvation involves the redemption of the whole man, and is offered freely to

IV. Salvation

Salvation involves the redemption of the whole man, and is offered freely to

mediatorial office of the Son of God, who by the Holy Spirit was born of the Virgin Mary and took upon him our nature, yet without sin; honored the divine law by his personal obedience and made atonement for our sins by his death. Being risen from the dead, he is now enthroned in Heaven, and, uniting in his person the tenderest sympathies with divine perfections, he is in every way qualified to be a compassionate and all-sufficient Saviour.

Col. 1:21–22; Eph. 1:7–10; Gal. 2:19–20; Gal. 3:13; Rom. 1:4; Eph. 1:20–23; Matt. 1:21–25; Luke 1:35; 2:11; Rom. 3:25.

V. Justification

Justification is God's gracious and full acquittal upon principles of righteousness of all sinners who believe in Christ. This blessing is bestowed, not in consideration of any works of righteousness which we have done, but through the

all who accept Jesus Christ as Lord and Saviour, who by His own blood obtained eternal redemption for the believer. In its broadest sense salvation includes regeneration, sanctification, and glorification.

1. Regeneration, or the new birth, is a work of God's grace whereby believers become new creatures in Christ Jesus. It is a change of heart wrought by the Holy Spirit through conviction of sin, to which the sinner responds in repentance toward God and faith in the Lord Jesus Christ.

Repentance and faith are inseparable experiences of grace. Repentance is a genuine turning from sin toward God. Faith is the acceptance of Jesus Christ and commitment of the entire personality to Him as Lord and Saviour. Justification is God's gracious and full acquittal upon principles of His righteousness of all sinners who repent and believe in Christ. Justification brings

all who accept Jesus Christ as Lord and Saviour, who by His own blood obtained eternal redemption for the believer. In its broadest sense salvation includes regeneration, justification, sanctification, and glorification. There is no salvation apart from personal faith in Jesus Christ as Lord.

A. Regeneration, or the new birth, is a work of God's grace whereby believers become new creatures in Christ Jesus. It is a change of heart wrought by the Holy Spirit through conviction of sin, to which the sinner responds in repentance toward God and faith in the Lord Jesus Christ. Repentance and faith are inseparable experiences of grace.

Repentance is a genuine turning from sin toward God. Faith is the acceptance of Jesus Christ and commitment of the entire personality to Him as Lord and Saviour.

B. Justification is God's gracious and full acquittal upon principles of His

redemption that is in and through Jesus Christ. It brings us into a state of most blessed peace and favor with God, and secures every other needed blessing.

Rom. 3:24; 4:2; 5:1–2; 8:30; Eph. 1:7; 1 Cor. 1:30–31; 2 Cor. 5:21.

VI. The Freeness of Salvation

The blessings of salvation are made free to all by the gospel. It is the duty of all to accept them by penitent and obedient faith. Nothing prevents the salvation of the greatest sinner except his own voluntary refusal to accept Jesus Christ as teacher, Saviour, and Lord.

Eph. 1:5; 2:4–10; 1 Cor. 1:30–31; Rom. 5:1–9; Rev. 22:17; John 3:16; Mark 16:16.

VII. Regeneration

Regeneration or the new birth is a change of heart wrought by the Holy Spirit, whereby we become partakers of the divine nature and a holy disposition is

the believer into a relationship of peace and favor with God.

2. Sanctification is the experience, beginning in regeneration, by which the believer is set apart to God's purposes, and is enabled to progress toward moral and spiritual perfection through the presence and power of the Holy Spirit dwelling in him. Growth in grace should continue throughout the regenerate person's life.

3. Glorification is the culmination of salvation and is the final blessed and abiding state of the redeemed.

Gen. 3:15; Ex. 3:14–17; 6:2–8; Matt. 1:21; 4:17; 16:21–26; 27:22–28:6; Luke 1:68–69; 2:28–32; John 1:11–14,29; 3:3–21,36; 5:24; 10:9,28–29; 15:1–16; 17:17; Acts 2:21; 4:12; 15:11; 16:30–31; 17:30–31; 20:32; Rom. 1:16–18; 2:4; 3:23–25; 4:3ff.; 5:8–10; 6:1–23; 8:1–18,29–39; 10:9–10,13; 13:11–14; 1 Cor. 1:18,30; 6:19–20; 15:10; 2 Cor. 5:17–20; Gal. 2:20;

righteousness of all sinners who repent and believe in Christ. Justification brings the believer unto a relationship of peace and favor with God.

C. Sanctification is the experience, beginning in regeneration, by which the believer is set apart to God's purposes, and is enabled to progress toward moral and spiritual maturity through the presence and power of the Holy Spirit dwelling in him. Growth in grace should continue throughout the regenerate person's life.

D. Glorification is the culmination of salvation and is the final blessed and abiding state of the redeemed.

Genesis 3:15; Exodus 3:14–17; 6:2–8; Matthew 1:21; 4:17; 16:21–26; 27:22–28:6; Luke 1:68–69; 2:28–32; John 1:11–14,29; 3:3–21,36; 5:24; 10:9,28–29; 15:1–16; 17:17; Acts 2:21; 4:12; 15:11; 16:30–31; 17:30–31; 20:32; Romans 1:16–18; 2:4; 3:23–25; 4:3ff.; 5:8–10; 6:1–23; 8:1–18,29–39;

given, leading to the love and practice of righteousness. It is a work of God's free grace conditioned upon faith in Christ and made manifest by the fruit which we bring forth to the glory of God.

John 3:1–8, 1:16–18; Rom. 8:2; Eph. 2:1,5–6,8,10; Eph. 4:30,32; Col. 3:1–11; Titus 3:5.

VIII. Repentance and Faith

We believe that repentance and faith are sacred duties, and also inseparable graces, wrought in our souls by the regenerating Spirit of God; whereby being deeply convinced of our guilt, danger, and helplessness, and of the way of salvation by Christ, we turn to God with unfeigned contrition, confession, and supplication for mercy; at the same time heartily receiving the Lord Jesus Christ as our Prophet, Priest, and King, and relying on him alone as the only and all-sufficient Saviour.

3:13; 5:22–25; 6:15; Ephes. 1:7; 2:8–22; 4:11–16; Phil. 2:12–13; Col. 1:9–22; 3:1ff.; 1 Thess. 5:23–24; 2 Tim. 1:12; Titus 2:11–14; Heb. 2:1–3; 5:8–9; 9:24–28; 11:1–12:8,14; James 2:14–26; 1 Peter 1:2–23; 1 John 1:6–2:11; Rev. 3:20; 21:1–22:5.

10:9–10,13; 13:11–14; 1 Corinthians 1:18,30; 6:19–20; 15:10; 2 Corinthians 5:17–20; Galatians 2:20; 3:13; 5:22–25; 6:15; Ephesians 1:7; 2:8–22; 4:11–16; Philippians 2:12–13; Colossians 1:9–22; 3:1ff.; 1 Thessalonians 5:23–24; 2 Timothy 1:12; Titus 2:11–14; Hebrews 2:1–3; 5:8–9; 9:24–28; 11:1–12:8,14; James 2:14–26; 1 Peter 1:2–23; 1 John 1:6–2:11; Revelation 3:20; 21:1–22:5.

*Luke 22:31–34; Mark
1:15; 1 Tim. 1:13;
Rom. 3:25,27,31;
Rom. 4:3,9,12,16–17;
John 16:8–11.*

X. Sanctification

Sanctification is the
process by which the
regenerate gradually
attain to moral and
spiritual perfection
through the presence
and power of the
Holy Spirit dwell-
ing in their hearts. It
continues throughout
the earthly life, and is
accomplished by the
use of all the ordinary
means of grace, and
particularly by the
Word of God.

*Acts 20:32; John
17:17; Rom. 6:5–6;
Eph. 3:16; Rom.
4:14; Gal. 5:24; Heb.
12:14; Rom. 7:18–
25; 2 Cor. 3:18; Gal.
5:16,25–26.*

IX. God's Purpose of Grace	V. God's Purpose of Grace	V. God's Purpose of Grace
Election is the gracious purpose of God, according to which he regenerates, sanctifies and saves sinners. It is perfectly consistent with the free agency of man, and comprehends all the means in connection with the end. It is	Election is the gracious purpose of God, according to which He regenerates, sanctifies, and glorifies sinners. It is consistent with the free agency of man and comprehends all the means in connection with the end. It	Election is the gracious purpose of God, according to which He regenerates, justifies, sanctifies, and glorifies sinners. It is consistent with the free agency of man, and comprehends all the means in connection with the end. It is

248

a most glorious display of God's sovereign goodness, and is infinitely wise, holy, and unchangeable. It excludes boasting and promotes humility. It encourages the use of means in the highest degree.

Rom. 8:30; 11:7; Eph. 1:10; Acts 26:18; Eph. 1:17–19; 2 Tim. 1:9; Psalm 110:3; 1 Cor. 2:14; Eph. 2:5; John 6:44–45,65; Rom. 10:12–15.

XI. Perseverance

All real believers endure to the end. Their continuance in well-doing is the mark which distinguishes them from mere professors. A special Providence cares for them, and they are kept by the power of God through faith unto salvation.

John 10:28–29; 2 Tim. 2:19; 1 John 2:19; 1 Cor. 11:32; Rom. 8:30; 9:11,16; Rom. 5:9–10; Matt. 26:70–75.

is a glorious display of God's sovereign goodness, and is infinitely wise, holy, and unchangeable. It excludes boasting and promotes humility.

All true believers endure to the end. Those whom God has accepted in Christ, and sanctified by His Spirit, will never fall away from the state of grace, but shall persevere to the end. Believers may fall into sin through neglect and temptation, whereby they grieve the Spirit, impair their graces and comforts, bring reproach on the cause of Christ, and temporal judgments on themselves, yet they shall be kept by the power of God through faith unto salvation.

Gen. 12:1–3; Ex. 19:5–8; 1 Sam. 8:4–7,19–22; Isa. 5:1–7; Jer. 31:31ff.; Matt. 16:18–19; 21:28–45; 24:22,31; 25:34; Luke 1:68–79; 2:29–32; 19:41–44; 24:44–48; John 1:12–14; 3:16; 5:24; 6:44–45,65; 10:27–29; 15:16;

the glorious display of God's sovereign goodness, and is infinitely wise, holy, and unchangeable. It excludes boasting and promotes humility.

All true believers endure to the end. Those whom God has accepted in Christ, and sanctified by His Spirit, will never fall away from the state of grace, but shall persevere to the end. Believers may fall into sin through neglect and temptation, whereby they grieve the Spirit, impair their graces and comforts, and bring reproach on the cause of Christ and temporal judgments on themselves; yet they shall be kept by the power of God through faith unto salvation.

Genesis 12:1–3; Exodus 19:5–8; 1 Samuel 8:4–7,19–22; Isaiah 5:1–7; Jeremiah 31:31ff.; Matthew 16:18–19; 21:28–45; 24:22,31; 25:34; Luke 1:68–79; 2:29–32; 19:41–44; 24:44–48; John 1:12–14; 3:16; 5:24; 6:44–45,65; 10:27–

17:6,12,17–18; Acts 20:32; Rom. 5:9–10; 8:28–39; 10:12–15; 11:5–7,26–36; 1 Cor. 1:1–2; 15:24–28; Ephes. 1:4–23; 2:1–10; 3:1–11; Col. 1:12–14; 2 Thess. 2:13–14; 2 Tim. 1:12; 2:10,19; Heb. 11:39–12:2; 1 Peter 1:2–5,13; 2:4–10; 1 John 1:7–9; 2:19; 3:2.

29; 15:16; 17:6, 12, 17–18; Acts 20:32; Romans 5:9–10; 8:28–39; 10:12–15; 11:5–7,26–36; 1 Corinthians 1:1–2; 15:24–28; Ephesians 1:4–23; 2:1–10; 3:1–11; Colossians 1:12–14; 2 Thessalonians 2:13–14; 2 Timothy 1:12; 2:10,19; Hebrews 11:39–12:2; James 1:12; 1 Peter 1:2–5,13; 2:4–10; 1 John 1:7–9; 2:19; 3:2.

XII. The Gospel Church

A church of Christ is a congregation of baptized believers, associated by covenant in the faith and fellowship of the gospel; observing the ordinances of Christ, governed by his laws, and exercising the gifts, rights, and privileges invested in them by his word, and seeking to extend the gospel to the ends of the earth. Its Scriptural officers are bishops, or elders, and deacons.

Matt. 16:18; Matt. 18:15–18; Rom. 1:7; 1 Cor. 1:2; Acts 2:41–42; 5:13–14; 2 Cor. 9:13; Phil.

VI. The Church

A New Testament church of the Lord Jesus Christ is a local body of baptized believers who are associated by covenant in the faith and fellowship of the gospel, observing the two ordinances of Christ, committed to His teachings, exercising the gifts, rights, and privileges invested in them by His Word, and seeking to extend the gospel to the ends of the earth.

This church is an autonomous body, operating through democratic processes under the Lordship of Jesus Christ. In

VI. The Church

A New Testament church of the Lord Jesus Christ is an autonomous local congregation of baptized believers, associated by covenant in the faith and fellowship of the gospel; observing the two ordinances of Christ, governed by His laws, exercising the gifts, rights, and privileges invested in them by His Word, and seeking to extend the gospel to the ends of the earth. Each congregation operates under the Lordship of Christ through democratic processes. In such a congregation each

1:1; 1 Tim. 4:14; Acts 14:23; Acts 6:3,5–6; Heb. 13:17; 1 Cor. 9:6,14.

such a congregation, members are equally responsible. Its Scriptural officers are pastors and deacons.

The New Testament speaks also of the church as the body of Christ which includes all of the redeemed of all the ages.

Matt. 16:15–19; 18:15–20; Acts 2:41–42,47; 5:11–14; 6:3–6; 13:1–3; 14:23,27; 15:1–30; 16:5; 20:28; Rom. 1:7; 1 Cor. 1:2; 3:16; 5:4–5; 7:17; 9:13–14; 12; Ephes. 1:22–23; 2:19–22; 3:8–11,21; 5:22–32; Phil. 1:1; Col. 1:18; 1 Tim. 3:1–15; 4:14; 1 Peter 5:1–4; Rev. 2–3; 21:2–3.

member is responsible and accountable to Christ as Lord. Its scriptural officers are pastors and deacons. While both men and women are gifted for service in the church, the office of pastor is limited to men as qualified by Scripture.

The New Testament speaks also of the church as the Body of Christ which includes all of the redeemed of all the ages, believers from every tribe, and tongue, and people, and nation.

Matthew 16:15–19; 18:15–20; Acts 2:41–42,47; 5:11–14; 6:3–6; 13:1–3; 14:23,27; 15:1–30; 16:5; 20:28; Romans 1:7; 1 Corinthians 1:2; 3:16; 5:4–5; 7:17; 9:13–14; 12; Ephesians 1:22–23; 2:19–22; 3:8–11,21; 5:22–32; Philippians 1:1; Colossians 1:18; 1 Timothy 2:9–14; 3:1–15; 4:14; Hebrews 11:39–40; 1 Peter 5:1–4; Revelation 2–3; 21:2–3.

XIII. Baptism and the Lord's Supper

Christian baptism is the immersion of a believer in water in the name of the Father, the Son, and the Holy Spirit. The act is a symbol of our faith in a crucified, buried and risen Saviour. It is prerequisite to the privileges of a church relation and to the Lord's Supper, in which the members of the church, by the use of bread and wine, commemorate the dying love of Christ.

Matt. 28:19–20; 1 Cor. 4:1; Rom. 6:3–5; Col. 2:12; Mark 1:4; Matt. 3:16; John 3:23; 1 Cor. 11:23–26; 1 Cor. 10:16–17,21; Matt. 26:26–27; Acts 8:38–39; Mark 1:9–11.

VII. Baptism and the Lord's Supper

Christian baptism is the immersion of a believer in water in the name of the Father, the Son, and the Holy Spirit. It is an act of obedience symbolizing the believer's faith in a crucified, buried, and risen Saviour, the believer's death to sin, the burial of the old life, and the resurrection to walk in newness of life in Christ Jesus. It is a testimony to his faith in the final resurrection of the dead. Being a church ordinance, it is prerequisite to the privileges of church membership and to the Lord's Supper.

The Lord's Supper is a symbolic act of obedience whereby members of the church, through partaking of the bread and the fruit of the vine, memorialize the death of the Redeemer and anticipate His second coming.

Matt. 3:13–17; 26:26–30; 28:19–20; Mark 1:9–11; 14:22–

VII. Baptism and the Lord's Supper

Christian baptism is the immersion of a believer in water in the name of the Father, the Son, and the Holy Spirit. It is an act of obedience symbolizing the believer's faith in a crucified, buried, and risen Saviour, the believer's death to sin, the burial of the old life, and the resurrection to walk in newness of life in Christ Jesus. It is a testimony to his faith in the final resurrection of the dead. Being a church ordinance, it is prerequisite to the privileges of church membership and to the Lord's Supper.

The Lord's Supper is a symbolic act of obedience whereby members of the church, through partaking of the bread and the fruit of the vine, memorialize the death of the Redeemer and anticipate His second coming.

Matthew 3:13–17; 26:26–30; 28:19–20; Mark 1:9–11; 14:22–

26; Luke 3:21–22; 22:19–20; John 3:23; Acts 2:41–42; 8:35–39; 16:30–33; Acts 20:7; Rom. 6:3–5; 1 Cor. 10:16,21; 11:23–29; Col. 2:12.

26; Luke 3:21–22; 22:19–20; John 3:23; Acts 2:41–42; 8:35–39; 16:30–33; 20:7; Romans 6:3–5; 1 Corinthians 10:16,21; 11:23–29; Colossians 2:12.

XIV. The Lord's Day

The first day of the week is the Lord's day. It is a Christian institution for regular observance. It commemorates the resurrection of Christ from the dead and should be employed in exercises of worship and spiritual devotion, both public and private, and by refraining from worldly amusements, and resting from secular employments, works of necessity and mercy only excepted.

Ex. 20:3–6; Matt. 4:10; Matt. 28:19; 1 Tim. 4:13; Col. 3:16; John 4:21; Ex. 20:8; 1 Cor. 16:1–2; Acts 20:7; Rev. 1:1; Matt. 12:1–13.

VIII. The Lord's Day

The first day of the week is the Lord's Day. It is a Christian institution for regular observance. It commemorates the resurrection of Christ from the dead and should be employed in exercises of worship and spiritual devotion, both public and private, and by refraining from worldly amusements, and resting from secular employments, work of necessity and mercy only being excepted.

Ex. 20:8–11; Matt. 12:1–12; 28:1ff.; Mark 2:27–28; 16:1–7; Luke 24:1–3,33–36; John 4:21–24; 20:1,19–28; Acts 20:7; 1 Cor. 16:1–2; Col. 2:16; 3:16; Rev. 1:10.

VIII. The Lord's Day

The first day of the week is the Lord's Day. It is a Christian institution for regular observance. It commemorates the resurrection of Christ from the dead and should include exercises of worship and spiritual devotion, both public and private. Activities on the Lord's Day should be commensurate with the Christian's conscience under the Lordship of Jesus Christ.

Exodus 20:8–11; Matthew 12:1–12; 28:1ff.; Mark 2:27–28; 16:1–7; Luke 24:1–3,33–36; John 4:21–24; 20:1,19–28; Acts 20:7; Romans 14:5–10; 1 Corinthians 16:1–2; Colossians 2:16; 3:16; Revelation 1:10.

XXV. The Kingdom

The Kingdom of God is the reign of God

IX. The Kingdom

The kingdom of God includes both His

IX. The Kingdom

The Kingdom of God includes both His

in the heart and life of the individual in every human relationship, and in every form and institution of organized human society. The chief means for promoting the Kingdom of God on earth are preaching the gospel of Christ, and teaching the principles of righteousness contained therein. The Kingdom of God will be complete when every thought and will of man shall be brought into captivity to the will of Christ. And it is the duty of all Christ's people to pray and labor continually that his Kingdom may come and his will be done on earth as it is done in heaven.

Dan. 2:37–44; 7:18; Matt. 4:23; 8:12; 12:25; 13:38,43; 25:34; 26:29; Mark 11:10; Luke 12:32; 22:29; Acts 1:6; 1 Cor. 15:24; Col. 1:13; Heb. 12:28; Rev. 1:9; Luke 4:43; 8:1; 9:2; 17:20–21; John 3:3; John 18:36; Matt. 6:10; Luke 23:42.

general sovereignty over the universe and His particular kingship over men who willfully acknowledge Him as King. Particularly the kingdom is the realm of salvation into which men enter by trustful, childlike commitment to Jesus Christ. Christians ought to pray and to labor that the kingdom may come and God's will be done on earth. The full consummation of the kingdom awaits the return of Jesus Christ and the end of this age.

Gen. 1:1; Isa. 9:6–7; Jer. 23:5–6; Matt. 3:2; 4:8–10,23; 12:25–28; 13:1–52; 25:31–46; 26:29; Mark 1:14–15; 9:1; Luke 4:43; 8:1; 9:2; 12:31–32; 17:20–21; 23:42; John 3:3; 18:36; Acts 1:6–7; 17:22–31; Rom. 5:17; 8:19; 1 Cor. 15:24–28; Col. 1:13; Heb. 11:10,16; 12:28; 1 Peter 2:4–10; 4:13; Rev. 1:6,9; 5:10; 11:15; 21–22.

general sovereignty over the universe and His particular kingship over men who willfully acknowledge Him as King. Particularly the Kingdom is the realm of salvation into which men enter by trustful, childlike commitment to Jesus Christ. Christians ought to pray and to labor that the Kingdom may come and God's will be done on earth. The full consummation of the Kingdom awaits the return of Jesus Christ and the end of this age.

Genesis 1:1; Isaiah 9:6–7; Jeremiah 23:5–6; Matthew 3:2; 4:8–10,23; 12:25–28; 13:1–52; 25:31–46; 26:29; Mark 1:14–15; 9:1; Luke 4:43; 8:1; 9:2; 12:31–32; 17:20–21; 23:42; John 3:3; 18:36; Acts 1:6–7; 17:22–31; Romans 5:17; 8:19; 1 Corinthians 15:24–28; Colossians 1:13; Hebrews 11:10,16; 12:28; 1 Peter 2:4–10; 4:13; Revelation 1:6,9; 5:10; 11:15; 21–22.

XV. The Righteous and the Wicked

There is a radical and essential difference between the righteous and wicked. Those only who are justified through the name of the Lord Jesus Christ and sanctified by the Holy Spirit are truly righteous in his sight. Those who continue in impenitence and unbelief are in his sight wicked and are under condemnation. This distinction between the righteous and the wicked holds in and after death, and will be made manifest at the judgment when final and everlasting awards are made to all men.

Gen. 3:19; Acts 13:36; Luke 23:43; 2 Cor. 5:1,6,8; Phil. 1:23; 1 Cor. 15:51–52; 1 Thess. 4:17; Phil. 3:21; 1 Cor. 6:3; Matt. 25:32–46; Rom. 9:22–23; Mark 9:48; 1 Thess. 1:7–10; Rev. 22:20.

XVI. The Resurrection

The Scriptures clearly teach that Jesus rose from the dead. His grave was

X. Last Things

God, in His own time and in His own way, will bring the world to its appropriate end. According to His promise, Jesus Christ will return personally and visibly in glory to the earth; the dead will be raised; and Christ will judge all men in righteousness. The unrighteous will be consigned to hell, the place of everlasting punishment. The righteous in their resurrected and glorified bodies will receive their reward and will dwell forever in heaven with the Lord.

Isa. 2:4; 11:9; Matt. 16:27; 18:8–9; 19:28; 24:27,30,36,44; 25:31–46; 26:64; Mark 8:38; 9:43–48; Luke 12:40,48; 16:19–26; 17:22–37; 21:27–28; John 14:1–3; Acts 1:11; 17:31; Rom. 14:10; 1 Cor. 4:5; 15:24–28,35–58; 2 Cor. 5:10; Phil. 3:20–21; Col. 1:5; 3:4; 1 Thess. 4:14–18; 5:1ff.; 2 Thess. 1:7ff.; 2; 1 Tim. 6:14; 2 Tim. 4:1,8; Titus 2:13; Heb. 9:27–28; James

X. Last Things

God, in His own time and in His own way, will bring the world to its appropriate end. According to His promise, Jesus Christ will return personally and visibly in glory to the earth; the dead will be raised; and Christ will judge all men in righteousness. The unrighteous will be consigned to Hell, the place of everlasting punishment. The righteous in their resurrected and glorified bodies will receive their reward and will dwell forever in Heaven with the Lord.

Isaiah 2:4; 11:9; Matthew 16:27; 18:8–9; 19:28; 24:27,30,36,44; 25:31–46; 26:64; Mark 8:38; 9:43–48; Luke 12:40,48; 16:19–26; 17:22–37; 21:27–28; John 14:1–3; Acts 1:11; 17:31; Romans 14:10; 1 Corinthians 4:5; 15:24–28,35–58; 2 Corinthians 5:10; Philippians 3:20–21; Colossians 1:5; 3:4; 1 Thessalonians 4:14–18; 5:1ff.; 2 Thessaloni-

emptied of its contents. He appeared to the disciples after his resurrection in many convincing manifestations. He now exists in his glorified body at God's right hand. There will be a resurrection of the righteous and the wicked. The bodies of the righteous will conform to the glorious spiritual body of Jesus.

1 Cor. 15:1–58; 2 Cor. 5:1–8; 1 Thess. 4:17; John 5:28–29; Phil. 3:21; Acts 24:15; John 20:9; Matt. 28:6.

XVII. The Return of the Lord

The New Testament teaches in many places the visible and personal return of Jesus to this earth. "This same Jesus which is taken up from you into heaven, shall so come in like manner as ye have seen him go into heaven." The time of his coming is not revealed. "Of that day and hour knoweth no one, no, not the angels in heaven, but my Father only" (Matt. 24:36). It is

5:8; 2 Peter 3:7ff.; 1 John 2:28; 3:2; Jude 14; Rev. 1:18; 3:11; 20:1–22:13.

ans 1:7ff.; 2; 1 Timothy 6:14; 2 Timothy 4:1,8; Titus 2:13; Hebrews 9:27–28; James 5:8; 2 Peter 3:7ff.; 1 John 2:28; 3:2; Jude 14; Revelation 1:18; 3:11; 20:1–22:13.

the duty of all believ-
ers to live in readi-
ness for his coming
and by diligence in
good works to make
manifest to all men
the reality and power
of their hope in
Christ.

*Matt. 24:36; Matt.
24:42–47; Mark
13:32–37; Luke
21:27–28; Acts
1:9–11.*

XXIII. Evangelism and Missions

It is the duty of every
Christian man and
woman, and the duty
of every church of
Christ to seek to
extend the gospel to
the ends of the earth.
The new birth of
man's spirit by God's
Holy Spirit means
the birth of love for
others. Missionary
effort on the part of
all rests thus upon a
spiritual necessity of
the regenerate life.
It is also expressly
and repeatedly com-
manded in the teach-
ings of Christ. It is
the duty of every
child of God to seek
constantly to win the

XI. Evangelism and Missions

It is the duty and
privilege of every fol-
lower of Christ and
of every church of the
Lord Jesus Christ to
endeavor to make dis-
ciples of all nations.
The new birth of
man's spirit by God's
Holy Spirit means the
birth of love for oth-
ers. Missionary effort
on the part of all rests
thus upon a spiri-
tual necessity of the
regenerate life, and is
expressly and repeat-
edly commanded
in the teachings of
Christ. It is the duty
of every child of God
to seek constantly to
win the lost to Christ

XI. Evangelism and Missions

It is the duty and
privilege of every fol-
lower of Christ and
of every church of the
Lord Jesus Christ to
endeavor to make dis-
ciples of all nations.
The new birth of
man's spirit by God's
Holy Spirit means
the birth of love for
others. Missionary
effort on the part of
all rests thus upon
a spiritual necessity
of the regenerate
life, and is expressly
and repeatedly com-
manded in the teach-
ings of Christ. The
Lord Jesus Christ
has commanded the
preaching of the gos-

lost to Christ by personal effort and by all other methods sanctioned by the gospel of Christ.

Matt. 10:5; 13:18–23; 22:9–10; 28:19–20; Mark 16:15–16; 16:19–20; Luke 24:46–53; Acts 1:5–8; 2:1–2,21,39; 8:26–40; 10:42–48; 13:2,30–33; 1 Thess. 1–8.

by personal effort and by all other methods in harmony with the gospel of Christ.

Gen. 12:1–3; Ex. 19:5–6; Isa. 6:1–8; Matt. 9:37–38; 10:5–15; 13:18–30,37,43; 16:19; 22:9–10; 24:14; 28:18–20; Luke 10:1–18; 24:46–53; John 14:11–12; 15:7–8,16; 17:15; 20:21; Acts 1:8; 2; 8:26–40; 10:42–48; 13:2–3; Rom. 10:13–15; Ephes. 3:1–11; 1 Thess. 1:8; 2 Tim. 4:5; Heb. 2:1–3; 11:39–12:2; 1 Peter 2:4–10; Rev. 22:17.

pel to all nations. It is the duty of every child of God to seek constantly to win the lost to Christ by verbal witness undergirded by a Christian lifestyle, and by other methods in harmony with the gospel of Christ.

Genesis 12:1–3; Exodus 19:5–6; Isaiah 6:1–8; Matthew 9:37–38; 10:5–15; 13:18–30, 37–43; 16:19; 22:9–10; 24:14; 28:18–20; Luke 10:1–18; 24:46–53; John 14:11–12; 15:7–8,16; 17:15; 20:21; Acts 1:8; 2; 8:26–40; 10:42–48; 13:2–3; Romans 10:13–15; Ephesians 3:1–11; 1 Thessalonians 1:8; 2 Timothy 4:5; Hebrews 2:1–3; 11:39–12:2; 1 Peter 2:4–10; Revelation 22:17.

XX. Education

Christianity is the religion of enlightenment and intelligence. In Jesus Christ are hidden all the treasures of wisdom and knowledge. All sound learning is therefore a part of our Christian heritage.

XII. Education

The cause of education in the kingdom of Christ is co-ordinate with the causes of missions and general benevolence and should receive along with these the liberal support of the churches. An

XII. Education

Christianity is the faith of enlightenment and intelligence. In Jesus Christ abide all the treasures of wisdom and knowledge. All sound learning is, therefore, a part of our Christian heritage. The new

The new birth opens all human faculties and creates a thirst for knowledge. An adequate system of schools is necessary to a complete spiritual program for Christ's people. The cause of education in the Kingdom of Christ is coordinate with the causes of missions and general benevolence, and should receive along with these the liberal support of the churches.

Deut. 4:1,5,9,13–14; Deut. 6:1,7–10; Psalm 19:7–8; Prov. 8:1–7; Prov. 4:1–10; Matt. 28:20; Col. 2:3; Neh. 8:1–4.

adequate system of Christian schools is necessary to a complete spiritual program for Christ's people.

In Christian education there should be a proper balance between academic freedom and academic responsibility. Freedom in any orderly relationship of human life is always limited and never absolute. The freedom of a teacher in a Christian school, college, or seminary is limited by the pre-eminence of Jesus Christ, by the authoritative nature of the Scriptures, and by the distinct purpose for which the school exists.

Deut. 4:1,5,9,14; 6:1–10; 31:12–13; Neh. 8:1–8; Job. 28:28; Psalms 19:7ff.; 119:11; Prov. 3:13ff.; 4:1–10; 8:1–7,11; 15:14; Eccl. 7:19; Matt. 5:2; 7:24ff.; 28:19–20; Luke 2:40; 1 Cor. 1:18–31; Eph. 4:11–16; Phil. 4:8; Col. 2:3,8–9; 1 Tim. 1:3–7; 2 Tim. 2:15;

birth opens all human faculties and creates a thirst for knowledge. Moreover, the cause of education in the Kingdom of Christ is co–ordinate with the causes of missions and general benevolence, and should receive along with these the liberal support of the churches. An adequate system of Christian education is necessary to a complete spiritual program for Christ's people.

In Christian education there should be a proper balance between academic freedom and academic responsibility. Freedom in any orderly relationship of human life is always limited and never absolute. The freedom of a teacher in a Christian school, college, or seminary is limited by the pre-eminence of Jesus Christ, by the authoritative nature of the Scriptures, and by the distinct purpose for which the school exists.

Deuteronomy 4:1,5,9,14; 6:1–10;

*3:14–17; Heb. 5:12–
6:3; James 1:5; 3:17.*

*31:12–13; Nehemiah
8:1–8; Job 28:28;
Psalms 19:7ff.;
119:11; Proverbs
3:13ff.; 4:1–10;
8:1–7,11; 15:14;
Ecclesiastes 7:19;
Matthew 5:2; 7:24ff.;
28:19–20; Luke
2:40; 1 Corinthians
1:18–31; Ephesians
4:11–16; Philippi-
ans 4:8; Colossians
2:3,8–9; 1 Timothy
1:3–7; 2 Timo-
thy 2:15; 3:14–17;
Hebrews 5:12–6:3;
James 1:5; 3:17.*

XXIV. Stewardship

God is the source of
all blessings, tem-
poral and spiritual;
all that we have and
are we owe to him.
We have a spiritual
debtorship to the
whole world, a holy
trusteeship in the
gospel, and a bind-
ing stewardship in
our possessions. We
are therefore under
obligation to serve
him with our time,
talents and material
possessions; and
should recognize all
these as entrusted to
us to use for the glory
of God and helping
others. Christians
should cheerfully,
regularly, systemati-

XIII. Stewardship

God is the source of
all blessings, tem-
poral and spiritual;
all that we have and
are we owe to Him.
Christians have a
spiritual debtorship
to the whole world,
a holy trusteeship
in the gospel, and a
binding stewardship
in their possessions.
They are therefore
under obligation
to serve Him with
their time, talents,
and material posses-
sions; and should
recognize all these as
entrusted to them to
use for the glory of
God and for helping
others. According
to the Scriptures,

XIII. Stewardship

God is the source of
all blessings, tem-
poral and spiritual;
all that we have and
are we owe to Him.
Christians have a
spiritual debtorship
to the whole world,
a holy trusteeship
in the gospel, and a
binding stewardship
in their possessions.
They are therefore
under obligation
to serve Him with
their time, talents,
and material posses-
sions; and should
recognize all these as
entrusted to them to
use for the glory of
God and for helping
others. According
to the Scriptures,

cally, proportionately, and liberally, contribute of their means to advancing the Redeemer's cause on earth.

Luke 12:42; 16:1–8; Titus 1:7; 1 Peter 4:10; 2 Cor. 8:1–7; 2 Cor. 8:11–19; 2 Cor. 12:1–15; Matt. 25:14–30; Rom. 1:8–15; 1 Cor. 6:20; Acts 2:44–47.

Christians should contribute of their means cheerfully, regularly, systematically, proportionately, and liberally for the advancement of the Redeemer's cause on earth.

Gen. 14:20; Lev. 27:30–32; Deut. 8:18; Mal. 3:8–12; Matt. 6:1–4,19–21; 19:21; 23:23; 25:14–29; Luke 12:16–21,42; 16:1–13; Acts 2:44–47; 5:1–11; 17:24–25; 20:35; Rom. 6:6–22; 12:1–2; 1 Cor. 4:1–2; 6:19–20; 12; 16:1–4; 2 Cor. 8–9; 12:15; Phil. 4:10–19; 1 Peter 1:18–19.

Christians should contribute of their means cheerfully, regularly, systematically, proportionately, and liberally for the advancement of the Redeemer's cause on earth.

Genesis 14:20; Leviticus 27:30–32; Deuteronomy 8:18; Malachi 3:8–12; Matthew 6:1–4,19–21; 19:21; 23:23; 25:14–29; Luke 12:16–21,42; 16:1–13; Acts 2:44–47; 5:1–11; 17:24–25; 20:35; Romans 6:6–22; 12:1–2; 1 Corinthians 4:1–2; 6:19–20; 12; 16:1–4; 2 Corinthians 8–9; 12:15; Philippians 4:10–19; 1 Peter 1:18–19.

XXII. Co-Operation

Christ's people should, as occasion requires, organize such associations and conventions as may best secure co-operation for the great objects of the Kingdom of God. Such organizations have no authority over each other or over the churches. They are voluntary and advisory bodies

XIV. Co-Operation

Christ's people should, as occasion requires, organize such associations and conventions as may best secure co-operation for the great objects of the kingdom of God. Such organizations have no authority over one another or over the churches. They are voluntary and advisory bodies designed

XIV. Cooperation

Christ's people should, as occasion requires, organize such associations and conventions as may best secure cooperation for the great objects of the Kingdom of God. Such organizations have no authority over one another or over the churches. They are voluntary and advisory bodies designed

designed to elicit, combine, and direct the energies of our people in the most effective manner. Individual members of New Testament churches should co-operate with each other, and the churches themselves should co-operate with each other in carrying forward the missionary, educational, and benevolent program for the extension of Christ's Kingdom. Christian unity in the New Testament sense is spiritual harmony and voluntary co-operation for common ends by various groups of Christ's people. It is permissable and desirable as between the various Christian denominations, when the end to be attained is itself justified, and when such co-operation involves no violation of conscience or compromise of loyalty to Christ and his Word as revealed in the New Testament.

Ezra 1:3–4; 2:68–69; 5:14–15; Neh. 4:4–6; 8:1–4; Mal. 3:10; Matt. 10:5–15; 20:1–

to elicit, combine, and direct the energies of our people in the most effective manner. Members of New Testament churches should co-operate with one another in carrying forward the missionary, educational, and benevelent ministries for the extension of Christ's kingdom. Christian unity in the New Testament sense is spiritual harmony and voluntary co-operation for common ends by various groups of Christ's people. Co-operation is desirable between the various Christian denominations, when the end to be attained is itself justified, and when such co-operation involves no violation of conscience or compromise of loyalty to Christ and his Word as revealed in the New Testament.

Ex. 17:12; 18:17ff.; Judg. 7:21; Ezra 1:3–4; 2:68–69; 5:14–15; Neh. 4; 8:1–5; Matt. 10:5–15; 20:1–16; 22:1–10; 28:19–20; Mark 2:3; Luke 10:1ff.; Acts 1:13–14; 2:1ff.; 4:31–37;

to elicit, combine, and direct the energies of our people in the most effective manner. Members of New Testament churches should cooperate with one another in carrying forward the missionary, educational, and benevolent ministries for the extension of Christ's Kingdom. Christian unity in the New Testament sense is spiritual harmony and voluntary cooperation for common ends by various groups of Christ's people. Cooperation is desirable between the various Christian denominations, when the end to be attained is itself justified, and when such cooperation involves no violation of conscience or compromise of loyalty to Christ and His Word as revealed in the New Testament.

Exodus 17:12; 18:17ff.; Judges 7:21; Ezra 1:3–4; 2:68–69; 5:14–15; Nehemiah 4; 8:1–5; Matthew 10:5–15; 20:1–16; 22:1–10; 28:19–20; Mark 2:3; Luke 10:1ff.;

16; 22:1–10; Acts
1:13–14; 1:21,26;
2:1,41–47; 1 Cor.
1:10–17; 12:11–12;
13; 14:33–34,40;
16:2; 2 Cor. 9:1–15;
Eph. 4:1–16; 3 John
5–8.

13:2–3; 15:1–35;
1 Cor. 1:10–17;
3:5–15; 12; 2 Cor.
8–9; Gal. 1:6–10;
Eph. 4:1–16; Phil.
1:15–18.

Acts 1:13–14; 2:1ff.;
4:31–37; 13:2–3;
15:1–35; 1 Cor-
inthians 1:10–17;
3:5–15; 12; 2 Corin-
thians 8–9; Galatians
1:6–10; Ephesians
4:1–16; Philippians
1:15–18.

XXI. Social Service

Every Christian is under obligation to seek to make the will of Christ regnant in his own life and in human society to oppose in the spirit of Christ every form of greed, selfishness, and vice; to provide for the orphaned, the aged, the helpless, and the sick; to seek to bring industry, government, and society as a whole under the sway of the principles of righteousness, truth and brotherly love; to promote these ends Christians should be ready to work with all men of good will in any good cause, always being careful to act in the spirit of love without compromising their loyalty to Christ and his truth. All means and methods used in social service for the

XV. The Christian and the Social Order

Every Christian is under obligation to seek to make the will of Christ supreme in his own life and in human society. Means and methods used for the improvement of society and the establishment of righteousness among men can be truly and permanently helpful only when they are rooted in the regeneration of the individual by the saving grace of God in Christ Jesus. The Christian should oppose in the spirit of Christ every form of greed, selfishness, and vice. He should work to provide for the orphaned, the needy, the aged, the helpless, and the sick. Every Christian should seek to bring industry, govern-

XV. The Christian and the Social Order

All Christians are under obligation to seek to make the will of Christ supreme in our own lives and in human society. Means and methods used for the improvement of society and the establishment of righteousness among men can be truly and permanently helpful only when they are rooted in the regeneration of the individual by the saving grace of God in Jesus Christ. In the spirit of Christ, Christians should oppose racism, every form of greed, self-ishness, and vice, and all forms of sexual immorality, including adultery, homosexu-ality, and pornog-raphy. We should work to provide for the orphaned, the

amelioration of society and the establishment of righteousness among men must finally depend on the regeneration of the individual by the saving grace of God in Christ Jesus.

Luke 10:25–37; Ex. 22:10,14; Lev. 6:2; Deut. 20:10; Deut. 4:42; Deut. 15:2; 27:17; Psalm 101:5; Ezek. 18:6; Heb. 2:15; Zech. 8:16; Ex. 20:16; James 2:8; Rom. 12–14; Col. 3:12–17.

ment, and society as a whole under the sway of the principles of righteousness, truth, and brotherly love. In order to promote these ends Christians should be ready to work with all men of good will in any good cause, always being careful to act in the spirit of love without compromising their loyalty to Christ and his truth.

Ex. 20:3–17; Lev. 6:2–5; Deut. 10:12; 27:17; Psalm 101:5; Micah 6:8; Zech. 8:16; Matt. 5:13–16,43–48; 22:36–40; 25:35; Mark 1:29–34; 2:3ff.; 10:21; Luke 4:18–21; 10:27–37; 20:25; John 15:12; 17:15; Rom. 12–14; 1 Cor. 5:9–10; 6:1–7; 7:20–24; 10:23–11:1; Gal. 3:26–28; Eph. 6:5–9; Col. 3:12–17; 1 Thess. 3:12; Philemon; James 1:27; 2:8.

needy, the abused, the aged, the helpless, and the sick. We should speak on behalf of the unborn and contend for the sanctity of all human life from conception to natural death. Every Christian should seek to bring industry, government, and society as a whole under the sway of the principles of righteousness, truth, and brotherly love. In order to promote these ends Christians should be ready to work with all men of good will in any good cause, always being careful to act in the spirit of love without compromising their loyalty to Christ and His truth.

Exodus 20:3–17; Leviticus 6:2–5; Deuteronomy 10:12; 27:17; Psalm 101:5; Micah 6:8; Zechariah 8:16; Matthew 5:13–16,43–48; 22:36–40; 25:35; Mark 1:29–34; 2:3ff.; 10:21; Luke 4:18–21; 10:27–37; 20:25; John 15:12; 17:15; Romans 12–14; 1 Corinthians 5:9–10; 6:1–7; 7:20–24; 10:23–11:1;

Galatians 3:26–28;
Ephesians 6:5–9;
Colossians 3:12–17;
1 Thessalonians
3:12; Philemon;
James 1:27; 2:8.

XIX. Peace and War

It is the duty of Christians to seek peace with all men on principles of righteousness. In accordance with the spirit and teachings of Christ they should do all in their power to put an end to war.

The true remedy for the war spirit is the pure gospel of our Lord. The supreme need of the world is the acceptance of his teachings in all the affairs of men and

XVI. Peace and War

It is the duty of Christians to seek peace with all men on principles of righteousness. In accordance with the spirit and teachings of Christ they should do all in their power to put an end to war.

The true remedy for the war spirit is the gospel of our Lord. The supreme need of the world is the acceptance of His teachings in all the affairs of men and

XVI. Peace and War

It is the duty of Christians to seek peace with all men on principles of righteousness. In accordance with the spirit and teachings of Christ they should do all in their power to put an end to war.

The true remedy for the war spirit is the gospel of our Lord. The supreme need of the world is the acceptance of His teachings in all the affairs of men and nations, and the practical application of his law of love.

We urge Christian people throughout the world to pray for the reign of the Prince of Peace, and to oppose everything likely to provoke war.

Matt. 5:9,13–14,43– 46; Heb. 12:14; James 4:1; Matt. 6:33; Rom. 14:17,19.

nations, and the practical application of His law of love.

Isa. 2:4; Matt. 5:9,38–48; 6:33; 26:52; Luke 22:36,38; Rom. 12:18–19; 13:1–7; 14:19; Heb.12:14; James 4:1–2.

nations, and the practical application of His law of love. Christian people throughout the world should pray for the reign of the Prince of Peace.

Isaiah 2:4; Matthew 5:9,38–48; 6:33; 26:52; Luke 22:36,38; Romans 12:18–19; 13:1–7; 14:19; Hebrews 12:14; James 4:1–2.

XVIII. Religious Liberty

God alone is Lord of the conscience, and he has left it free from the doctrines and commandments of men which are contrary to his Word or not contained in it. Church and state should be separate. The state owes to the church protection and full freedom in the pursuit of its spiritual ends. In providing for such freedom no ecclesiastical group or denomination should be favored by the state more than others. Civil government being ordained of God, it is the duty of Christians to render loyal obedience thereto in all things

XVII. Religious Liberty

God alone is Lord of the conscience, and He has left it free from the doctrines and commandments of men which are contrary to His Word or not contained in it. Church and state should be separate. The state owes to every church protection and full freedom in the pursuit of its spiritual ends. In providing for such freedom no ecclesiastical group or denomination should be favored by the state more than others. Civil government being ordained of God, it is the duty of Christians to render loyal obedience

XVII. Religious Liberty

God alone is Lord of the conscience, and He has left it free from the doctrines and commandments of men which are contrary to His Word or not contained in it. Church and state should be separate. The state owes to every church protection and full freedom in the pursuit of its spiritual ends. In providing for such freedom no ecclesiastical group or denomination should be favored by the state more than others. Civil government being ordained of God, it is the duty of Christians to render loyal obedience

not contrary to the revealed will of God. The church should not resort to the civil power to carry on its work. The gospel of Christ contemplates spiritual means alone for the pursuit of its ends. The state has no right to impose penalties for religious opinions of any kind. The state has no right to impose taxes for the support of any form of religion. A free church in a free state is the Christian ideal, and this implies the right of free and unhindered access to God on the part of all men, and the right to form and propagate opinions in the sphere of religion without interference by the civil power.

Rom. 13:1–7; 1 Peter 2:17; 1 Tim. 2:1–2; Gal. 3:9–14; John 7:38–39; James 4:12; Gal. 5:13; 2 Peter 2:18–21; 1 Cor. 3:5; Rom. 6:1–2; Matt. 22:21; Mark 12:17.

———

Source: Annual,
SBC, 1925, 71–76;

thereto in all things not contrary to the revealed will of God. The church should not resort to the civil power to carry on its work. The gospel of Christ contemplates spiritual means alone for the pursuit of its ends. The state has no right to impose penalties for religious opinions of any kind. The state has no right to impose taxes for the support of any form of religion. A free church in a free state is the Christian ideal, and this implies the right of free and unhindered access to God on the part of all men and the right to form and propagate opinions in the sphere of religion without interference by the civil power.

Gen. 1:27; 2:7; Matt. 6:6–7; 24:16:26; 22:21; John 8:36; Acts 4:19–20; Rom. 6:1–2; 13:1–7; Gal. 5:1,13; Phil. 3:20; 1 Tim. 2:1–2; James 4:12; 1 Peter 2:12–17; 3:11–17; 4:12–19.

———

Annual, SBC, 1963, 269–81;

thereto in all things not contrary to the revealed will of God. The church should not resort to the civil power to carry on its work. The gospel of Christ contemplates spiritual means alone for the pursuit of its ends. The state has no right to impose penalties for religious opinions of any kind. The state has no right to impose taxes for the support of any form of religion. A free church in a free state is the Christian ideal, and this implies the right of free and unhindered access to God on the part of all men, and the right to form and propagate opinions in the sphere of religion without interference by the civil power.

Genesis 1:27; 2:7; Matthew 6:6–7, 24; 16:26; 22:21; John 8:36; Acts 4:19–20; Romans 6:1–2; 13:1–7; Galatians 5:1,13; Philippians 3:20; 1 Timothy 2:1–2; James 4:12; 1 Peter 2:12–17; 3:11–17; 4:12–19.

XVIII. The Family

God has ordained the family as the foundational institution of human society. It is composed of persons related to one another by marriage, blood, or adoption.

Marriage is the uniting of one man and one woman in covenant commitment for a lifetime. It is God's unique gift to reveal the union between Christ and His church and to provide for the man and the woman in marriage the framework for intimate companionship, the channel of sexual expression according to biblical standards, and the means for procreation of the human race.

The husband and wife are of equal worth before God, since both are created in God's image. The marriage relationship models the way God relates to His people. A husband is to love his wife as Christ loved the church. He has the God-given responsibility to provide for, to protect, and to lead his family. A wife is to submit herself graciously to the servant leadership of her husband even as the church willingly submits to the headship of Christ. She, being in the image of God as is her husband and thus equal to him, has the God-given responsibility to respect her husband and to serve as his helper in managing the household and nurturing the next generation.

Children, from the moment of conception, are a blessing and heritage from the Lord. Parents are to demonstrate to their children God's pattern for marriage. Parents are to teach their children spiritual and moral values and to lead them, through consistent lifestyle example and loving discipline, to make choices based on biblical truth. Children are to honor and obey their parents.

Genesis 1:26–28; 2:15–25; 3:1–20; Exodus 20:12; Deuteronomy 6:4–9; Joshua 24:15;

*1 Samuel 1:26–28;
Psalms 51:5; 78:1–8;
127; 128; 139:13–
16; Proverbs 1:8;
5:15–20; 6:20–22;
12:4; 13:24; 14:1;
17:6; 18:22; 22:6,15;
23:13–14; 24:3;
29:15,17; 31:10–31;
Ecclesiastes 4:9–12;
9:9; Malachi
2:14–16; Matthew
5:31–32; 18:2–5;
19:3–9; Mark
10:6–12; Romans
1:18–32; 1 Corinthi-
ans 7:1–16; Ephesi-
ans 5:21–33; 6:1–4;
Colossians 3:18–21;
1 Timothy 5:8,14;
2 Timothy 1:3–5;
Titus 2:3–5; Hebrews
13:4; 1 Peter 3:1–7.*

———

Annual, SBC,
2000, 30–36.

SUBJECT INDEX

Scripture Index